Raising Student Learning in Latin America

Raising Student Learning in Latin America

The Challenge for the 21st Century

Emiliana Vegas and
Jenny Petrow

THE WORLD BANK
Washington, D.C.

Cover design: ULTRAdesigns, Silver Spring, MD

ISBN-13: 978-0-8213-7082-7
eISBN: 0-8213-7083-9
DOI: 10.1596/978-0-8213-7082-7
e-ISBN-13: 978-0-8213-7083-4

Library of Congress Cataloging-in-Publication Data
Vegas, Emiliana.
    Raising student learning in Latin America : the challenge for the 21st century / Emiliana Vegas and Jenny Petrow.

    p. cm.—(Latin American development forum series)
  Includes bibliographical references and index.
  ISBN-13: 978-0-8213-7082-7
  ISBN-10: 0-8213-7082-0
  ISBN-13: 978-0-8213-7083-4 (epub 13)
  ISBN-10: 0-8213-7083-9 (epub 10)
  1. Academic achievement—Latin America. 2. Basic education—Latin America—Evaluation.
  I. Petrow, Jenny. II. Title.
  LB1062.6.V43 2007
  379.8—dc22

                                                                    2007030104

Latin American Development Forum Series

This series was created in 2003 to promote debate, disseminate information and analysis, and convey the excitement and complexity of the most topical issues in economic and social development in Latin America and the Caribbean. It is sponsored by the Inter-American Development Bank, the United Nations Economic Commission for Latin America and the Caribbean, and the World Bank. The manuscripts chosen for publication represent the highest quality in each institution's research and activity output and have been selected for their relevance to the academic community, policy makers, researchers, and interested readers.

Advisory Committee Members

Other Titles in the Latin American Development Forum Series

New Titles

Innovative Experiences in Access to Finance: Market-Friendly Roles for the Visible Hand? (2008), Augusto de la Torre, Juan Carlos Gozzi, and Sergio L. Schmukler.

China's and India's Challenge to Latin America: Opportunity or Threat? (2008), Daniel Lederman, Marcelo Olarreaga, and Guillermo Perry, editors

Fiscal Policy, Stabilization, and Growth: Prudence or Abstinence? (2007), Guillermo Perry, Luis Servén, and Rodrigo Suescún, editors

Remittances and Development: Lessons from Latin America (2007), Pablo Fajnzylber and J. Humberto López, editors

Published Titles

Investor Protection and Corporate Governance: Firm-Level Evidence Across Latin America (2007), Alberto Chong and Florencio López-de-Silanes, editors

The State of State Reform in Latin America (2006), Eduardo Lora, editor

Emerging Capital Markets and Globalization: The Latin American Experience (2006), Augusto de la Torre and Sergio L. Schmukler

Beyond Survival: Protecting Households from Health Shocks in Latin America (2006), Cristian C. Baeza and Truman G. Packard

Natural Resources: Neither Curse nor Destiny (2006), Daniel Lederman and William F. Maloney, editors

Beyond Reforms: Structural Dynamics and Macroeconomic Vulnerability (2005), José Antonio Ocampo, editor

Privatization in Latin America: Myths and Reality (2005), Alberto Chong and Florencio López-de-Silanes, editors

Keeping the Promise of Social Security in Latin America (2004), Indermit S. Gill, Truman G. Packard, and Juan Yermo

Lessons from NAFTA: For Latin America and the Caribbean (2004), Daniel Lederman, William F. Maloney, and Luis Servén

The Limits of Stabilization: Infrastructure, Public Deficits, and Growth in Latin America (2003), William Easterly and Luis Servén, editors

Globalization and Development: A Latin American and Caribbean Perspective (2003), José Antonio Ocampo and Juan Martin, editors

Is Geography Destiny? Lessons from Latin America (2003), John Luke Gallup, Alejandro Gaviria, and Eduardo Lora

About the Authors

Emiliana Vegas is a senior education economist in the World Bank's Human Development Department of the Latin America and the Caribbean Region. Her fields of interest include the economics of education, teacher labor markets, and the relationship between education policy and student outcomes. In her current position, she is responsible for producing research as well as leading the World Bank's education operations and technical assistance activities in Chile and Uruguay. She is the author of several articles in peer-reviewed journals and institutional reports, and she is the editor of *Incentives to Improve Teaching: Lessons from Latin America* (World Bank 2005). Dr. Vegas holds a Doctor of Education degree from Harvard University, where her concentration was in the economics of education. She has a master's degree in public policy studies from Duke University and a bachelor's degree in journalism from Andrés Bello Catholic University in Caracas, Venezuela. She has worked at the Research Triangle Institute's Center for International Development.

Jenny Petrow is a Foundation Representative at the Inter-American Foundation, where she manages a portfolio of grants to nongovernmental and community-based organizations in Haiti, the Dominican Republic, and the Eastern Caribbean. Previously, she worked at the World Bank's Human Development Department of the Latin America and the Caribbean Region as an education consultant where, in addition to her capacity as researcher and writer, she provided technical assistance to education operations in Bolivia and Panama. Her areas of interest include education quality, nonformal education, and civil society strengthening. Ms. Petrow holds a bachelor's degree in humanities from Yale University and a master's degree in international development studies from George Washington University, Washington, D.C., where she focused on international education policy. She has a background in educational curriculum development and is the author of *Spanish Demystified*, recently published by McGraw-Hill.

Contents

Acknowledgments

This book is based on an extensive review of the literature, as well as on original research conducted for this study by Samuel Berlinski, Javier Corrales, Yael Duthilleul, Sebastián Galiani, Marco Manacorda, Patrick J. McEwan, Daniel Ortega, Chris Sakellariou, and Miguel Urquiola.

The authors are grateful to Pedro Cerdán-Infantes, William Lorie, Erika Molina, Milagros Nores, Joseph Olchefske, Domenec Ruiz Devesa, Ilana Umansky, Christel Vermeersch, and Amy Walter, who contributed sections of this book. Guillermo Perry (Chief Economist, Latin America and the Caribbean Region); Eduardo Vélez-Bustillo (Education Sector Manager, Latin America and the Caribbean Region); Ariel Fiszbein (Adviser to the Vice President, Development Economics Research Group); and Jennie Litvack (Lead Economist, Human Development Department, Latin America and the Caribbean Region) provided overall guidance. Juan Carlos Navarro, Inter-American Development Bank; Lant Pritchett; and Christopher Thomas served as peer reviewers.

The authors also benefited from helpful comments from Elizabeth King, Patrick McEwan, Harry Patrinos, Jeff Puryear, Alberto Rodriguez, Lucrecia Santibáñez and Joseph Shapiro.

Abbreviations

AGE	Apoyo a la Gestión Escolar
ANEP-CODICEN	Administración Nacional de la Educación Pública y Consejo Directivo Central
ANEP/MEMFOD	Administración Nacional de la Educación Pública y Programa de Modernización de la Educación Media y Formación Docente
ANMEB	Acuerdo Nacional para la Modernización de la Educación Básica
APRENDO	Sistema Nacional de Medición de Logros Académicos
CONAFE	Consejo Nacional de Fomento Educativo
CRECER	Evaluación Nacional
DE	Department for Education
DfEE	Department for Education and Employment
DfES	Department for Education and Skills
DFID	U.K. Department for International Development
DfTE	Department for Training and Education
ECAES	Exámenes de Calidad de la Educación Superior
ECCE	Early Childhood Care and Education
ECLAC	Economic Commission for Latin America and the Caribbean (United Nations)
EDUCO	Programa de Educación de la Comunidad
ENEM	Exame Nacional do Ensino Médio
ENLACE	Evaluación Nacional del Logro Académico en Centros Escolares
EXCALE	Examen de la Calidad y el Logro Educativos
FNBE	Finnish National Board of Education
FORMABIAP	Programa de Formación de Maestros Bilingûes de la Amazonia Peruana
FSD	Full School Day

FTS	Full-Time School
FUNDEF	Fundo de Manutenção e Desenvolvimento do Ensino Fundamental e de Valorização do Magistério
GDP	gross domestic product
GRADE	Grupo de Análisis para el Desarrollo
IALS	International Adult Literacy Survey
ICFES	Instituto Colombiano para el Fomento de la Educación Superior
ICT	information and communication technologies
IDB	Inter-American Development Bank
IEA	International Association for the Evaluation of Educational Achievement
IIEP	International Institute for Educational Planning
IIS	Institute for Statistics
IZA	Institute for the Study of Labor
KERIS	Korea Education & Research Information Service
LLECE	Latin American Evaluation Laboratory for the Evaluation of Education Quality
MDGs	Millennium Development Goals
MECE	Proyecto de Mejoramiento de la Calidad Educativa (Chile)
MINEDUC	Ministerio de Educación
NGO	nongovernmental organization
NICHD	National Institute for Child and Human Development
OECD	Organisation for Economic Co-operation and Development
ONE	Operativo Nacional de Evaluación
OREALC	Oficina Regional de Educación para América Latina y el Caribe
P-900	Program for the Improvement of Quality in Poor Area Basic Schools
PACES	Programa de Ampliación de Cobertura de la Educación Secundaria
PAES	Prueba de Aprendizaje para Egresados de Educación Media
PIRLS	Progress in International Reading Literacy Study
PISA	Programme for International Student Assessment
PREAL	Partnership for Educational Revitalization in the Americas
PROHECO	Proyecto Hondureño de Educación Comunitaria
PRONERE	Programa Nacional de Evaluación del Rendimiento Escolar
SABE	Strengthening Achievement in Basic Education
SABER	Sistema de Evaluación de la Calidad de la Educación
SAEB	Sistema de Avaliação da Educação Básica
SECE	Sistema de Evaluación de la Calidad de la Educación

SIMCE	Sistema de Medición de la Calidad Educación
SIMECAL	Sistema de Medición de la Calidad
SINEA	Sistema Nacional de Medición y Evaluación del Aprendizaje
SINECE	Sistema Nacional de Evaluación de la Calidad Educativo
SNE	Sistema Nacional de Evaluación
SNED	Sistema Nacional de Evaluación del Desempeño de los Establecimientos Subvencionados
SNEPE	Sistema Nacional de Evaluación del Proceso Educativà
TIMSS	Third International Mathematics and Science Study
UIS	UNESCO Institute for Statistics
UMCE	Unidad Externa de Medición de la Calidad de la Educación
UN	United Nations
UNESCO	United Nations Educational, Scientific, and Cultural Organization
UNICEF	United Nations Children's Fund
USAC	Universidad de San Carlos de Guatemala
USAID	U.S. Agency for International Development

Executive Summary

Countries in Latin America and the Caribbean consistently perform poorly in international assessments: even after controlling for per capita GDP, the region's students perform far below students in OECD and East Asian countries. Performance is not only weak; it is also declining relative to other countries with similar income levels. In 1960, 7 percent of adults in Latin America and 11 percent of adults in East Asia had completed upper-secondary school. Forty years later, this figure had quadrupled to 44 percent in East Asia and risen to just 18 percent in Latin America and the Caribbean. The region has fallen even further behind Spain and the Scandinavian countries—countries that had comparable levels of educational attainment in 1960.

In the face of poor student performance, understanding what and how students are learning have emerged as salient issues. What and how much students learn are policy concerns for various reasons, ranging from ensuring human rights to reducing inequality to improving individual life outcomes, competitiveness, economic growth, and development outcomes. Evidence from developing countries suggests that returns to learning may be even higher in developing countries than in developed countries. As the region embarks on a series of reforms addressing quality and equity in basic education, identifying policies and programs that can improve learning will be vital, especially as more and more of the most marginalized and vulnerable children enter the system.

Improving student learning is the key challenge for education in Latin America and the Caribbean, for several reasons:

- Students in the region are among the lowest performers on international assessments of skills. Poor and nonwhite students have a higher probability of achieving low scores than white students of higher socioeconomic status, but even those students underperform students from OECD countries, dispelling the myth that the region's most privileged students receive a good education.
- A high percentage of students achieve far below minimum skill levels in all subjects.
- Within countries, the achievement gap across students is large, perpetuating or exacerbating the region's already high level of inequality.

- Expansion of educational opportunities has not markedly reduced income inequality, underdevelopment, and poverty, possibly because of the poor quality of education.

As political and educational authorities turn their attention toward the task of improving learning, standardized tests have become a more important—and more controversial—element in the policy debate. Although these instruments are not without problems, testing methodologies have improved, making these assessments the best indicator available for measuring performance.

Standardized test results are very useful for policy makers, for a variety of reasons:

- They provide a quantitative measure of certain skills and knowledge that can be tracked and compared, allowing success in meeting learning goals to be tracked across time and across schools.
- They can provide teachers and schools with information about their own strengths and weaknesses and alert them to areas that need improvement.
- They can provide parents and students with information about areas in which students are excelling or struggling.

Since the 1990s, virtually all countries in the region have experimented with national standardized tests, with varying success. In some countries, such as Ecuador and Guatemala, assessment programs were funded by international organizations, then abandoned soon after external funding ended. In other countries, such as Chile and Uruguay, national assessments have been implemented regularly and have had important effects on education policy making. A few Latin American countries have also participated in international assessments.

Learning hinges on myriad factors, from a parent's education and societal values regarding education to school infrastructure and the agricultural calendar. These factors can be grouped into three categories—student-side factors, school-side factors, and systemwide factors—which interact to produce student learning. In order to craft policies that raise both the quality and the equity of education, policy makers need to understand how these three sets of factors affect student learning.

Ensuring that all students learn requires both a theory of action for providing education and strong alignment of the roles and responsibilities of all participants in the education system to ensure education quality. International evidence suggests that at least three different institutional visions—quality contracts, differentiated instruction, and managed instruction—can help improve the quality of education. The challenge for countries in the region is to adopt an institutional vision that is appropriate given their individual historical, social, and political contexts and to consistently apply that vision to ensure that all students achieve at their potential.

Introduction

Education has long been viewed as wielding powerful transformative powers. Governments often regard education as a path to nationhood and citizenship building. Economists view education as an engine for increasing and equalizing income. Sociologists such as Paulo Freire see education as an engine for social transformation and for consciousness-raising among the "oppressed" classes. The United Nations and human rights activists consider education a basic human right that allows people to take part in society and enjoy full, meaningful lives. In sum, education is seen as a p olitical, economic, and social necessity and obligation.

Achieving universal primary education has been on the global agenda since the Universal Declaration of Human Rights affirmed children's right to free and compulsory education in 1948. Over the past 20 years, it has developed into an international priority. In 2000 the United Nations adopted the Millennium Declaration and laid out a road map for achieving the Millennium Development Goals (MDGs), a series of development targets for countries around the world. These goals include achieving "universal primary education" to "ensure that all boys and girls complete a full course of primary schooling"—a target that is often measured through primary-school enrollment, primary-school completion, and the literacy rate among 15- to 24-year-olds.

In 2000 the Dakar Framework for Action renewed the pledge to Education for All first set out in 1990 in Jomtien, Thailand. Jomtien's commitment to meet students' "basic learning needs" affirmed the right to education and recognized the inherent differences among learners. The Dakar Framework echoed this commitment to quality as well as coverage and included goals such as "ensuring that by 2015 all children, particularly girls, children in difficult circumstances and those belonging to certain ethnic groups, have access to and complete free and compulsory primary education of good quality" (UNESCO 1999).

Progress and Challenges in Latin America and the Caribbean

Almost all countries in the region have achieved universal primary enrollment, and access to secondary and higher education is also on the rise in many countries. Average public spending on education has also increased, rising from 2.7 percent of the gross domestic product (GDP) in 1990 to 4.3 percent in 2003 (World Bank Edstats online database).

These accomplishments are impressive, but in their effort to achieve universal primary education, many countries have left other goals—including learning—behind. Primary education is only a first step. Policy makers in the region now need to focus on equalizing access to secondary and tertiary education; reducing socioeconomic and ethnic inequalities; and, above all, ensuring that all children learn.

Many challenges remain. Countries in Latin America consistently perform poorly in international assessments: even after controlling for per capita GDP, the region's students perform far below students in the Organisation for Economic Co-operation and Development (OECD) and East Asian countries. Performance is not only weak, it is also declining relative to other countries with similar income levels. In 1960, 7 percent of adults in Latin America and 11 percent of adults in East Asia had completed upper-secondary school. Forty years later, this figure had quadrupled to 44 percent in East Asian and risen to just 18 percent in Latin America and the Caribbean (Di Gropello 2006). The region has fallen even farther behind Spain and the Scandinavian countries—countries that had comparable levels of educational attainment in 1960.

Millions of students are failing to meet minimum learning requirements and to acquire basic skills and competencies. Almost one-fifth of children who enter primary school repeat grades or drop out of school. Among those who begin secondary or higher education, many do not finish.

All of these outcomes are worse for the poor, who are less likely to attend school, to complete school, or to have access to good education and more likely to repeat a grade or drop out than their nonpoor peers. The region's unequal learning outcomes underscore the fact that poor children face many barriers to receiving a good education, of which poor schools are only one. Other obstacles range from malnutrition to lack of preparation to the high opportunity costs of schooling. Policy makers need to understand what can be done to improve the quality of service disadvantaged students receive, to ensure that they are stimulated in the classroom, and to identify how these students can learn to their full potential.

Scope of the Book

This book examines the state of student learning in Latin America and the Caribbean. It summarizes recent evidence and provides new evidence on the impact on student learning of policies and programs, and it presents policy options for increasing learning among all students in the region.

One of the advantages of examining learning is that techniques have been developed for assessing it, as measured by standardized-test results.

While standardized tests are an imperfect and incomplete measure of student achievement, they are the best tool available for comparing how students and schools are performing. This volume therefore relies primarily on indicators from national and international assessments of subject matter (usually language and math) knowledge. Where such data are not available, it examines intermediate learning indicators, such as dropout and completion rates.

The book is divided into three parts. Part I focuses on the central role of student learning in education. Chapter 1 examines why student learning outcomes are important. Chapter 2 analyzes the extent to which learning takes place in schools in the region. Chapter 3 discusses some of the advantages and disadvantages of generating and using information on student learning to raise the quality of education.

Part II reviews the evidence on the factors and policies that affect student learning. It first presents a conceptual framework that facilitates understanding of the factors that influence student learning. It then reviews the evidence on the impact on student learning of economic, political, and social conditions (chapter 4); student endowments and behaviors (chapter 5); school endowments and behaviors (chapter 6); and institutional factors and policies (chapter 7).

Part III focuses on quality assurance and beyond. Chapter 8 examines evidence from countries that have succeeded in achieving high levels of learning among most, if not all, students, in order to present policy options on education quality assurance. Chapter 9 summarizes the book's main messages and discusses unanswered questions.

References

Di Gropello, E. 2006. *Meeting the Challenges of Secondary Education in Latin America and East Asia. Improving Efficiency and Resource Mobilization.* Washington, DC: World Bank.

Edstats database. Available at http://www1.worldbank.org/education/edstats.

UNESCO (United Nations Educational, Scientific, and Cultural Organization), and United Nations Committee on Economic, Social and Cultural Rights. 1999. *Right to Education: Scope and Implementation.* http://portal.unesco.org/education/en/file_download.php/c144c1a8d6a75ae8dc55ac385f58102erighteduc.pdf

Part I

The Central Role of Student Learning

Public education systems have multiple objectives. They can include ensuring that all individuals have the skills to learn throughout their lives; providing individuals with the necessary skills to access good jobs; and transferring social values considered critical to fostering a national identity. To attain any of these objectives, students need to learn. Part I examines the central role of student learning in education.

1

Why Does Student Learning Matter?

What and how much students learn is a policy concern for reasons that range from ensuring human rights to improving individual life outcomes; raising competitiveness, economic growth, and development outcomes; and reducing inequality. This chapter examines how learning contributes to each of these goals.

The Opportunity to Learn as a Human Right

Education was recognized as a human right in the Universal Declaration of Human Rights in 1948, a right subsequently established as binding international law in the 1966 International Covenant on Economic, Social and Cultural Rights and the 1989 UN Convention on the Rights of the Child. Reasserted in the Jomtien and Dakar Declarations, this right has since been incorporated into most national constitutions.

Most of these agreements focus on the right to free and compulsory education. The Convention on the Rights of the Child goes beyond this guarantee to describe the purpose of education, which includes "the development of the child's personality, talents and mental and physical abilities to their fullest potential" (Article 29). The United Nations considers education a prerequisite for exercising other civil, political, economic, and social rights, viewing it as "the primary vehicle by which economically and socially marginalized adults and children can lift themselves out of poverty and obtain the means to participate fully in their communities" (UNESCO and UN Committee on Economic, Social, and Cultural Rights 1999).

Universal education is a prerequisite for reducing poverty. But ensuring a child's right to education goes beyond simply providing access to schools. It involves guaranteeing all students an equal opportunity to learn.

Effect of Learning on Individuals' Labor Market Outcomes

Education has been shown to be inextricably related to individuals' labor market outcomes. Until recently, most studies on the returns to education focused on the relation between the quantity of education and income. These studies find a strong link between years of schooling and personal economic returns. Following the work of Jacob Mincer (1974), such studies show that on average, an additional year of education is associated with about a 10 percent increase in wages and that the estimated returns to education differ substantially across countries and income levels, with returns to education higher in low-income countries (Psacharopoulos and Patrinos 2004; see also Psacharopoulos 1994; Card 1999; Harmon, Oosterbeek, and Walker 2003). Krueger and Lindahl (2001) interpret the findings from the literature as indicating that the returns to investments in education are higher for more-disadvantaged individuals, contributing to the postulate that education may be an important factor in promoting equity.

The literature has speculated on the potential causes of the salary differential between educated and uneducated workers. Methodologically, understanding this causality is tricky, because of the difficulty in attributing differences in wages to differences in years of schooling rather than to other unobservable characteristics, such as motivation or innate ability. It could be argued, for instance, that people who obtain more education are more motivated and would therefore have earned more even without the effects of schooling. Researchers have found a number of ways to address this issue (as discussed below), establishing the effects of schooling and in some cases showing larger returns to schooling than originally postulated (Hanushek and Woessmann 2007).

Do returns to education reflect the increase in skills acquired in school? Is student learning correlated with performance in the labor market? The answers to these questions are critical, because if differences in wages are partially attributable to different skill sets that can be acquired in school—especially for students from disadvantaged backgrounds—improving student learning may prove essential to increasing the income of poor households.

Several studies have shown a relation between student learning and labor market returns, moving beyond previous research that used years of education as a proxy for schooling. Information on years of schooling is a crude measure of what students actually learn, as recent results on international tests highlight. In Latin America many students who have made their way through the school system are barely literate. Because what students learn both within and across countries varies substantially, using years of education as a proxy for skills is inadequate when estimating the effects of skills on labor market outcomes.

To deal with this problem, researchers have started focusing on the relation between "cognitive skills" and income. This research uses student test scores as a proxy for cognitive skills, much in the way that this volume looks at student performance on standardized assessments as a measure of student learning.

A number of studies report a strong correlation between test scores and wages (UNESCO 2004). Three studies conducted in the United States show a 12 percent increase in earnings for every one standard deviation increase in math test scores (Mulligan 1999; Murnane and others 2000; Lazear 2003). This impact is thought to increase with work experience; that is, educational attainment may help workers get hired, but it is the recognition of their skill-related performance that may cause their earnings to rise once they are on the job (Altonji and Pierret 2001).

Using the International Adult Literacy Survey (IALS) (applied in 15 countries, including Canada, Chile, the United States, and 12 countries in Europe), Leuven, Oosterbeek, and van Ophen (2004) show that differences in wages across countries are explained in part by differences in skills, as defined by cognitive ability. These differences persist even after controlling for average years of schooling, meaning that students reap returns from what they have learned, not just from additional years of education. Green and Riddell (2003) find that skills influence differences in wages across workers in Canada.

The returns to skills are especially great in fast-growing countries with open economies that enable the absorption of highly skilled workers. Indeed, recent research indicates that increases in education quality appear to raise an individual's income level by increasing a country's rate of technological progress (Jamison, Jamison, and Hanushek 2006).

Hanushek and Woessmann (2007) show that returns to learning in developing countries—including Ghana, Kenya, Morocco, Pakistan, South Africa, and Tanzania—may be even higher than in developed countries. Using data from Chile, Sakellariou (2006) shows that a one standard deviation increase in test scores on the IALS is associated with higher earnings of 15–20 percent—a substantial difference. He finds that while skills have positive returns for people at all income levels, the returns to additional years of education after controlling for skills varies across income levels. For low-income individuals, especially those in the bottom 25 percent of the earnings distribution, cognitive ability is more important than years of education. In contrast, higher-income people, especially the richest 25 percent, benefit very little from acquiring more skills but benefit significantly from acquiring more schooling. These results suggest that returns to better skills are the key to higher earnings in Chile for the majority of the population, especially the poor.

Patrinos, Ridao-Cano, and Sakellariou (2006) estimate the returns to education for different skills groups in 16 East Asian and Latin American countries. They show that the returns to education in lower-income countries are higher for low-skilled individuals than for highly skilled individuals. This finding represents a strong argument for investing in education in developing countries in order to promote economic equality.[1]

Effect of Learning on Society as a Whole

Both educational attainment and learning are tied to a number of development outcomes beyond individual incomes. Education has been shown to affect health outcomes (especially mother and child outcomes), maternal and infant mortality, fertility, migration, age of marriage, civil participation, and violent and risky behaviors. The social returns to education thus exceed the private returns.

Researchers have established the relation between a variety of health and well-being outcomes on the one hand and both educational attainment and learning on the other. Higher reading and math scores are associated with lower fertility rates in Ghana (Oliver 1999) and South Africa (Thomas 1999). As with individual economic returns, on which test scores show an even stronger impact than mere educational attainment, cognitive skills have stronger effects on the number of children per household than do mere years of schooling. In Africa education has also been associated with lower prevalence of HIV and greater use of condoms, among both men and women (UNESCO 2004).

A mother's education also has a strong impact on her child's health. The link between a mother's years of schooling and her children's health is well established empirically (Behrman 1996; Strauss and Thomas 1998; Cutler and Lleras-Muney 2006). Although it is not clear which aspects of education account for this relation, studies from developing countries have associated it with health knowledge and math scores (Glewwe 2002).

Research also indicates that more-educated people are more likely to participate in civil life and influence decisions that may affect their lives (Dee 2003). Using U.S. data, Heckman (2006) presents new evidence on the relation between both cognitive and noncognitive skills on the one hand and the reduction in risky behavior, such as criminality, drug use, and teen pregnancy, on the other. How cognitive skills and test scores relate to all of these social outcomes is an important area for future research.

Effect of Learning on Economic Development

The relation between education and economic growth can imply even greater gains for society as a whole.[2] Although the exact relation between educational attainment and growth is unclear, the gains are thought to occur through the accumulation of benefits to individuals, the increase in rates of invention and innovation, and the introduction of new technologies and improved production methods.

Most studies examining the relation between education and economic growth have focused on educational attainment, or the quantity of education. Almost all of these studies have found a positive relation between education attainment and growth rates—a relation that is widely accepted in development circles.

It is not clear, however, whether years of education lead to economic growth or economically healthy countries tend to prioritize education. Pritchett's (2001) research on the relation between educational attainment and economic growth suggests that the quality of education—not just the quantity—may play a key role. His findings—which suggest that mere schooling without acquisition of cognitive skills does not contribute to increased economic growth, because schooling generates higher wages while not generating higher productivity or skills—are seen as a mandate to improve the quality of education.

Indeed, new research on the relation between education quality and growth suggests that years of education may be a less important contributing factor to economic growth than the quality of education, as represented by scores on international assessments (Lee and Lee 1995; Hanushek and Kimko 2000; Barro 2001). Using cross-country data from 1960 to 1990, Hanushek and Kimko (2000) examine what they call "the quality of the labor force," as measured by math and science scores. They find that a one standard deviation difference in test scores is associated with a 1 percent difference in annual growth rates of per capita GDP. As this added growth compounds, it can lead to large increases in national income (Hanushek 2004).

Using data on 15 countries in the Organisation for Economic Co-operation and Development (OECD) from the IALS survey, Coulombe and Tremblay (2006) confirm these findings. They conclude that the quality of education, as expressed by student test scores, is more important for overall economic growth than years of schooling and that returns for improving literacy skills are higher for women than for men. They argue that improving the overall literacy skills of society has a greater effect on growth than does concentrating on developing a highly educated elite.

Hanushek and Woessmann (2007) distinguish between the impact on growth of improving the average basic skills of the population and the effect of raising the skills of the most highly skilled workers in the population in developing countries. Using results from the Programme for International Student Assessment (PISA) that draws on OECD and developing-country data, they find that both basic skills and the skills of highly trained workers are important for economic development.

In examining the relation between cognitive skills and economic outcomes, it is important to remember that cognitive skills do not stem only from schooling. Some cognitive skills are innate; others are developed in the home, from family and friends, and through the media. Schooling is only one way in which people acquire knowledge—but it is the one that policy makers can most readily influence.[3]

Furthermore, the relation between education and growth can be affected by a number of factors other than schooling, including a country's economic institutions. Pritchett (2001) posits that when educated labor is devoted to unproductive or low-productivity activities, what may appear to be low returns to schooling may in fact be a low-quality environment for applying cognitive skills. Hanushek and Woessmann (2007) find that income growth rates are higher in countries that have policies that favor openness to trade and a regulatory environment that protects against expropriation. Although ample research has documented the important role that the institutional framework of the economy plays in economic growth, Hanushek and Woessmann find that the inclusion of these variables does not significantly reduce the effect of education quality (as measured by test scores) on economic growth. Indeed, it appears that education quality bolsters the impact of an open institutional environment on economic growth.

For education quality to lead to increased wages, a strong macroeconomic and labor market environment seems to be necessary. Because the impact of cognitive skills on incomes appears to take place as a result of the ability of workers to adopt new technologies, an environment that fosters innovation is probably a necessary condition for education quality to affect wages. Extensive research has documented the impact of openness of the economy on growth.[4] More recent work shows that the effects of education quality on labor market returns are stronger in countries in which trade barriers are not substantial (Jamison, Jamison, and Hanushek 2006).

Effect of Learning on Inequality

The relation between education and inequality is complex, for while education has the capacity to offset economic, social, and political inequalities, it can also perpetuate them. Sociologist Paulo Freire saw education as the center of Latin America's power struggle between rich and poor, as well as its antidote (Freire 1970). Insofar as student learning is tied to positive social and economic outcomes, providing all children with the opportunity to learn should prove especially beneficial to those most in need.

Student achievement in Latin America is below the world average, and within-country variations often fall along socioeconomic and ethnic or racial lines. Although countries in the region have expanded education, offering the majority of children equal access to learning opportunities, income inequalities, underdevelopment, and poverty persist (DeFerranti and others 2004).

Evidence is increasingly showing that education quality, not just quantity, may be responsible for perpetuating income inequalities; improvement in the quality of education of the poor could thus potentially reduce them. Consider, for example, the evidence on private returns to education. If one additional year of education is associated with about a 10 percent increase in wages, as Psacharopoulos and Patrinos (2004) have established, why has increased access to education not helped reduce economic disparities? Factors beyond educational attainment (including differences in labor market opportunities, corruption, and discrimination) may be playing a role (DeFerranti and others 2004). Latin America's large within-country disparities in learning outcomes may also imply that not all children are receiving the same quality of education. Ensuring that children learn—not just attend school—is a necessary condition for guaranteeing equality of opportunities (Reimers 2000).

Access to basic education has improved drastically over the past 20 years; ensuring that students complete their secondary education and promoting equitable access to tertiary education remain two of the region's main challenges. Uneven access to tertiary education, which yields the largest economic gains, may play a large role in perpetuating inequality.

Many of the most successful educational interventions for improving the quality of education have above-average success rates with students of low socioeconomic status. If higher test scores do indeed raise personal income, spur overall economic growth, and raise social indicators, a strong argument can be made that spending on education that targets the poor can contribute to reducing social and economic inequalities in the region.

Notes

1. To estimate the returns to skills, and not just educational attainment, Patrinos, Ridao-Cano, and Sakellariou (2006) use quantile regression, which allows the estimation of the return to education at any arbitrary quantile of the wage distribution. As they explain (p. 7), "The idea behind quantile regression is to look at the returns at one part of the distribution, say the bottom quintile, so as to facilitate a comparison with returns at another part, say the top quintile. The comparison then allows us to infer the extent to which education exacerbates or reduces underlying inequality in wages due to other, perhaps unobservable, factors."

2. For a review of the relation between cognitive skills, individual earnings, and economic growth, see Hanushek and Woessmann (2007).

3. Home and community environments may also be influenced by policy makers, albeit to a lesser extent.

4. Sachs and Warner (1997), DeFerranti and others (2003), and Perry and others (2006) provide evidence that a countries' openness to trade is positively related to macroeconomic growth.

References

Altonji, J. G., and C. R. Pierret. 2001. "Employer Learning and Statistical Discrimination." *Quarterly Journal of Economics* 116 (1): 313–50.

Barro, R. J. 2001. "Human Capital and Growth." *American Economic Review, Papers and Proceedings* 91 (2): 12–17.

Behrman, J. 1996. "The Impact of Health and Nutrition on Education." *World Bank Research Observer* 11 (1): 23–37.

Card, D. 1999. "The Causal Effect of Education on Earnings." In *Handbook of Labor Economics,* ed. Orley Ashenfelter and David Card, 1801–63. Amsterdam: North-Holland.

Coulombe, S., and J-F. Tremblay. 2006. "Literacy and Growth." *Topics in Macroeconomics* 6 (2). Berkeley Electronic Press. http://www.bepress.com/bejm/topics/vol6/iss2/art4/

Cutler, D., and A. Lleras-Muney. 2006. "Education and Health: Evaluating Theories and Evidence." NBER Working Paper 12352, National Bureau of Economic Research, Cambridge, MA.

Dee, T. 2003. "Are There Civic Returns to Education?" NBER Working Paper 9588, National Bureau of Economic Research, Cambridge, MA.

DeFerranti, D., G. E. Perry, F. H. G. Ferreira, and M. Walton. 2004. *Inequality in Latin America and the Caribbean: Breaking with History?* Washington, DC: World Bank.

DeFerranti, D., G. E. Perry, I. Gill, J. Luis Guasch, W. Maloney, C. Sánchez-Párama and N. Schady. 2003. *Closing the Gap in Education and Technology.* World Bank Latin American and Caribbean Studies, World Bank, Washington, DC.

Freire, P. 1970. *Pedagogy of the Oppressed.* New York: Continuum Publishing Co.

Glewwe, P. 2002. "Schools and Skills in Developing Countries: Education Policies and Socioeconomic Outcomes." *Journal of Economic Literature* 40 (2): 436–82.

Green, David A., and W. Craig Riddell. 2003. "Literacy and Earnings: An Investigation of the Interaction of Cognitive and Unobserved Skills in Earnings Generation." *Labour Economics* 10 (2): 165–84

Hanushek, E. A. 2004. "Some Simple Analytics of School Quality." NBER Working Paper 10229, National Bureau of Economic Research, Cambridge, MA.

Hanushek, E. A., and D. D. Kimko. 2000. "Schooling, Labor-Force Quality, and the Growth of Nations." *American Economic Review* 90 (5): 1184–1208.

Hanushek, E. A., and L. Woessmann. 2007. "The Role of Education Quality in Economic Growth." World Bank Policy Research Working Paper 4122, Washington, DC.

Harmon, C., H. Oosterbeek, and I. Walker. 2003. "The Returns to Education: Microeconomics." *Journal of Economic Surveys* 17 (2): 115–55.

Heckman, J. 2006. "The Effects of Cognitive and Noncognitive Abilities on Labor Market Outcomes and Social Behavior." NBER Working Paper 12006, National Bureau of Economic Research, Cambridge, MA.

Jamison, E. A., D. T. Jamison, and E. A. Hanushek. 2006. "The Effects of Education Quality on Income Growth and Mortality Decline." NBER Working Paper 12652, National Bureau for Economics Research, Cambridge, MA.

Krueger, A. B., and M. Lindahl. 2001. "Education for Growth: Why and For Whom?" *Journal of Economic Literature* 39 (4): 1101–36.

Lazear, E. P. 2003. "Teacher Incentives." *Swedish Economic Policy Review* 10 (3): 179–214.

Lee, D-W., and T-H. Lee. 1995. "Human Capital and Economic Growth: Tests Based on the International Evaluation of Educational Achievement." *Economics Letters* 47 (2): 219–25.

Leuven, E., H. Oosterbeek, and H. van Ophen. 2004. "Explaining International Differences in Male Skill Wage Differentials by Differences in Demand and Supply of Skill." *Economic Journal* 114 (495): 466–86.

Mincer, J. 1974. *Schooling, Experience, and Earnings*. New York: National Bureau of Economic Research Press.

Mulligan, C. B. 1999. "Galton versus the Human Capital Approach to Inheritance." *Journal of Political Economy* 107 (6): S184–S224.

Murnane, R. J., J. B. Willett, Y. Duhaldeborde, and J. H. Tyler. 2000. "How Important Are the Cognitive Skills of Teenagers in Predicting Subsequent Earnings?" *Journal of Policy Analysis and Management* 19 (4): 547–68.

Oliver, R. 1999. "Fertility and Women's Schooling in Ghana." In *The Economics of School Quality Investments in Developing Countries,* ed. P. Glewwe, 327–44. New York: St. Martin's.

Patrinos, H. A., C. Ridao-Cano, and C. Sakellariou. 2006. "Heterogeneity in Ability and Returns to Education: Multi-country Evidence from Latin America and East Asia." World Bank Policy Research Working Paper 4040, Washington DC.

Perry, G., O. S. Arias, J. H. López, W. F. Maloney, and L. Servén. 2006. *Poverty Reduction and Growth: Virtuous and Vicious Circles*. Washington, DC: World Bank.

Pritchett, L. 2001. "Where Has All the Education Gone?" *World Bank Economic Review* 15 (3): 367–91.

Psacharopoulos, G. 1994. "Returns to Investment in Education: A Global Update." *World Development* 22 (9): 1325–44.

Psacharopoulos, G., and H. A. Patrinos. 2004. "Returns to Investment in Education: A Further Update." *Education Economics* 12 (2): 111–34.

Reimers, Fernando. 2000. "Educational Opportunity and Policy in Latin America." In *Unequal Schools, Unequal Chances,* ed. Fernando Reimers. Cambridge, MA: Harvard University Press.

Sachs, J., and A. Warner. 1997. "Fundamental Sources of Long-Run Growth." *American Economic Review Papers and Proceedings* 87: 184–88.

Sakellariou, C. 2006. "Cognitive Ability and Returns to Schooling in Chile." Background paper prepared for this report. World Bank, Washington, DC.

Strauss, J., and D. Thomas. 1998. "Health, Nutrition, and Economic Development." *Journal of Economic Literature* 36 (2): 766–817.

Thomas, D. 1999. "Fertility, Education and Resources in South Africa." In *Critical Perspectives on Schooling and Fertility in the Developing World,* ed. C. H. Bledsoe, J. B. Casterline, J. A. Johnson-Kuhn, and J. G. Haaga. Washington, DC: National Academy Press.

UNESCO (United Nations Educational, Scientific. and Cultural Organization). 2004. *2005 EFA Global Monitoring Report. Education for All: The Quality Imperative*. Paris.

UNESCO, and United Nations Committee on Economic, Social and Cultural Rights. 1999. *Right to Education: Scope and Implementation*. http://portal. unesco.org/education/en/file_download.php/c144c1a8d6a75ae8dc55ac385f58 102erighteduc.pdf

2

How Much Are Students in the Region Learning?

Improving student learning is the key challenge for education in Latin America and the Caribbean, for several reasons. First, the region's countries are among the lowest performers on international assessments of student skills. Second, a high percentage of students in the region are achieving well below minimum skill levels in all subjects. Third, in many countries, differences in learning outcomes of students from different backgrounds are large.

This book uses student test scores as a measure of student learning. It examines the performance of Latin America and the Caribbean based on international assessments, such as the Programme for International Student Assessment (PISA), which tests 15-year-olds in a number of cross-curricular competencies; the Trends in International Mathematics and Science Study (TIMSS), which tests fourth and eighth graders in math and science; and the Progress in International Reading Literacy Study (PIRLS), which tests fourth graders in reading. While PISA is administered to 15-year-olds and thus focuses on secondary-school achievement, PISA scores are a good indication of the quality of educational services students received at the primary level (although the results may overstate the quality of primary education, because students reaching secondary school are likely to be higher performers). The analysis also draws on a regional assessment, the Latin American Evaluation Laboratory for the Evaluation of Education Quality (LLECE), which tests language, math, and associated skills among third and fourth graders. (Descriptions of these tests appear in appendix 1.) While only a few Latin American countries participate in these assessments, the limited results provide some insights into student learning in the region. National assessments also provide information on patterns of student learning.

Weak Average Performance on International Assessments

Educational performance indicators in the region are exceedingly low.[1] Latin American countries are among the lowest-performing countries on the PISA (table 2.1). In 2000 and 2003, the participating Latin American countries scored between one (Argentina, Chile, and Uruguay) and almost three (Peru) standard deviations below the international average. Among participating countries, Mexico, Argentina, Chile, Brazil, and Peru ranked 34th, 35th, 36th, 37th, and 41st (last), respectively, in reading in 2000 (OECD, UNESCO, and UIS 2003). Math results were similar.

Table 2.1 Mean PISA 2003 Math, Language, and Science Scores, by Country

Economy	Math	Language	Science
Hong Kong (China)	550	510	539
Finland	544	543	548
Korea, Rep. of	542	534	538
Japan	534	498	548
New Zealand	523	522	521
OECD average	500	494	500
Poland	490	497	498
Spain	485	481	487
United States	483	495	491
Portugal	466	478	468
Greece	445	472	481
Turkey	423	441	434
Uruguay	422	434	438
Thailand	417	420	429
Mexico	385	400	405
Brazil	356	403	390

Source: OECD 2003.

Educational performance in the region is low even compared with countries with similar per capita GDP (figure 2.1). With the exception of Uruguay, countries in the region perform considerably worse than expected given their average income per capita. Thus, not only is the region performing well below OECD standards, as could be expected of countries with per capita GDPs that are significantly lower, it is also falling behind countries with similar levels of GDP. Only Uruguay is on par with countries at similar income levels (Thailand and Tunisia).

Not surprisingly, given their lower per capita GDP, Latin American countries invest significantly less on education per student than other countries that participate in the PISA. Strikingly, however, mean scores in the region are below those predicted given per pupil expenditure levels (figure 2.2). In contrast, countries such as Finland, Hungary, Japan, the Republic of Korea, and Poland have mean scores that are much higher than the average scores of countries that spend the same amount per student.

Latin American countries have a disproportionately high number of students who perform poorly on the PISA. Peru, Brazil, Mexico, Argentina, Uruguay, and Chile have the highest percentages of students at Level 2, Level 1, and below Level 1 (the lowest levels) in math. (See appendixes 2 and 3 for a description of these levels.) Countries in the region also have very few students achieving at the highest levels (4 and 5), with Peru

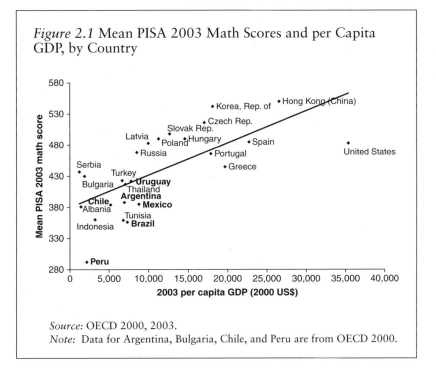

Figure 2.1 Mean PISA 2003 Math Scores and per Capita GDP, by Country

Source: OECD 2000, 2003.
Note: Data for Argentina, Bulgaria, Chile, and Peru are from OECD 2000.

Figure 2.2 Mean PISA 2000 Math Scores and per-Student Expenditure on Education, by Country

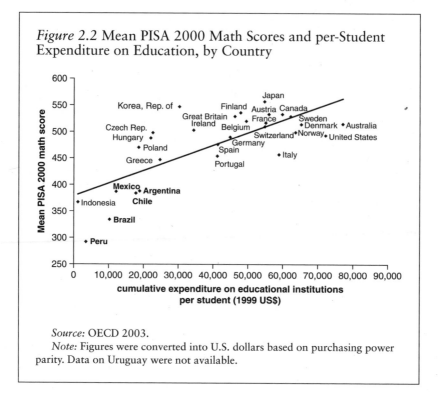

Source: OECD 2003.

Note: Figures were converted into U.S. dollars based on purchasing power parity. Data on Uruguay were not available.

and Mexico having almost no students performing at these levels. Reading results are similar, with no Latin American country exhibiting more than 1.9 percent of students at Level 5 (figure 2.3). Peru stands out as an outlier, with more than half of its students achieving below Level 1.

Comparison of the top performer on the PISA (Finland) with Chile (an average Latin American performer) highlights the striking differences between the two (figure 2.4). Finland is top heavy, with a majority of students performing at the highest achievement levels. Chile is bottom heavy, with a majority of students performing at the lowest achievement levels. The fact that 78 percent of Chilean students perform at Level 2 or below underscores the main challenges facing Latin America: reaching adequate learning levels for a large majority of youth (box 2.1).

Latin American countries performed exceptionally poorly (one to three standard deviations below the mean) on the PISA 2003 math and reading assessment. In contrast, high-performing countries performed one to 1–1.5 standard deviations above the mean (figure 2.5).[2] Low-performing countries are thus significantly farther from the mean than high-performing countries.

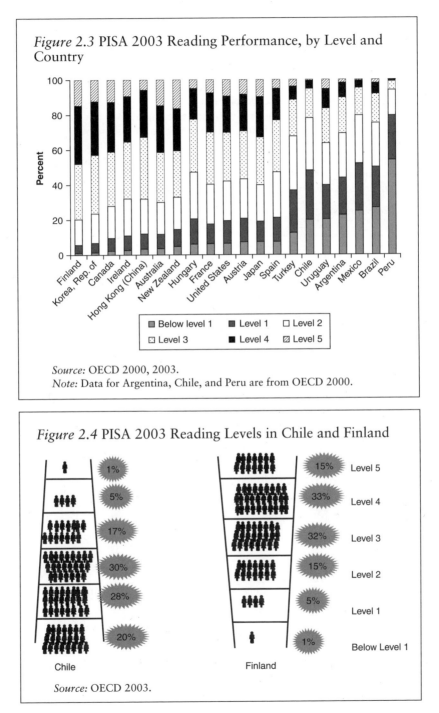

Figure 2.3 PISA 2003 Reading Performance, by Level and Country

Source: OECD 2000, 2003.
Note: Data for Argentina, Chile, and Peru are from OECD 2000.

Figure 2.4 PISA 2003 Reading Levels in Chile and Finland

Chile

Finland

Source: OECD 2003.

Box 2.1 Lagging Performance despite Universal Secondary Education in Chile

Chile is currently the only country in Latin America to have achieved universal secondary education. Despite the extraordinary increase in enrollment, however, performance on national assessments has not improved over time, and Chilean students continue to perform well below students from OECD countries on international assessments. In 2006 Chile made international headlines when more than half a million secondary students went on strike, demanding an overhaul of the education system in order to ensure education quality in all public and private schools.

Source: Authors.

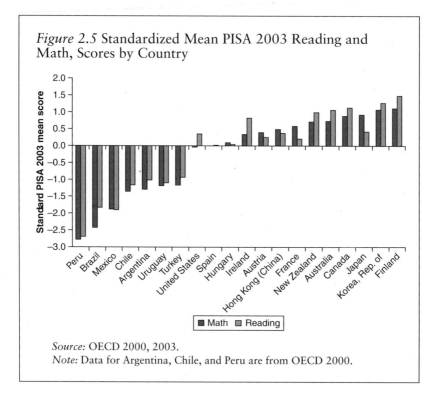

Figure 2.5 Standardized Mean PISA 2003 Reading and Math, Scores by Country

Source: OECD 2000, 2003.
Note: Data for Argentina, Chile, and Peru are from OECD 2000.

Similar trends are evident in the TIMSS results. Chile and Colombia were two of the lowest-scoring countries in math and science in 1995 and 1999 (figure 2.6). In 1999 Chilean students outperformed only students from the Philippines and Morocco—countries with per capita GDPs of less than half that of Chile—performing at the level of students from

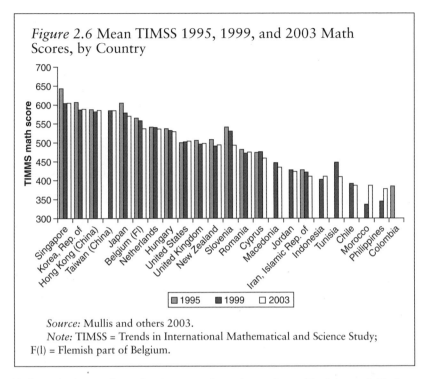

Figure 2.6 Mean TIMSS 1995, 1999, and 2003 Math Scores, by Country

Source: Mullis and others 2003.

Note: TIMSS = Trends in International Mathematical and Science Study; F(l) = Flemish part of Belgium.

Indonesia in math and science and students from Tunisia and Turkey in science (Martin and others 2000; Mullis and others 2000), countries with much lower per capita GDPs. Among countries complying with the TIMSS guidelines, Colombia ranked last in 1995. In 2003 Chilean students performed well below average in math (ranking 35th out of 40), outperforming only Botswana, Saudi Arabia, Ghana, and South Africa (Martin, Mullis, and Gonzalez 2004).[3]

PIRLS also finds substantial differences in performance across and within the 35 participating countries (IEA 2002). Students from Argentina (with an average score of 420) and Colombia (with an average score of 422) performed below the international average (500), ranking 30th and 31st out of 35 countries. Their performance was comparable to that of students from Iran, Macedonia, and Turkey.

Large Within-Country Differences in Performance

It is important to understand not only how the average student in a country does relative to the average student in other countries but also how the distributions of each country compare. In PISA 2000 and 2003 and TIMSS 1999 and 2003, only about one-tenth of total

student variation in performance was between countries: most variation occurred within countries (between education systems, schools,
or students within schools). Within-country variation in results ranges
from relatively low to very high (in Argentina, Brazil, and Uruguay)
(Casassus and others 2000; IEA 2002; Martin, Mullis, and Gonzalez
2004; Mullis and others 2004; OECD 2004; OECD, UNESCO, and UIS
2003; Woessmann 2005).

The dispersion of test scores is a good measure of inequality within
countries. Peru, Brazil, and Uruguay show the lowest average test scores
and the largest dispersion (figure 2.7). The fact that countries with high
average scores also tend to have low test-score inequality suggests that
there is no trade-off between education quality and equity.

Within-country differences in both learning outcomes and educational
attainment are often related to socioeconomic differences. In most countries in the region, the richest adults 21–30 have at least four more years
of schooling than the poorest adults the same age (table 2.2). As access
has grown, the gap has increased in most countries. Only Chile, Colombia,
and El Salvador reduced this disparity between 1995 and 2000.

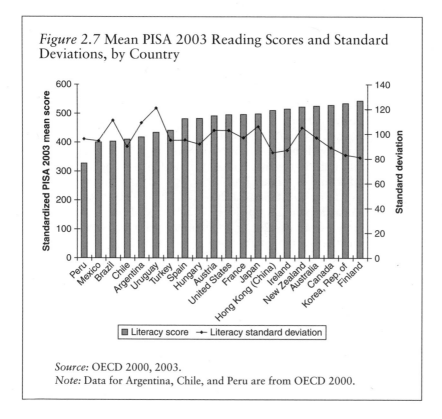

Figure 2.7 Mean PISA 2003 Reading Scores and Standard
Deviations, by Country

Source: OECD 2000, 2003.
Note: Data for Argentina, Chile, and Peru are from OECD 2000.

Table 2.2 Difference in Average Number of Years of Schooling of Richest and Poorest Quintiles of 21- to 30-Year-Olds in Selected Countries in Latin America and the Caribbean, 1990–2000

Country	1990	1995	2000
Argentina	4.6	4.6	5.1
Bolivia	—	6.7	7.4
Brazil	7.1	6.9	6.9
Chile	4.8	5.3	5.0
Colombia	—	5.6	5.0
Costa Rica	4.9	5.3	6.0
Dominican Republic	—	3.8	—
Ecuador	—	5	5.2
El Salvador	6.5	7.5	5.0
Guatemala	—	—	7.1
Honduras	5.4	4.9	6.0
Jamaica	1.1	1.2	1.2
Mexico	6.6	6	6.9
Nicaragua	—	4.9	5.2
Panama	5.5	5.5	5.9
Paraguay	—	5.4	5.9
Peru	—	4.9	5.1
Uruguay	4.1	4.5	5.0
Venezuela, R. B. de	4.0	3.9	4.6

Source: DeFerranti and others 2004.
— Not available.
Note: Data are for most recent year within two years of date indicated.

In most countries in the region, individuals from socioeconomically disadvantaged backgrounds are not spending as many years in the system as their wealthier counterparts, despite having almost equal access to primary education. Poorer students leave school earlier than socioeconomically advantaged students. While this gap in dropout rates may be attributable in part to the effects of socioeconomic status and household factors, there is evidence that the poor have access to lower-quality schools and are therefore less inclined to stay in the system.[4]

Student achievement also varies by socioeconomic background. "PISA constructed an index of socioeconomic background that includes indicators of: parental occupational status; parents' level of education converted into years of schooling; possessions related to "classical" culture; family structure; students' nationality and that of their parents; and the language spoken at home. This index was used to calculate socioeconomic quartiles for this figure." Average test scores of students in the bottom income quartiles are lower than those of students in higher income quartiles (figure 2.8).

Mean sixth-grade language test scores in Uruguay illustrate the effect of socioeconomic background on performance. Despite rising test scores

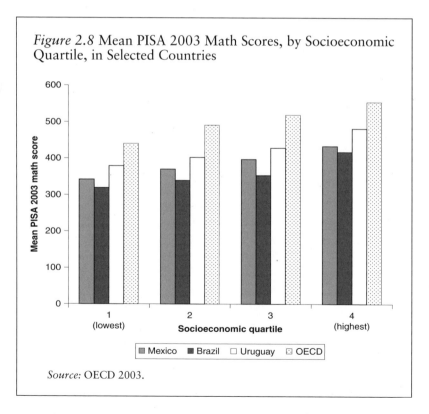

Figure 2.8 Mean PISA 2003 Math Scores, by Socioeconomic Quartile, in Selected Countries

Source: OECD 2003.

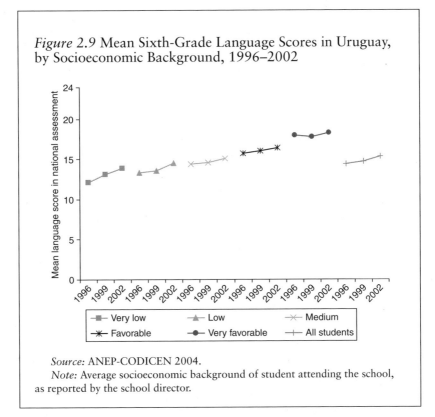

Figure 2.9 Mean Sixth-Grade Language Scores in Uruguay, by Socioeconomic Background, 1996–2002

Source: ANEP-CODICEN 2004.
Note: Average socioeconomic background of student attending the school, as reported by the school director.

over time among all socioeconomic groups and a reduction in the gap in learning between students of high- and low-income backgrounds, the gap in achievement between children from advantaged and disadvantaged socioeconomic backgrounds persists (figure 2.9). Only 39 percent of secondary students who attended schools in low socioeconomic areas obtained high scores on the math test in 1999, whole 85 percent of those in high socioeconomic areas did so. On the language test, the corresponding figures were 46 and 87 percent (ANEP/MEMFOD 2003). In 2002, 88 percent of sixth graders from "favorable" backgrounds but just 55 percent of sixth graders from "very unfavorable" backgrounds passed the language test. On the math test, the corresponding figures were 72 percent and 36 percent (ANEP-CODICEN 2002). The results of the 2005 assessments suggest stagnating test averages, especially among children from disadvantaged backgrounds.[5]

Ethnic and racial inequalities also exist, especially in ethnically diverse countries. Indigenous students are less likely than their nonindigenous classmates to finish primary school. In Bolivia, a country with an indigenous majority that has made great strides in primary access, 38 percent of indigenous students and 11 percent of nonindigenous students 15–19 did not complete primary school in 2002. In Guatemala, another country with a high percentage of indigenous students, more than half of indigenous students and 32 percent of nonindigenous failed to complete primary school. In Panama 45 percent of indigenous and just 6 percent of nonindigenous students did not complete primary school (ECLAC 2005).

Indigenous students and students of African descent also achieve at lower levels than their white classmates, even after controlling for income. This difference is particularly large in Guatemala (figure 2.10) (see McEwan 2004; Hernandez-Zavala and others 2006; McEwan and Trowbridge 2007).

In Brazil, home to Latin America's highest percentage of people of African descent, large disparities are evident in the performance of students who self-identify as black, mixed, or white. Test scores of nonwhite students are considerably lower than those of white students, with black students performing worse than students of mixed race (figure 2.11). Socioeconomic status and race are closely tied in Brazil, and between a third and a half of variation in these results are attributable to socioeconomic and school conditions. Even when controlling for these two factors, however, nonwhite students still score 0.15–0.25 standard deviations lower than white students (DeFerranti and others 2003).

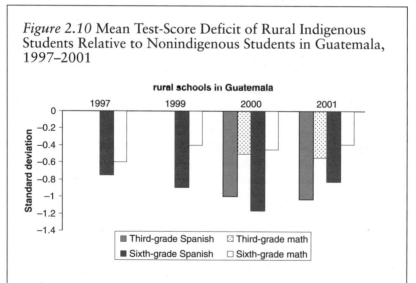

Figure 2.10 Mean Test-Score Deficit of Rural Indigenous Students Relative to Nonindigenous Students in Guatemala, 1997–2001

Source: McEwan and Trowbridge 2007.
Note: Figures are based on performance on Guatemala's Programa Nacional de Evaluación del Rendimiento Escolar (PRONERE), unadjusted for income. All differences shown are statistically significant.

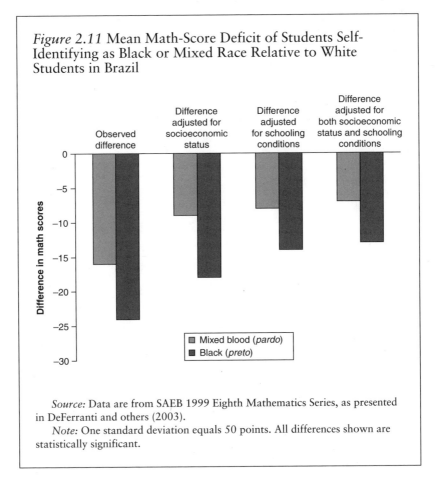

Figure 2.11 Mean Math-Score Deficit of Students Self-Identifying as Black or Mixed Race Relative to White Students in Brazil

Source: Data are from SAEB 1999 Eighth Mathematics Series, as presented in DeFerranti and others (2003).
Note: One standard deviation equals 50 points. All differences shown are statistically significant.

Weak Performance by Students from Favorable Socioeconomic and Racial Backgrounds

Even students from "favorable" socioeconomic backgrounds are achieving well below students from OECD countries on all international assessments of student achievement, dispelling the myth that the region's most privileged students receive a high-quality education. Average test scores of students from the most-advantaged socioeconomic backgrounds in Brazil and Mexico are lower than those of disadvantaged students in OECD countries (see figure 2.8). Fifteen-year-olds from the wealthiest quartile in Uruguay are the only group in the region to outperform the poorest quartile of students from OECD countries.

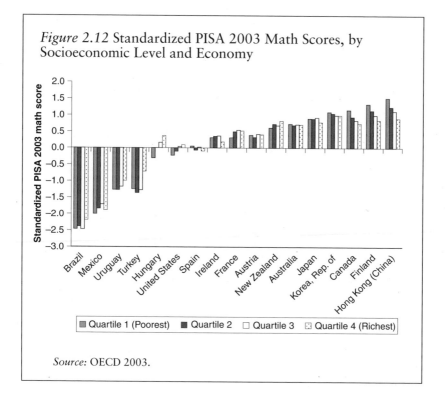

Figure 2.12 Standardized PISA 2003 Math Scores, by Socioeconomic Level and Economy

Source: OECD 2003.

Across socioeconomic status groups, students in the region have below-average PISA 2003 scores (figure 2.12).[6] The average score of a poor child in Brazil is almost 2.5 standard deviations below the international mean, while the average score of a poor child in the Republic of Korea is 1.5 standard deviations above the mean. A rich child in Brazil performs about four standard deviations below a rich child in Hong Kong (China), underscoring the fact that while rich children outperform poor children in the region, they do so at levels that are almost consistently substandard.

Notes

1. Many poor countries do not participate in international education assessments, because the financial and political costs of doing so are substantial. The results can nevertheless help evaluate how some countries in the region fare compared with similar or higher-income OECD countries. Given that the Latin American countries participating in international assessments include the region's most economically developed nations, the results likely overstate performance by the region as a whole.

2. Argentina, Chile, and Peru participated in the 2000 assessment but not in the 2003 assessment, but these two tests are directly comparable (OECD 2004).

3. Chile's performance in science was slightly higher (average score of 413), although even there it ranked 33rd out of 40, performing at the level of the Arab Republic of Egypt and Indonesia and outperforming only Morocco, Saudi Arabia, and South Africa (Martin, Mullis, and Gonzalez 2004).

4. Hanushek, Lavy, and Hitomi (2006) use panel data on primary-school students in the Arab Republic of Egypt to examine the relation between school quality and dropout rates. They show that holding student ability and achievement constant, a student is less likely to remain in a school of low quality than a school of high quality.

5. Although the 2005 assessments employed a different methodology (item response theory), the test designs ensure comparability of results across years.

6. The PISA measures socioeconomic status as a composite of maternal education, occupation, and an index of home possessions and family wealth.

References

ANEP-CODICEN (Administración Nacional de la Educación Pública y Consejo Directivo Central). 2002. *Los niveles de desempeño al inicio de la educación primaria. Primer informe.* Montevideo.

———. 2004. *Panorama de la educación en Uruguay: Una década de transformaciones 2004.* Programa de Evaluación de la Gestión Educativa, Gerencia de Investigación y Evaluación, Gerencia General de Planeamiento y Gestión Educativa, Montevideo.

ANEP/MEMFOD (Administración Nacional de la Educación Pública y Programa de Modernización de la Educación Media y Formación Docente). 2003. *Informe anual de actividades y resultados: Año 2003.* Montevideo.

Casassus, J., S. Cusato, J. E. Froemel, and J. C. Palafox. 2000. *First International Comparative Study of Language, Mathematics, and Associated Factors for Students in the Third and Fourth Years of Primary School. Second Report.* LLECE, UNESCO–SANTIAGO, Santiago.

DeFerranti, D., G. E. Perry, I. Gill, J. L, Guasch, W. F. Maloney, C. Sánchez-Páramo, and N. Schady. 2003. *Closing the Gap in Education and the Technology.* Washington, DC: World Bank.

DeFerranti, D., G. E. Perry, F. H. G. Ferreira, and M. Walton. 2004. *Inequality in Latin America and the Caribbean: Breaking with History?* Washington, DC: World Bank.

ECLAC (Economic Commission for Latin America and the Caribbean). 2005. *The Millennium Development Goals: A Latin American and Caribbean Perspective.* Santiago: United Nations.

Hanushek, E. A., V. Lavy, and K. Hitomi. 2006. "Do Students Care about School Quality? Determinants of Dropout Behavior in Developing Countries." NBER Working Paper 12737, National Bureau of Economic Research, Cambridge, MA.

Hernandez-Zavala, M., H. Patrinos, C. Sakellariou, and J. Shapiro. 2006. "Quality of Schooling and Quality of Schools for Indigenous Students in Guatemala, Mexico, and Peru." World Bank Policy Research Working Paper 3982, Washington, DC.

IEA (International Association for the Evaluation of Educational Achievement). 2002. *PIRLS 2001 International Report.* Chestnut Hill, MA.

Martin, M. O., I. V. S. Mullis, and E. J. Gonzalez. 2004. "Home Environments Fostering Children's Reading Literacy: Results from the PIRLS 2001 Study of Reading Literacy Achievement in Primary Schools in 35 Countries." Paper pre-.sented at the First International Association for the Evaluation of Educational Achievement International Research Conference, Lefkosia, Cyprus.

Martin, M. O., I. V. S. Mullis, E. J. Gonzalez, K. D. Gregory, T. A. Smith, and S. J. Chrostowski. 2000. *TIMSS 1999 International Science Report.* Chestnut Hill, MA: Boston College.

McEwan, P. 2004. "The Indigenous Test Score Gap in Bolivia and Chile." *Economic Development and Cultural Change* 53: 157–90.

McEwan, P. J., and M. Trowbridge. 2007. "The Achievement of Indigenous Students in Guatemalan Primary Schools." *International Journal of Educational Development* 27: 61–76.

Mullis, I. V. S., M. O. Martin, E. J. Gonzalez, K. D. Gregory, R. A. Garden, K. M. O'Connor, et al. 2000. *TIMSS 1999 International Mathematics Report.* Chestnut Hill, MA: Boston College.

Mullis, I. V. S., M. O. Martin, E. J. Gonzalez, and A. M. Kennedy. 2003. *PIRLS 2001 International Report: IEA's Study of Reading Literacy Achievement in Primary Schools.* Chestnut Hill, MA: Boston College.

Mullis, I. V. S., M. O. Martin, E. J. Gonzalez, and S. J. Chrostowski. 2004. *Findings from IEA'S Trends in International Mathematics and Science Study at the Fourth and Eighth Grades.* Chestnut Hill, MA: TIMSS & PIRLS International Study Center, Boston College.

OECD (Organisation for Economic Co-operation and Development). 2000. Programme for International Student Assessment (PISA) database. http://www.pisa.oecd.org/

———. 2003. Programme for International Student Assessment (PISA) database. http://www.pisa.oecd.org

———. 2004. *Learning for Tomorrow's World: First Results from PISA 2003.* Paris: OECD.

OECD, UNESCO (United Nations Educational, Scientific, and Cultural Organization), and IIS (Institute for Statistics). 2003. *Literacy Skills for the World of Tomorrow: Further Results from PISA 2000: Publications 2000.* Paris: OECD/UNESCO–IIS.

Woessmann, Ludger. 2005. "Families, Schools, and Primary-School Learning: Evidence for Argentina and Colombia in an International Perspective." Policy Research Paper 3537, World Bank, Washington, DC.

3

Benefits and Challenges of Measuring Student Learning

As standardized tests have become the prevailing measure of student learning and school quality, they have become a controversial element of the policy debate. Use of such tests—by policy makers, researchers, or teachers—to measure what students know has its benefits and pitfalls.

Before the advantages and disadvantages of standardized assessments can be weighted, it is important to understand what assessment systems are meant to accomplish. Among international assessments, PISA focuses on reasoning skills, while TIMSS emphasizes subject matter knowledge. The OECD, which administers PISA, describes the knowledge and skills it tests as "defined not primarily in terms of a common denominator of national school curricula, but in terms of what skills are deemed to be essential for future life" (OECD 2003: 14). TIMSS measures learning differently, focusing on content standards based on the specific objectives embodied in the curricula of a number of countries.

Assessment results are made available to a variety of stakeholders, including school administrators, education policy makers, students, and parents. The usefulness of the information depends, of course, on the quality of the information. If, for example, a test is applied to all students in the country; the data are collected and analyzed; and school, regional, and national reports are distributed to all stakeholders in the educational system (parents, school staff, and policy makers), the information should help improve learning outcomes through a variety of channels. In contrast, if only a small, unrepresentative sample of children is tested and only national reports are published, the channels of transmission may be limited, reducing the usefulness of the testing information.

The use of standardized assessments to measure student learning presents some disadvantages. Standardized tests measure only a small part of what students learn in school, usually assess only mathematics, language, and science, excluding other subject areas. Nonacademic knowledge and behaviors, such as life skills, ethical and moral values, artistic and creative abilities, and a sense of civic or social responsibility, are harder to quantify and therefore often lie outside the scope of standardized testing. Even "objective" knowledge, such as facts and basic reasoning skills, can vary across cultural or values systems and can therefore be difficult to assess. Furthermore, tests can be "noisy," limiting their institutional utility unless such "noise" is accounted for (Kane and Staiger 2001, 2002; Koretz 2002; Chay, McEwan, and Urquiola 2005; Mizala, Romaguera, and Urquiola 2006; Urquiola and Vegas 2006).[1] Problems arise when tests are used as the only instrument holding teachers and schools accountable, especially when results or methodology may be flawed.

Testing methodologies have improved over time, and they continue to do so. Despite their flaws, they remain the best indicator available of performance. They provide a quantitative measure of certain skills and knowledge that can be tracked and compared, allowing policy makers to assess their success in meeting learning goals across years and schools. They can provide information to teachers and schools about their own strengths and weaknesses and alert them to areas that need improvement. They can provide information to parents and students about areas in which students are excelling or struggling.

Translating Information on Student Performance into Better Learning Outcomes

Information can contribute to improved learning through three channels (figure 3.1). The first is by providing information to schools and teachers to improve classroom instruction. To the extent that standardized tests measure learning and results are available at the school level, administrators and

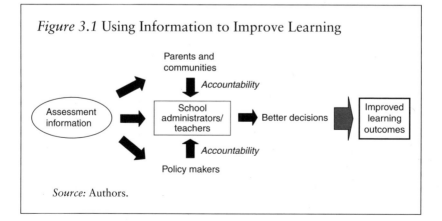

Figure 3.1 Using Information to Improve Learning

Parents and communities

Accountability

Assessment information

School administrators/ teachers

Better decisions

Improved learning outcomes

Accountability

Policy makers

Source: Authors.

teachers can benefit from a test that allows them to compare their results with those of other schools or relative to their own institution in years past. Test results can help identify the subjects in which a school is lagging or areas in which certain students are having trouble. This information allows school administrators and teachers to make decisions that may translate into better learning outcomes.

The second channel provides policy makers with information on the status of the educational system and student learning. Analysis of trends and breakdowns of results may allow them to identify actions that can improve the educational system. Results can be used to identify schools that may need technical assistance, supplemental services, or extra resources. Such use of assessments can also create a positive feedback loop, in which the assessment information leads to improvements and is therefore viewed positively by both policy makers and school-level actors. Results are often used in conjunction with a system of sanctions for low-performing schools or, as is more often the case, rewards for high-performing schools.

The third channel by which assessment information can translate into better learning outcomes is by providing information to parents and communities, which can use the information to hold schools accountable. This direct relation between families and schools is what the 2004 *World Development Report* (World Bank 2003) refers to as the "short route" to accountability. The positive effects of this type of parental and community participation in education have been well documented. El Salvador's Programa de Educación de la Comunidad (EDUCO) used community monitoring to help reduce teacher and student absenteeism through this "short route." Schools participating in the Proyecto Hondureño de Educación Comunitaria (PROHECO) in Honduras also reported improved educational indicators. Parents are often best able to provide teachers with information about their children, and the proximity of communities to schools and teachers allows them to better monitor what is happening in the classroom (World Bank 2003). Providing parents with access to information from assessments adds a new dimension to participation, in that parents have a way to monitor educational results and demand change when they are poor. This type of influence of educational institutions from within is what Albert Hirschman (1970) refers to as "voice"—parents expressing dissatisfaction and demanding change.

A second way in which this short route to accountability operates is through what Hirschman calls "exit." This is the basic premise of school choice: parents transfer their children to other schools when they are dissatisfied, thereby exerting pressure on poorly managed schools to improve. In practice, there are few documented cases of parents successfully using information to pressure education systems or schools to improve their services by exiting schools with which they are unhappy (or choosing better alternatives). Moreover, many students, especially in rural areas, do not have the option of changing to another school.

Elacqua and Fabrega (2004) show how difficult it is in practice to create the short route of accountability or an exit strategy. They examine how parents used (or did not use) information during 23 years of school choice in Chile. They conclude that in general, parents access few sources of information, rely on sources of poor quality, and are rarely well informed about the schools they choose. Furthermore, parents tend to base their decisions on practical reasons—such as proximity of a school to home or work, costs, or security—rather than on information on a school's performance. When parents are not savvy consumers of information, they have little motivation to pressure schools to improve (Jimenez and Sawada 1999, King and Ozler 2000, Di Gropello and Marshall 2005, Sawada and Ragatz 2005).

It is unclear what types of mechanisms would encourage parents to take a more active role in advocating for better education for their children. Research shows that institutionalizing parental participation at the school level can contribute to improving various aspects of school management.

In addition to these three channels for improving student learning is the so-called "long route" to accountability—the traditional route, in which the public pressures policy makers to improve educational services. These demands may influence the decision making of both policy makers and school administrators, which may improve learning outcomes. Better information from national assessments may help policy making at different levels and increase accountability in the educational system, so that better decisions are carried out in the educational system. However, the effectiveness of these systems depends greatly upon the quality of the data and the analysis and distribution of results.

Challenges of Using Assessment Information to Raise Student Learning Outcomes

In theory, the measurement of student learning and the dissemination of information rests on a systematic framework within which information flows freely; citizens have a voice; and policy makers, school administrators, and teachers are responsible and responsive. The reality, however, is much more complex, for a number of reasons. First, politics—both national and local—can intervene. Under clientelistic systems of patronage, which describe the distribution of selective benefits to individuals or clearly defined groups in exchange for political support—accountability mechanisms can backfire (Hopkin 2006). In addition, the voices of the poor and disenfranchised are rarely heard as loudly as those of the rich and influential. The instruments of assessment themselves can vary in their ability to accurately measure what students really know, how schools are improving (or deteriorating), or how schools compare with one another, especially when the populations they serve are diverse.

The presence of "noise" in school-level test data can have serious policy consequences when a single year of test scores is used to rank schools. Sources of error include the level of distraction of students on a given testing day (a dog barking, a disruptive student); the weather on the day the assessment is given (a particularly hot or rainy day); the sample of items on the test; or changes in curricula and instruction that affect students' understanding of the test questions. In order to make inferences about year-to-year changes in successive cohorts of students, those changes cannot, without additional information, be validly attributed solely to instructional or other social environmental factors. Furthermore, because mean scores are often the primary indices for making comparisons, having just a few students achieve at the high or low end of the distribution can affect mean scores of small schools significantly.

Kane and Staiger (2002), who have extensively researched accountability measures and testing noise in the United States, caution policy makers of the possible pitfalls of using test scores for school accountability systems. They present three cases of accountability systems run awry as a result of a reliance on unreliable measures. In one example, a local newspaper published a story about an area school with the most-improved test scores, outlining the changes the school had undertaken to achieve such results. In fact, only 22 students at the school took the test. With such a small sample, it is only natural for test scores to fluctuate dramatically. The authors warn that as a result of such fluctuations, it is common for "two steps forward" to be followed by "one step back." They recommend that policy makers look at trends over several years as one way of avoiding such misattribution.

In Chile a reexamination of the P-900 compensatory school program shows how testing noise and the methodology for choosing recipient schools based on test-score cutoffs may have led to an overestimation of program impact. The P-900 program treated schools with the lowest scores, providing them with infrastructure improvements, materials, teacher training, and after-school tutoring for low-performing students. When, after program implementation, average test scores rose among these treatment schools, evaluators naturally attributed this improvement to the program, lauding its success.

A more recent evaluation asserts that the rise in test scores may have had more to do with the natural tendency of reversion to the mean than the effects of the P-900 program. Chay, McEwan, and Urquiola (2005) argue that simply comparing test scores from year to year may paint an inaccurate picture of what is really happening in a single school, because schools with especially poor results in one year would be expected to improve the following year even without an intervention, as a result of reversion to the mean, as measurement error is usually transitory and not correlated over time. To avoid mistakenly attributing changes to program effects, the authors recommend using a regression-discontinuity design to control for reversion to the mean. Using this methodology, they find the P-900 program produced results only after the first of operation and that the improvements were minor.[2]

Mizala, Romaguera, and Urquiola (2006) build on this research, documenting the challenges of using assessment-based evaluations of schools to provide information for a school-choice program. They show that in Chile the rankings of schools based on achievement and socioeconomic status are almost identical, implying that schools that perform better do so because they are enrolling students from higher socioeconomic backgrounds. Rewarding or sanctioning schools based on test-score cutoffs could thus disproportionately punish schools that enroll poor students.

Urquiola and Vegas (2006) explore whether test-score noise, which creates problems in establishing accountability mechanisms at the school level, also affects evaluation of educational performance at the district level. Using 1990–2002 test-score data from Chile, they show that small municipalities are more likely to experience large changes in test scores from one year to the next. Ranking municipalities by their mean test scores in a given period can thus be similar to assigning rankings by lottery.

Given this evidence, assessment systems need to be developed—and used—with care. As Kane and Staiger note, "The problem resides not with the measures themselves, but with the way that these measures are often used" (2002: 100). Student assessment information can be useful. It needs to be exercised with care, however, in comparing performance across schools or districts.

One policy option for improving the usefulness of student assessments is to collect information on student performance for a cohort of students across time. Known as "value-added assessment," this methodology allows educators and policy makers to track student achievement over time and to assess student achievement based on the rate of progress rather than on a single, absolute standard (Sanders 2001).[3]

Another policy implication of this research is the need to continue improving methodologies for distinguishing the true measures of student learning from noise. Psychometricians, researchers, and other experts offer a variety of sophisticated methodologies to account for measurement error and noise and to more effectively use test instruments to make inferences about the effectiveness of educational environments.

How Is Performance Assessed?

Since the 1990s, virtually all countries in the region have experimented with national standardized tests—with varying success (table 3.1). In some cases, such as Ecuador's Sistema Nacional de Medición de Logros Académicos (APRENDO) or Guatemala's Programa Nacional de Evaluación del Rendimiento Escolar (PRONERE), assessment programs were funded by international organizations, then abandoned soon after external funding ended. In other countries, such as Chile, policy makers have placed

Table 3.1 National Assessment Systems in Latin American Countries

Country	Name of assessment	Name of assessment	Years	Frequency	Grades tested	Census or samples	Based on curriculum	High stakes[a]
Argentina	Yes	Operativo Nacional de Evaluación (ONE)	1993–2005	Annually, except 2001	3, 6, 7, 12	Census and samples	Yes	No
Bolivia	No	Sistema de Medición de la Calidad (SIMECAL)	1996–2000	Annually, for varying grades[b]	First two assessments: 3, 6, 8 Third assessment: 12 for all students, 3 for bilingual students	Census and samples	Yes	Yes
Brazil	Yes	Sistema de Avaliação da Educação Básica (SAEB)	Since 1990	Every other year	4, 8, 11	Sample	Yes	No
		Exame Nacional do Ensino Médio (ENEM)	Since 1998	Annually	High school exit	Universal[c] (Voluntary)	Yes	No
		Prova Brasil	Since 2005	Every three years	4, 8	Census	No	No

(continued)

Table 3.1 National Assessment Systems in Latin American Countries *(continued)*

Country	Name of assessment	Name of assessment	Years	Frequency	Grades tested	Census or samples	Based on curriculum	High stakes
Chile	Yes	Sistema de Medición de la Calidad Educación (SIMCE)	Since 1988	Annually	4, 8, 10 in different years	Census and samples	Yes	Yes
Colombia	Yes	Sistema de Evaluación de la Calidad de la Educación (SABER)	1991, 1992, 1997, 1998, 2002, 2003	Some years	5, 9 in all regions; 3, 5, 7, 9 in some regions	Samples until 1999, census 2002–03	Since 1999	No
		Instituto Colombiano para el Fomento de la Educación Superior (ICFES)	Since 1980	Annually	11, high school exit	Universal[c] (voluntary)	Yes	Yes
		Exámenes de Calidad de la Educación Superior (ECAES)	Since 2003	Annually	College exit (degree specific)	Universal[c]	Yes	Yes

(continued)

Table 3.1 National Assessment Systems in Latin American Countries *(continued)*

Country	Name of assessment	Name of assessment	Years	Frequency	Grades tested	Census or samples	Based on curriculum	High stakes[a]
Costa Rica	Yes	Pruebas Nacionales	1986, 1987, 1989, 1990 1996, 1997	Some years	6, 9, *bachillerato* (high school)	Sample	Yes	No
			Since 1988	Annual	High school exit	Census	Yes	Yes
Cuba	Yes	Sistema de Evaluación de la Calidad de la Educación (SECE)	1996, 1998 2000, 2002	Every second year	6, 9, 12	Census (schools), sample of students	Yes	No
Dominican Republic	Yes	Pruebas Nacionales	Since 1991	Annually	8, 12, and basic adult education	Census	Yes	Yes
Ecuador	No	APRENDO	1996, 1997	Annually	3, 7, 10	Sample	No	No
El Salvador	Yes	Sistema Nacional de Evaluación de los Aprendizajes (SINEA)	Since 2001	Every second year	3, 6, 9	Sample	Yes	No
		Strengthening Achievement in Basic Education (SABE)	1993–98	Annually	K, 3, 4, 5, 6, 9 in different years	Sample	Yes	No

(continued)

Table 3.1 National Assessment Systems in Latin American Countries *(continued)*

Country	Name of assessment	Name of assessment	Years	Frequency	Grades tested	Census or samples	Based on curriculum	High stakes[a]
		Prueba de Aprendizaje para Egresados de Educación Media (PAES)	1997	Annually	10, 12	Census	Yes	Yes
Guatemala	Yes[d]	Programa Nacional de Evaluación del Rendimiento Escolar (PRONERE)	1998–2001	Annually	3, 6	Sample	No	No
			Since 2004	Annually	1, 3	Sample	No	No
			Since 2005	Annually	9	Census[e]	No	No
Honduras	Yes	Unidad Externa de Medición de la Calidad de la Educación (UMCE)	1997, 2000, 2004	Some years	3, 6	Sample	No	No
Mexico	Yes	Estándares Nacionales	1997–2004	Annually	2, 3, 4, 5, 6, 7, 8, 9 in different years	Sample	Yes	No

(continued)

Table 3.1 National Assessment Systems in Latin American Countries (continued)

Country	Name of assessment	Name of assessment	Years	Frequency	Grades tested	Census or samples	Based on curriculum	High stakes[a]
		Examen de la Calidad y el Logro Educativos (EXCALE)	2005	Annually	3, 5, 6, 7, 8, 9 in different years	Sample	Yes	No
		Evaluación Nacional del Logro Académico en Centros Escolares (ENLACE)	Since 2006	Annually	3, 4, 5, 6, 9	Census	Yes	No[f]
Nicaragua	Yes	Sistema Nacional de Evaluación (SNE)	1996–97, 2002, 2006	Some years	3, 6	Sample	Yes	No
Panama	Yes	Sistema Nacional de Evaluación de la Calidad Educativa (SINECE)	Since 1996	Every second year	3, 6, 9, 12	Sample	Yes	No

(continued)

Table 3.1 National Assessment Systems in Latin American Countries *(continued)*

Country	Name of assessment	Name of assessment	Years	Frequency	Grades tested	Census or samples	Based on curriculum	High stakes[a]
Paraguay	Yes	Sistema Nacional de Evaluación del Proceso Educativo (SNEPE)	Since 1996	Annually	3, 6, 9, 12 in different years	Sample (census in 2001 in Escuela Viva)	Since 2006	No
Peru	Yes	Evaluación Nacional (initially named CRECER)	1996, 1998, 2001, 2004	Every second or third year	4, 6, 11	Sample	No	No
		Second-grade reading assessment	Since 2006	Pilot	2	Census[g]	No	No
Uruguay	Yes	Programa de Evaluación de Aprendizajes	Since 1996	Every third year	6	Sample plus voluntary option for other schools	Yes	No

(continued)

Table 3.1 National Assessment Systems in Latin American Countries *(continued)*

Country	Name of assessment	Name of assessment	Years	Frequency	Grades tested	Census or samples	Based on curriculum	High stakes[a]
Venezuela, R. B. de	No	Sistema Nacional de Medición y Evaluación del Aprendizaje (SINEA)	1998	Once	6	Sample	Yes	No

Source: Ferrer 2006 and questionnaires completed by evaluation offices in each country.

a. "High stakes" means that test results have direct implications for students for passing a grade level, being admitted to university, or being eligible for other benefits.

b. Although SIMECAL was originally meant to be administered annually, limited funding has meant that testing has been conducted sporadically, each time at different grade levels.

c. "Universal" refers to exit exams that test all school leavers but not all students in the system.

d. Primary school assessments were carried out by MINEDUC/PRONERE in 1998–2001 and by USAID/MINEDUC/PRONERE in 2004. Secondary assessments were carried out by MINEDUC/USAC.

e. The 2005 application was intended to be a census, but it ended up being a sample, although not necessarily a representative one, as a result of the nonparticipation of a number of schools.

f. ENLACE is low stakes for students but high stakes for teachers, as it replaced the achievement tests that were part of the Carrera Magesterial.

g. The second-grade reading assessment was piloted in 2006. Although meant to be a census, it reached only about half of the population.

great emphasis on implementing and publicizing national assessments, which have become influential in policy making.

Most countries in Latin America and the Caribbean administer standardized tests. Some countries administer the tests infrequently, however, or have modified or discontinued the tests. República Bolivariana de Venezuela applied its standardized test only once, in 1998, as a pilot. In contrast, Chile has applied its national assessment system, the *Sistema de Medición de la Calidad Educativa* (SIMCE), annually since 1988. Other countries fall between these two extremes, applying tests every second year (Brazil and Peru) or every third year (Uruguay).

An important factor in the testing practices that determines the level of detail of statistical reports is whether only a sample of students or all students are tested. Most countries choose a sample of students to be nationally or, at most, regionally representative of the student population. Selecting a sample of students to be tested is less expensive than testing all students, but it limits the possibility of producing school-level reports of test results, thus limiting the use of the assessments for improving instructional practices in all schools.

Some countries apply testing at different grades in different years, usually covering both primary and secondary school. Other countries, such as Colombia or Costa Rica, focus their efforts on key years, such as the final years of primary, middle, or secondary school. Virtually all countries that test elementary or secondary school students test mathematics and language.

A few Latin American countries have taken part in international assessments (described in chapter 2). Such assessments allow for comparison of achievement across countries and monitoring of achievement at the national and international levels. Countries in the region perform poorly relative to East Asian and OECD countries on these assessments.

International assessments apply context questionnaires, collecting information on families, schools, and resources available to children. PIRLS administers a lengthy set of questionnaires to parents, school administrators, teachers, and students. TIMSS administers questionnaires to teachers, principals, and students but not to parents. PISA surveys neither teachers nor parents. Because it is administered to older students, however, some of the information that other assessments collect through questionnaires to parents and guardians is collected from students themselves. (Appendix 1 provides a detailed description of each international assessment.)

Brazil and Mexico are the only countries in the region that participated in two consecutive applications of any of these tests. Brazil showed a significant improvement in performance between PISA 2000 and PISA 2003; performance in Mexico declined. The decline in Mexico may have been partially caused by the strong emphasis on increasing secondary access (OECD 2004).

Measuring Institutional Capacity for
Using Assessment Information

The use of the information collected by student assessments varies greatly across countries in the region (box 3.1). Some countries limit the circulation of results to policy makers; others write school-specific reports and organize workshops to counsel schools on how to take advantage of the information (table 3.2).

Most Latin American countries established evaluation offices in the 1980s, but there is great variation across countries in their use of student assessment information. Ravela (2002, 2003); Ferrer (2006); and Galiani and Corrales (2006) evaluate the institutional capacity of evaluation offices throughout the region.

Most countries do not provide sufficient information to interpret student test scores, such as methodologies employed, information on response rates, estimates of margins of error, or information on students' socioeconomic status (Ravela 2002, 2003). Moreover, few countries engage in systematic efforts to reach stakeholders, such as policy makers, parents, and education activists.

Box 3.1 Using Standardized Assessments to Increase School Accountability in Chile and Uruguay

Chile and Uruguay provide examples of two different approaches to standardized assessments. Basic-education students in Chile have been assessed regularly since 1988. Student assessment information is publicized, with the goal of informing parents of the quality of public and private schools. Since 1980 Chile has provided a nationwide per student subsidy, which channels resources to schools based on student attendance. Information on school quality is provided regularly to parents, in order to inform their school choices. Mean test scores at the school level have been made public since 1988, and schools are often ranked based on their mean test scores.

Basic-education students in Uruguay have been assessed every three years since 1996. Detailed information on the performance of each classroom and school, in both absolute terms and relative to similar schools, is provided to teachers and principals in booklets, which also include information on improving performance in areas in which test scores are low. School-level information is not made public, although nationwide trends are published. In contrast to Chile, assessment information is collected and analyzed with the goal of informing education providers so that they can improve their teaching practices.

Source: Authors.

Table 3.2 Reporting Practices in Latin America and the Caribbean, by Country

Country	National assessment	Name	Distribution of results[a]	Products	Lowest level of analysis	Direct implications?[b]
Argentina	Yes	Operativo Nacional de Evaluación (ONE)	Internal	National remedial booklets; datasets released since 2000	Province	No
Bolivia	Yes	Sistema de Medición de la Calidad (SIMECAL)	Both	External: Basic statistics Internal: School analysis	Internal: Schools External: Department	No
Brazil	Yes	Sistema de Avaliação da Educação Básica (SAEB)	Mostly internal	Ministerial documents	Municipality	Unclear
		Exame Nacional do Ensino Médio (ENEM)	External	Student reports	Student	Yes
		Prova Brasil	Both	School reports and other analyses	School	Yes

(continued)

Table 3.2 Reporting Practices in Latin America and the Caribbean, by Country *(continued)*

Country	National assessment	Name	Distribution of results[a]	Products	Lowest level of analysis	Direct implications?[b]
Chile	Yes	Sistema de Medición de la Calidad Educación (SIMCE)	Both	School reports until 2006, then student and school reports	School, student	Yes
		Sistema Nacional de Evaluación de Desempeño de los Establecimientos Subvencionados (SNED)	Both	School and classroom reports	Classroom	Yes
Colombia	Yes	Sistema de Evaluación de la Calidad de la Educación (SABER)	Internal	School reports	Department	No
		Instituto Colombiano para el Fomento de la Educación Superior (ICFES)	Both	Student reports	School, student	Yes

(continued)

Table 3.2 Reporting Practices in Latin America and the Caribbean, by Country *(continued)*

Country	National assessment	Name	Distribution of results[a]	Products	Lowest level of analysis	Direct implications?[b]
		Exámenes de Calidad de la Educación Superior (ECAES)	External	Student reports	Student	Yes
Costa Rica	Yes	Pruebas Nacionales	Both	School and student reports	National	No
		Pruebas Nacionales	Both	Student reports and ministerial analyses	Student	Yes
Cuba	Yes	Sistema de Evaluación de la Calidad de la Educación (SECE)	Both	School and student reports	Municipality	No
Dominican Republic	Yes	Pruebas Nacionales	Both	School and student reports	Student	No
Ecuador	No	APRENDO	Both	School and national reports	Region	No
El Salvador	Yes	Strengthening Achievement in Basic Education (SABE)	Internal	School reports	Department	No

(continued)

Table 3.2 Reporting Practices in Latin America and the Caribbean, by Country (*continued*)

Country	National assessment	Name	Distribution of results[a]	Products	Lowest level of analysis	Direct implications?[b]
		Prueba de Aprendizaje para Egresados de Educación Media (PAES)	External	Student reports	Student	Yes
Guatemala	Yes	Programa Nacional de Evaluación del Rendimiento Escolar (PRONERE)	Both	Basic statistics	National and department	No
Honduras	Yes	Unidad Externa de Medición de la Calidad de la Educación (UMCE)	Internal	Statistical reports at national level	Department	No
Mexico	Yes	Estándares Nacionales	Both	Statistical reports at national level	Region; some regions provide additional reports at the school level	Yes

(continued)

Table 3.2 Reporting Practices in Latin America and the Caribbean, by Country (*continued*)

Country	National assessment	Name	Distribution of results[a]	Products	Lowest level of analysis	Direct implications?[b]
		Examen de la Calidad y el Logro Educativos (EXCALE)	Both	Data on Instituto Nacional de Evaluación de la Educación, accessible on Web site; school reports	Student	Yes
		Evaluación Nacional del Logro Académico en Centros Escolares (ENLACE)	Both	Public Web site accessible to parents, teachers, and other stakeholders; school-level reports; special reports for Carrera Magisterial	Student	Yes
Nicaragua	No	Sistema Nacional de Evaluación (SNE)	Both	School reports	Department	No

(*continued*)

Table 3.2 Reporting Practices in Latin America and the Caribbean, by Country *(continued)*

Country	National assessment	Name	Distribution of results[a]	Products	Lowest level of analysis	Direct implications?[b]
Panama	Yes	Sistema Nacional de Evaluación de la Calidad Educativa (SINECE)	Both	Reports for Ministry of Education, politicians, researchers, school administrators, and teachers	Region	No
Paraguay	No; assessment conducted only in Escuela Nueva)	Sistema Nacional de Evaluación del Proceso Educativo (SNEPE)	Both	Statistical reports, school reports	National; school for those in sample	No
Peru	Yes	Evaluación Nacional (initially named CRECER)	Mostly internal (external with delay)	Online documents and data sets (*Revista CRECER y Boletines Informativos*)	National	No
Uruguay	Yes	Programa de Evaluación de Aprendizajes	Mostly internal; also national report	School reports, national report	School	No

(continued)

Table 3.2 Reporting Practices in Latin America and the Caribbean, by Country *(continued)*

Country	National assessment	Name	Distribution of results[a]	Products	Lowest level of analysis	Direct implications?[b]
Venezuela, R. B. de	No	Sistema Nacional de Medición y Evaluación del Aprendizaje (SINEA)	Internal	Internal reports on school, state and national performance levels	State	No

Source: Ferrer 2006 and questionnaires completed by evaluation offices in each country.

a. Internal publications are those shared only within the ministry of education or similar institutions.

b. "Direct implications" refers to whether any government actions, such as rewarding or sanctioning schools or implementing programs in certain schools, depend on the results of the test.

In a comprehensive review of education offices in 19 Latin American countries, Ferrer (2006) reviews the institutional and legal framework, the existence of curricular standards, the types of instruments used and populations tested, the degree of participation in international student assessments, the types of reports produced on student learning outcomes, and the dissemination efforts of student learning information.

Galiani and Corrales (2006) use the Ferrer review; a review of published information on student assessments in Latin America; and a detailed survey of education information offices in several countries to construct a quantitative index of student assessment institutional capacity in Latin American countries. They focus on three components of public policy:

- Stability (the extent to which policies are stable over time)
- Coherence and coordination (the degree to which policies are consistent with related policies and result from well-coordinated actions by the actors participating in their design and implementation)
- Quality of implementation (the extent to which different aspects of the policy are well executed).

They create three indices of institutional capacity, each more comprehensive than the previous one. First, they combine the three categories of public policy into a preliminary index of institutional capacity, called the Ferrer-derived index (table 3.3). This index varies widely across countries. They identify three clusters of countries:

- Top performers (institutional capacity index of 0.68–0.79) include Mexico, Chile, Brazil, Colombia, and Peru.
- Medium performers (institutional capacity index of 0.28–0.50) include Argentina, El Salvador, and Honduras.
- Low performers (institutional capacity index of −0.12–0.08) include the Dominican Republic, Bolivia, Paraguay, Uruguay, República Bolivariana de Venezuela, Ecuador, Nicaragua, Cuba, Costa Rica, Guatemala, and Panama.

Within the top cluster, countries have relatively high scores in each of the categories evaluated. Among intermediate performers, performance is less consistent, with some categories (stability in Argentina, quality of implementation in El Salvador, coherence and coordination in Honduras) exhibiting very low indexes. Among low-performing countries, inconsistencies are largest in stability, with values ranging from 0.04 in Cuba to 0.34 in Guatemala. Indexes for the other two measures are relatively low in all countries in this cluster.

Galiani and Corrales (2006) posit that their Ferrer-derived index is an insufficient, and possibly distorted, measure of institutional capacity,

Table 3.3 Ferrer-Derived Indexes of Institutional Capacity for
Assessment in Latin America and the Caribbean, by Country

Country	Stability	Coherence and coordination	Quality of implementation	Ferrer index (2005)
Mexico	0.75	1.00	0.62	0.79
Chile	0.88	0.51	0.93	0.77
Brazil	0.89	0.56	0.77	0.74
Colombia	0.66	0.77	0.62	0.69
Peru	0.53	0.86	0.64	0.68
Argentina	0.34	0.67	0.50	0.50
El Salvador	0.37	0.52	0.11	0.33
Honduras	0.59	−0.03	0.29	0.28
Dominican Republic	0.10	0.05	0.13	0.09
Bolivia	0.29	−0.25	0.14	0.06
Paraguay	0.31	−0.25	0.07	0.04
Uruguay	0.05	−0.08	0.13	0.03
Venezuela, R. B. de	0.26	−0.25	0.07	0.03
Ecuador	0.29	−0.25	0.00	0.01
Nicaragua	0.29	−0.25	0.00	0.01
Cuba	0.04	−0.25	0.07	−0.05
Costa Rica	0.11	−0.64	0.17	−0.12
Guatemala	0.34	−0.70	0.00	−0.12
Panama	0.30	−0.75	0.00	−0.15

Source: Galiani and Corrales 2006.

because it does not incorporate many of these offices' functions and dimensions. One missing component is the quality of dissemination efforts, a crucial activity in any evaluation. To assess the extent to which raw data are made readily available for analysts and the public in general, the authors explored two areas: whether the offices upload datasets online and whether they upload analyses by external authors of these datasets or make them available on the Internet. With this information, they developed an index of the quality of dissemination, which, combined with the other indexes, produced the first consolidated index of institutional capacity for student assessments in the region (table 3.4).

Table 3.4 Consolidated Index of Institutional Capacity for Assessment in Latin America and the Caribbean, by Country

| Country | Ferrer-derived categories | | | Review of online information | First consolidated index |
	Stability	Coherence and coordination	Quality of implementation	Quality of dissemination	
Chile	0.88	0.51	0.93	1.00	0.83
Colombia	0.66	0.77	0.62	1.00	0.76
Mexico	0.75	1.00	0.62	0.63	0.75
Brazil	0.89	0.56	0.77	0.58	0.70
Peru	0.53	0.86	0.64	0.63	0.66
Argentina	0.34	0.67	0.50	1.00	0.63
El Salvador	0.37	0.52	0.11	0.50	0.38
Honduras	0.59	−0.03	0.29	0.25	0.28
Dominican Republic	0.10	0.05	0.13	0.50	0.19
Bolivia	0.29	−0.25	0.14	0.50	0.17
Paraguay	0.31	−0.25	0.07	0.50	0.16
Uruguay	0.05	−0.08	0.13	0.50	0.15

(continued)

Table 3.4 Consolidated Index of Institutional Capacity for Assessment in Latin America and the Caribbean, by Country *(continued)*

Country	Ferrer-derived categories			Review of online information		First consolidated index
	Stability	Coherence and coordination	Quality of implementation	Quality of dissemination		
Ecuador	0.29	−0.25	0.00	0.50		0.13
Nicaragua	0.29	−0.25	0.00	0.25		0.07
Venezuela, R. B. de	0.26	−0.25	0.07	0.00		0.02
Costa Rica	0.11	−0.64	0.17	0.25		−0.03
Cuba	0.04	−0.25	0.07	0.00		−0.03
Guatemala	0.34	−0.70	0.00	0.13		−0.06
Panama	0.30	−0.75	0.00	0.00		−0.11

Source: Galiani and Corrales 2006.

This index yields several changes in country rankings. The range of variation shrinks, because most scores of the lower-ranked countries in the Ferrer-derived index rise. Argentina, Chile, and Colombia register large increases in scores, pushing Argentina closer to the category of a top performer, on par with Peru and pushing Bolivia, the Dominican Republic, Ecuador, Paraguay, and Uruguay into the intermediate category.

Though more comprehensive than the Ferrer-based index, the first consolidated index lacks crucial data that are relevant for analyzing the performance of evaluation offices. These data include

- Turnover rates of directors and technical experts
- Political interference (the extent to which recent operational changes have been the result of decisions made by political actors—ministers, presidents, legislatures—rather than in-house technical experts)
- International independence (the extent to which recent operational changes have been the result of decisions made by political actors rather than in-house technical experts)
- Financial stability (the extent to which the offices have experienced major changes in budgets in the past few years)
- Regularity of publications (whether the office issues official reports with some degree of regularity, governed by legal norms indicating periodicity).

To obtain information on each of these categories, Galiani and Corrales, with support from the World Bank, asked countries to fill out a questionnaire. Based on the answers, they developed a more encompassing index of institutional capacity, henceforth referred to as the survey-based index (table 3.5). The survey-based index provides a more complete assessment of institutional capacity than the first consolidated index, but it is based on data on only seven countries.

Despite this disadvantage, the index illustrates two types of variations. First, like the first consolidated index, the survey-based index shows wide variation, ranging from 0.20 (in Panama) to 0.80 (in Chile). Second, there is great variation within countries: even countries with high overall scores display room for improvement in some subcategories. Chile, for instance, scores poorly on coherence and coordination; Colombia scores poorly on quality of implementation; and Argentina, Peru, and Uruguay score poorly on stability. Nicaragua and Panama, both low performers overall, exhibit better performance in coherence and coordination than in other areas. No country has a consistently excellent or consistently deficient student assessment office.

Quantitative comparisons of the institutional capacity to evaluate education performance can be made based on the work of Galiani and Corrales. The first consolidated index covers many countries, but it does not provide information on a number of relevant factors (turnover rates of

Table 3.5 Consolidated Survey-Based Index in Selected Latin American Countries

Country	Stability	Coherence and coordination	Quality of implementation	Quality of dissemination	Consolidated index
Chile	0.70	0.73	0.86	0.92	0.80
Colombia	0.38	1.00	0.45	0.79	0.66
Peru	0.02	0.63	0.72	0.85	0.55
Argentina	−0.01	0.83	0.63	0.42	0.47
Uruguay	−0.05	0.58	0.34	0.92	0.45
Nicaragua	−0.01	0.58	0.30	0.69	0.39
Panama	0.12	0.25	0.20	0.22	0.20

Source: Galiani and Corrales 2006.

directors and technical experts, political interference, international independence, financial stability, regularity of publications). The survey-based index provides information on these categories, but it covers only a small group of countries. Neither index includes assessments of other very relevant issues, such as whether the offices conduct assessments that are adequate for the country's level of educational development or whether the tests are valid (that is, do they capture everything that they must capture or do they capture irrelevant factors?) (Braun and Kanjee 2006).

Despite these limitations, Galiani and Corrales (2006) offer the most comprehensive, verifiable, and replicable comparative assessment of institutional capacity. Their indexes reveal which countries are performing better or worse than other countries in various areas. The results suggest that the failure to stimulate societal demand for education quality may partly reflect the inadequacy of mechanisms for providing the information necessary to create such demand.

Notes

1. "Noise" refers to the transitory factors that can positively or negatively affect test scores, showing high volatility of test scores from one testing occasion to the next, especially among small schools whose sample sizes are small and therefore more affected by measurement error.

2. Earlier evaluations suggested that P-900 increased test scores by 0.4–0.7 standard deviations between 1988 and 1992. Chay, McEwan, and Urquiola (2005) show that similar improvements occurred before the program was in operation. Using the regression-discontinuity approach, they find no test-score gains between 1988 and 1990 but increases of about 0.2 standard deviations for the 1988–92 period. They suggest using similar strategies for programs that use test-score cutoffs to allocate funding.

3. Proponents of value-added assessment assert that it helps estimate academic progress in a way that is less confounded by socioeconomic factors. While teachers cannot control the achievement level of students when they arrive in the classroom, they can control the rate of academic achievement of their students once in their classroom (Sanders 2001). This does not mean that data collection and analysis is simple or straightforward. Questions remain as to how to define multidimensional academic progress as students progress from grade to grade.

References

Braun, H., and A. Kanjee. 2006. "Using Assessment to Improve Education in Developing Nations." In *Improving Education through Assessment, Innovation, and Evaluation*, ed. H. Braun, A. Kanjee, E. Bettinger, and M. Kremer. Cambridge, MA: American Academy of Arts and Sciences.

Chay, K. Y., P. J. McEwan, and M. S. Urquiola. 2005. "The Central Role of Noise in Evaluating Interventions that Use Test Scores to Rank Schools." *American Economic Review* 95 (4): 1237–58.

Di Gropello, E., and J. Marshall. 2005. "Teacher Effort and Schooling Outcomes in Rural Honduras." In E. Vegas, (ed.), *Incentives to Improve Teaching. Lessons from Latin America*, Washington, DC: World Bank.

Elacqua, G., and R. Fabrega. 2004. "El consumidor de la educación: Actor olvidado de la elección de colegios." Universidad Adolfo Ibáñez, Santiago.

Ferrer, G. 2006. *Estado de situación de los sistemas nacionales de evaluación de logros de aprendizaje en América Latina*. Partnership for Educational Revitalization in the Americas (PREAL), Santiago.

Galiani, S., and J. Corrales. 2006. "Academic Evaluation Offices in Latin America: An Index of Institutional Capacity." Background paper prepared for this report. World Bank, Washington, DC.

Hirschman, A. O. 1970. *Exit, Voice, and Loyalty: Responses to Decline in Firms, Organizations, and States*. Cambridge, MA: Harvard University Press.

Hopkin, Jonathan. 2006. "Conceptualizing Political Clientelism: Political Exchange and Democratic Theory." Department of Government, London School of Economics and Political Science, London. Paper prepared for American Political Science Association annual meeting, Philadelphia, August 31–September 3.

Jimenez, E., and Y. Sawada. 1999. "Do Community-Managed Schools Work? An Evaluation of El Salvador's EDUCO Program." *The World Bank Economic Review* 13(3): 415–41.

Kane, T., and D. Staiger. 2001. "Improving School Accountability Measures." NBER Working Paper W8156, National Bureau of Economic Research, Cambridge, MA. http://ssrn.com/abstract=262111

———. 2002. "The Promise and Pitfalls of Using Imprecise School Accountability Measures." *Journal of Economic Perspectives* 16 (4): 91–114.

King, E., and B. Ozler. 2000. "What's Decentralization Got to Do with Learning? The Case of Nicaragua's School Autonomy Reform." Working Paper Series on Impact Evaluation of Education Reforms. World Bank Development Research Group, Washington, DC.

Koretz, D. M. 2002. "Limitations in the Use of Achievement Tests as Measures of Educators' Productivity." *Journal of Human Resources* 37 (4): 752–77.

Mizala, A., P. Romaguera, and M. Urquiola. 2006. "Socioeconomic Status or Noise? Tradeoffs in the Generation of School-Quality Information." Documentos de Trabajo 225, Centro de Economía Aplicada, Universidad de Chile.

OECD (Organisation for Economic Co-operation and Development). 2003. *The PISA 2003 Assessment Framework*. Paris: OECD.

———. 2004. *Learning for Tomorrow's World. First Results from PISA 2003*. Programme for International Student Assessment, Paris.

Ravela, P. 2002. "¿Cómo presentan sus resultados los sistemas nacional de evaluación educativa en América Latina?" PREAL Boletín 22 (February), Partnership for Educational Revitalization in the Americas, Santiago and Washington, DC.

———. 2003. "¿Cómo aparecen los resultados de las evaluaciones educativas en la prensa?" PREAL Boletín 17 (July), Partnership for Educational Revitalization in the Americas, Santiago and Washington, DC.

Sanders, W. L. 2001. "Value-Added Assessment from Student Achievement Data: Opportunities and Hurdles. Create National Evaluation Institute." *Journal of Personnel Evaluation in Education* 14 (4): 329–39.

Sawada, Y. and A. Ragatz. 2005. "Decentralization of Education, Teacher Behavior, and Outcome: The Case of El Salvador's EDUCO Program." In E. Vegas, (ed.), *Incentives to Improve Teaching. Lessons from Latin America,* Washington, DC: World Bank.

Urquiola, M., and E. Vegas. 2005. "Arbitrary Variation in Teacher Salaries." In *Incentives to Improve Teaching: Lessons from Latin America,* ed. E. Vegas. Washington, DC: World Bank.

———. 2006. "¿Cómo lo ha hecho su alcalde? Estableciendo el desempeño educativo comunal." Background paper prepared for this report. World Bank, Washington, DC.

World Bank. 2003. *World Development Report 2004: Making Services Work for Poor People.* Washington, DC: World Bank.

Part II

A Framework for Understanding Student Learning

Acknowledging the significance of student learning is only the first step toward improving it. The real challenge lies in understanding how student learning is achieved and identifying policies that can improve it. Learning hinges on myriad factors that can touch on seemingly unrelated variables, from a parent's education and societal values regarding education to school infrastructure and the agricultural calendar. Policy, of course, can address only a small number of these factors.

Historically, education policy has focused on providing easily quantifiable inputs (money, infrastructure, textbooks) to schools and systems. This approach is popular because such inputs can be tracked and controlled relatively easily, are often highly visible, and are therefore politically viable. But improving educational inputs does not necessarily guarantee that learning will take place. These easy-to-measure resources may have very small effects on student achievement.

Empirically identifying the extent to which (and how) different variables contribute to student learning is difficult, for multiple reasons (Umansky 2005) reviews the challenges that researchers have faced in empirically identifying determinants of student learning). Factors influencing learning may fall on the student side or the school side, or they may be part of the education system as a whole. These factors are numerous and complex and may affect students differently depending on their race, socioeconomic background, gender, or other characteristics. Moreover, they may interact with one another to produce unexpected outcomes. The impact of resources on student learning may be limited, because resources are not necessarily allocated with the purpose of improving student learning. Schools and schools systems are highly politicized places, where decisions are made for a number of reasons, of which improving student learning may be only one (IDB 2006).

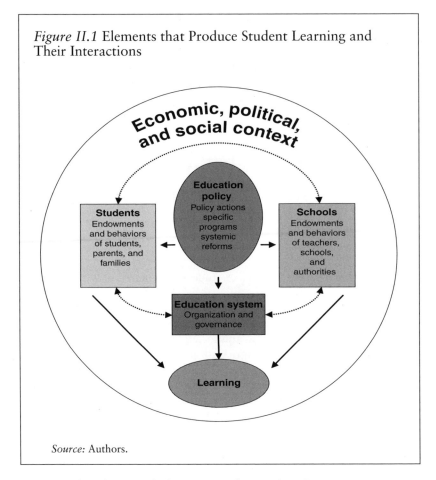

Figure II.1 Elements that Produce Student Learning and Their Interactions

Source: Authors.

Researchers have used education production functions to try to measure the complex relations between individual, family, school, and institutional characteristics on the one hand and endowments and learning outcomes on the other. Under this analytical framework, education systems are seen as productive systems in which school inputs are converted into outcomes, such as student learning. The production function model has been widely adopted as a way of investigating the inner workings of schools; it has provided clues as to why some schools and some students are more successful than others. Production functions allow researchers to investigate how different school inputs, such as classroom supplies, teacher characteristics, or class size independently relate to school outputs, such as test scores, graduation rates, or future earnings.

By identifying which school inputs, or combination of inputs, may be most effective at improving school quality and outputs, this research has great potential utility for education policy makers. To date, however, it has not offered as much guidance to policy makers as originally hoped. Little consensus has emerged over how to create accurate models for education quality. Debates continue over which inputs should be included, how they should be measured, and what form the production function should take (Hedges, Laine, and Greenwald 1994). As a result, the literature on the effects of inputs on student achievement is extensive but not conclusive.

Several models have been developed to try to explain educational quality and effectiveness (see Lockheed and Verspoor 1991; Heneveld and Craig 1995). This report approaches the issue of raising student learning by examining student-side, school-side, and systemwide variables, recognizing that the interactions among them jointly produce student learning (figure II.1). Students arrive at school with a series of endowments and behaviors that influence their learning. The endowments and behaviors of schools affect what they provide students. Organizational factors and the organization of the system as a whole also affect how and what students learn. The endowments and behaviors of students are influenced by their families and households; those of schools are affected by teachers and administrative authorities. The economic, social, and political context of a country provides the backdrop for these interactions.

The framework in figure II.1 distinguishes between the processes that produce learning, the actors and institutions that take part in these processes, and the policies that influence them. It highlights the fact that the quality of learning is a product of the interactions between students and schools, which is affected by organizational factors and education policy as well as by the social, economic, and political context. Understanding how these factors affect student learning is important for crafting policies to raise education quality and equity.

References

Hedges, L. V., R. D. Laine, and R. Greenwald. 1994. "Does Money Matter? A Meta-Analysis of Studies of the Effects of Differential School Inputs on Student Outcomes." *Education Researcher* 23: 5–14.

Heneveld, W., and H. Craig. 1995. *Schools Count: World Bank Project Designs and the Quality of Primary Education in Sub-Saharan Africa.* World Bank Technical Paper 303, Washington, DC.

IDB (Inter-American Development Bank). 2006. *The Politics of Policies: Economic and Social Progress in Latin America*, ed. E. Stein, M. Tommasi, K. Echebarría, E. Lora, and M. Payne. Washington, DC: Inter-American Development Bank.

Lockheed, M. E., and A. M. Verspoor. 1991. *Improving Primary Education in Developing Countries.* New York: Oxford University Press.

Umansky, I. 2005. "What Have We Learned? Revisiting the Education Production Function as a Tool for Understanding Education Quality in Latin America." Latin America and the Caribbean Region, Human Development Department, World Bank, Washington, DC.

4

Economic, Political, and Social Conditions

A country's overall economic, social, and political context serves as a backdrop to its education system. All three environments heavily influence students, schools, and institutions and the education policies affecting them.

The Investment and Economic Environment

Economic resources can determine a country's potential investment in education, which may affect achievement levels. Comparisons of educational outcomes in different countries need to take account of differences in resources.

Public investment in education in Latin America and the Caribbean has increased in recent years, to about 4 percent of GDP 2004 (figure 4.1). It still remains well below OECD levels, however.

Investment in Education

Student performance tends to be higher in wealthier countries (see figure 2.1), but the relation between GDP and average scores is not very strong. The relation between educational spending (as a percentage of GDP) and student performance is also weak (see figure 2.2). Chile has been increasing the share of its public expenditure on education—by more than 150 percent in primary and almost 200 percent in secondary since 1990 (Cox 2006)— but its results on national assessments remained stagnant.[1] Guatemala's spending on education is one of the lowest in the region, and its learning outcomes are dismal. Uruguay commits a relatively small percentage of its GDP to education spending (3.6 percent), but its students outperform those in neighboring countries on PISA. In short, countries commit very different

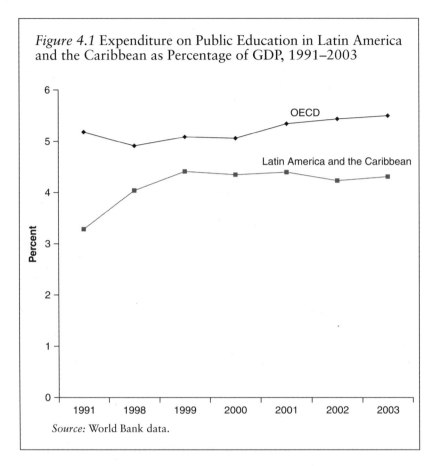

Figure 4.1 Expenditure on Public Education in Latin America and the Caribbean as Percentage of GDP, 1991–2003

Source: World Bank data.

levels of resources to education, independent of their income levels, with very different results. The lesson to be drawn from this evidence is that how resources are spent on education seems to be much more important than how much is spent.

International policy discussions of options for improving the quality of learning are often based on the assumption that expanding budgets is both necessary and sufficient, even though this assumption is not supported by the evidence (Hanushek 1995, 2003; Pritchett and Filmer 1997; Gundlach, Woessmann, and Gmelin 2001; Woessmann 2001; Pritchett 2004). In fact, the literature suggest that student performance bears little relation to patterns of educational expenditures across countries (Hanushek and Kimko 2000).

Using the International Education Association (IEA)'s cross-country assessments between 1965 and 1991, Hanushek and Kimko (2000) find that school resources have no strong relation with student test scores.

Using TIMSS 1995 cross-country data, Woessmann (2003) estimates the effects on student performance of the standard factors usually analyzed in the educational production function literature (family background and resources) and a multitude of institutional arrangements used by different schooling systems. He finds no relation between per student expenditure and student performance (the correlations between per student expenditure and average TIMSS test score are 0.13 for primary and 0.16 for secondary education), although GDP per capita is positively related with student achievement. Woessmann concludes that differences in resources do not explain differences in student performance across countries.

Hanushek and Luque (2003) find no relation between test scores and expenditures after controlling for differences in family background over time. Their estimations of a "global" education production function include measures of per-student spending and educational expenditure as a percentage of GDP, all of which they find to be negatively associated with student performance.[2] Across the sampled TIMSS countries, the authors find that the strength of resources in explaining better student performance appears limited. There are exceptions: in some countries, they find significant effects of resources on student outcomes, which they conclude should be investigated in more detail. Although the relation between resources and student performance is stronger in low-income countries, Hanushek and Luque maintain that these results do not allow any generalizations to be made about the link between school resources and income levels across countries.[3]

Using PISA 2000 data, Fuchs and Woessmann (2007) include educational expenditure per student in their measures of resources. They find the level of resources to be related to better performance in math and science. The effect is small, however, and disappears in math once low-spending countries are excluded from the sample, suggesting that the expenditure effect is driven largely by a few countries at the bottom of the distribution.

Research using international assessments supports the conclusion that there is no obvious relation between expenditure and standardized test achievement. The only patterns that come out of these studies are that low-performing countries tend to be low-spending countries (developing countries); among these countries there appears to be weak evidence of a slight positive relation between expenditure and educational achievement.

The debate on education financing underscores the difficulty researchers have had in identifying exactly what contributes to students learning. Some still hold fast to the notion that money must matter. Of course, students need access to a minimum standard of resources and materials. But studies drawing on cross-country data from international assessments show a weak, if any, relation between overall educational spending and student learning, even when controlling for other family and school factors (Hanushek and Kimko 2000; Hanushek and Luque 2003; Woessmann 2003; Hanushek 2005; Fuchs and Woessmann 2007). These findings are

---

Box 4.1 The Changing Demand for Skills in the
United States

Levy and Murnane (2004) explore the recent changes in the U.S. labor
market. They find that the jobs that are growing in number share two
types of general skills: (a) expert thinking, which they define as the ability
to solve new problems that cannot be solved by rules, and (b) complex
communication, the ability not only to transmit information but to convey
a particular interpretation of information to others. The authors explain
that while today's schools need to ensure that students master the critical
literacy and math skills needed to acquire the knowledge to become an
expert thinker in any field, they also need to provide students with complex communication and expert thinking skills in subject areas such as
language, history, and science.

Source: Authors, based on Levy and Murnane 2004.

---

also true when individual countries are examined over time. The results
indicate that merely increasing overall educational spending, without
making changes in how different institutions and education actors behave,
does not improve student learning outcome (Pritchett 2004; Fuchs and
Woessman 2007).

Overall Economic Environment

A country's economic environment can affect student learning outcomes.
In countries with open and growing economies, globalization raises the
demand for skills. Without a well-defined system of property rights and an
open economy, education and skills may not have the desired impact on economic outcomes, as Hanushek and Woessmann (2007) note. Cuba, which
has a closed economy, has comparatively high student learning outcomes
but lower than desired rates of economic development. Chile, an open economy that is the fastest growing in the region, has experienced social unrest as
a result of the perceived low quality of its public schools. Indeed, it appears
that the economic context maximizes both the impact of skills on economic
development and the demand for better-quality education (box 4.1).

The Political Environment

Political commitment to student learning outcomes affects not only funding
but also the types of educational policies put into place. Elected officials
often care about showing results while they are in office. While progress
in expanding access to schools can be achieved in relatively short periods

of time, improving student learning outcomes is a medium- to long-term proposition. Thus, unless they are under pressure from the electorate, elected officials are not often willing to be held accountable for improving student learning. Furthermore, political decisions regarding education do not necessarily focus on maximizing outcomes, such as improved student learning, or equal access to good-quality learning opportunities. Instead, decisions to make potentially inefficient educational investments often rest on the relative power of stakeholders in the education system (students, teachers, parents, administrators, politicians, and bureaucrats) (Pritchett and Filmer 1997).

The politics of education reform can be particularly thorny where improving student learning is concerned. Researchers have argued that educational reforms addressing the quality of education are often more difficult to implement than those addressing the quantity of or access to education, because they face more unfavorable political conditions and are more complicated by definition (Corrales 1999; IDB 2006).

"Quality reforms" are those that are most likely to influence student learning. They focus on improving the efficiency of investments to improve students' academic performance, reduce dropout or repetition rates, or increase teacher productivity. These reforms contrast with "access reforms," which expand educational coverage and opportunities.

Corrales identifies a number of political obstacles to quality reforms. One is the concentrated cost and diffused benefits of these reforms. These costs are often limited to a small number of people that can include extremely well-organized groups, such as teachers' unions, or powerful figures, such as government bureaucrats who are prepared to contest policies to which they object. In contrast, the benefits of quality reforms are spread out over various actors—parents, students, and society in general—who often have little political clout or are poorly organized. A second obstacle is the fact that the benefits of quality reforms are often intangible, general, and long term (in the form of long-term economic growth and rising incomes.[4]

In contrast to quality reforms, access reforms are relatively easy to implement, because their costs are dispersed across taxpayers and they provide tangible benefits to students, parents, teachers, and teachers' unions, builders and construction companies, and bureaucrats. Those stakeholders need sacrifice only a little to achieve success in the form of new or improved schools, more teachers, or increased enrollments (Corrales 1999). Furthermore, quality reforms may be hindered by other factors, such as high turnover within ministries of education and the weakness of ministries in the face of teachers' unions, as well as weak or insincere commitment to decentralization on the part of states (Corrales 1999).

Both Corrales (1999) and IDB (2006) emphasize the role of teachers' unions, especially their veto power in the policy-making process. Corrales is more optimistic than the IDB about the ability to overcome union opposition and involve unions in the policy-making process. Both studies note that a weak state and high turnover in education ministries often hinder policy making across administrations; consistency in these areas is necessary to promote and sustain policies that address education quality.

Experiences from East Asia, notably Hong Kong (China) and the Republic of Korea, suggest that a trade-off between quality and quantity of education does not necessarily exist (di Gropello 2006). In an examination of secondary education in East Asia and Latin America, di Gropello and the contributors to her book argue that such a dichotomy is false, that policy options exist to address both quality and quantity at the secondary level. Their analysis shows that at the secondary level, Brazil and Mexico have made raised quality indicators over the past decade—as measured by 2000 and 2003 PISA scores rose in Brazil and completion rates rose in Mexico—while simultaneously expanding enrollments. Both countries continue to struggle with equity and learning outcomes, and most Latin American countries with above-average access still have below-average test scores.

The decision to support national systems of assessment may be politically motivated as well. Often, policy makers introduce—and eliminate—national assessments of student performance based on political pressures rather than technical reasons. Examples of this abound in Latin America, where changes in the political party in power or the ideological slant of elected officials directly influence the continuity of student assessments.

Political commitment to student learning can reach beyond the country level to the international arena. International institutions such as UNICEF and UNESCO have already stepped up their commitment to student learning as part of Education for All (UNESCO 2004). A report by the World Bank's Independent Evaluation Group (World Bank 2006) has drawn attention to the importance of focusing on learning outcomes in World Bank lending. International pressure for focusing on student learning outcomes is rising.

Participating in international assessments is a tricky business for national governments. On the one hand, taking part in a PISA or TIMSS can demonstrate a political commitment to reaching internationally recognized student learning benchmarks. On the other hand, low achievement on such tests may publicly confirm the weakness of a country's education system. Argentina participated in PISA in 2003 but chose not to disseminate the results. Mexico participated in TIMSS in 1995 but did not publish its results. In contrast, in Germany the results of international assessments served as a catalyst for reform (box 4.2).

The Social Environment

Education systems are a mirror of society: Latin America's social inequities are reflected in who gets educated, what students learn, and how students

---

Box 4.2 PISA and the Education Policy Process in Germany

PISA was a wake-up call for Germany, drawing the flaws of the German education to the attention of all stakeholders. According to a report by the government, the results of PISA and TIMSS initiated fundamental changes in thinking about educational policy, changing the focus from input to outcome-driven reform (Klieme and others 2004).

In response to the PISA results, Chancellor Gerhard Schröder and Education Minister Edelgard Bulmahn called for a national effort to improve Germany's education systems. While education is traditionally under the jurisdiction of each state, Schröder called for an end to this fragmented approach. He suggested developing national educational standards, promoting preschool education, shifting financial priorities by correcting the imbalance between primary schools and academic-stream secondary schools, developing full-day schools, integrating immigrants into the education systems, and allowing more school autonomy in terms of teaching strategies, staff management, and finance. All of these reforms were subsequently implemented.

Source: Koda 2004.

---

and teachers interact. Income inequality and educational inequality, as reflected by differences in test scores, are positively related: countries with greater income inequality also tend to have greater inequality in test scores (figure 4.2).

How parents and communities value education can affect how decisions are made at the school level and beyond. As school systems in Latin America experiment with devolving responsibility to local actors, parents have begun to play a larger role not only in advocating for their children's education but also in taking part in it. Parents' and students' appreciation of good-quality education cannot be taken for granted, however. As Elacqua and Fabrega (2004) show for Chile, parents do not always educate themselves about their children's schooling or necessarily value school quality (as represented by test scores) over other factors, such as school proximity or social connections. Some studies conducted in the United States reach similar conclusions, suggesting that parents care more about school proximity and racial/ethnic makeup than test scores (Glazerman 1998).

The value that parents place on test scores versus other aspects of schooling may change according to minority status or socioeconomic status. A study of teacher preferences in the United States shows that on average, parents prefer teachers who can promote student satisfaction over those that may raise standardized test scores. In contrast, parents from

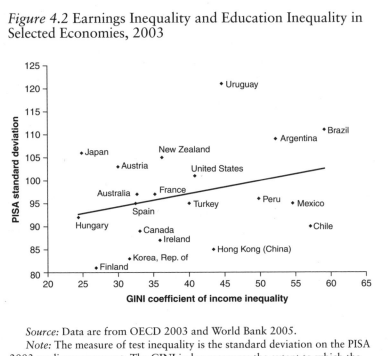

Figure 4.2 Earnings Inequality and Education Inequality in Selected Economies, 2003

Source: Data are from OECD 2003 and World Bank 2005.

Note: The measure of test inequality is the standard deviation on the PISA 2003 reading assessment. The GINI index measures the extent to which the distribution of income among individuals or households within an economy deviates from a perfectly equal distribution. A GINI index of 0.0 represents perfect equality, while an index of 100.0 implies perfect inequality.

low-income and minority schools value student achievement over student satisfaction. They are less likely to actively advocate for their children by expressing teacher preference than are parents from higher-income, non-minority schools, however (Jacob and Lefgren 2005). Furthermore, student learning may be second or third on the list of parental priorities, and parents who do value learning outcomes will not necessarily be vocal or active about their preferences.

The social value of education is also reflected in the value placed on the teaching profession, the prestige of teachers in the community, and, in turn, the training and salaries teachers receive and the profile and number of people entering the teaching profession. In Latin America the teaching profession carries very little prestige, and the academic preparation teachers receive is generally poor, except in rural areas and in some countries, such as Guatemala (Navarro 2002).

Notes

1. These figures are for 1990–2002. Chile's expenditure has increased even more since 2002, but test scores continue to stagnate.

2. As the authors caution, these estimations do not include measures of organizational or structural differences in the school systems of the various countries. If structural differences are correlated with resources, they would bias the coefficients (estimation of the relation).

3. Analyses by country suggest that differential effects of resources across countries by current level of development are not key. In general, the data provide little support for the idea that diminishing marginal returns drive the results (Hanushek and Luque 2003).

4. Many of these sentiments are echoed in a report by the Inter-American Development Bank entitled *The Politics of Policies: Economic and Social Progress in Latin America*, which describes two types of policies, "the politics of expansion and growing enrollments, and the politics of quality and efficiency improvements" (IDB 2006: 221).

References

Corrales, J. 1999. "The Politics of Education Reform: Bolstering the Supply and Demand; Overcoming Institutional Blocks." *Education Reform and Management Series* II (1). Washington, DC: World Bank.

Cox, C. 2006. "Policy Formation and Implementation in Secondary Education Reform: The Case of Chile at the Turn of the Century." Education Working Paper Series 3, World Bank, Washington, DC.

Di Gropello, E., ed. 2006. *Meeting the Challenges of Secondary Education in Latin America and East Asia*. Washington, DC: World Bank.

Elacqua, G. and R. Fábrega. 2004. "El Consumidor de la Educación: El Actor Olvidado de la Libre Elección de Colegios en Chile." Universidad Adolfo Ibáñez, Escuela de Gobierno, Santiago, Chile.

Fuchs, T., and L. Woessmann. 2007. "What Accounts for International Differences in Student Performance? A Re-Examination Using PISA Data." *Empirical Economics* 32 (2–3): 433–64.

Glazerman, S. 1998. "Determinants and Consequences of Parental School Choice." Ph.D. diss., Harris School of Public Policy, University of Chicago.

Gundlach, E., L. Woessmann, and J. Gmelin. 2001. "The Decline of Schooling Productivity in OECD Countries." *Economics Journal* 111 (May): C135–47.

Hanushek, E. A. 1995. "Interpreting Recent Research on Schooling in Developing Countries." *World Bank Research Observer* 10: 227–46.

———. 2003. "The Failure of Input-Based Schooling Policies." *Economic Journal* 113 (February): F64–F98.

———. 2005. "Why Quality Matters in Education." *Finance and Development*.

Hanushek, E. A., and D. D. Kimko. 2000. "Schooling, Labor-Force Quality, and the Growth of Nations." *American Economic Review* 90 (5): 1184–1208.

Hanushek, E. A., and J. A. Luque. 2003. "Efficiency and Equity in Schools around the World." *Economics of Education Review* 22: 481–502.

Hanushek, E. A., and L. Woessmann. 2007. "The Role of Education Quality in Economic Growth." World Bank Policy Research Working Paper 4122, Washington, DC.

IDB (Inter-American Development Bank). 2006. *The Politics of Policies: Economic and Social Progress in Latin America,* ed. E. Stein, M. Tommasi, K. Echebarría, E. Lora, and M. Payne. Washington, DC: Inter-American Development Bank.

Jacob, B. A., and L. Lefgren. 2005. "What Do Parents Value in Education? An Empirical Investigation of Parents' Revealed Preferences for Teachers." NBER Working Paper 11494, National Bureau of Economic Research, Cambridge, MA.

Klieme, E., H. Avenarius, W. Blum, P. Döbrich, H. Gruber, M. Prenzel, K. Reiss, K. Riquarts, J. Rost, H-E. Tenorth, and H. J. Vollmer. 2004. *The Development of National Educational Standard: An Expertise.* Federal Ministry of Education and Research, Berlin.

Koda, Y. 2004. "The Media Coverage on the Programme for International Student Assessment (PISA)." Paper prepared for the World Bank. Korea Education & Research Information Service (KERIS). http://www.keris.or.kr/english/index.jsp.

Levy, F., and R. Murnane. 2004. *The New Division of Labor: How Computers Are Creating the Next Job Market.* New York: Russell Sage Foundation.

Navarro, J. C., ed. 2002. *¿Quienes son los maestros? Carreras e incentivos docentes en América Latina.* Inter-American Development Bank, Washington, DC.

OECD, UNESCO (United Nations Educational, Scientific, and Cultural Organization). 2004. *2005 EFA Global Monitoring Report. Education for All: The Quality Imperative.* Paris.

Pritchett, L. 2004. "Towards a New Consensus for Addressing the Global Challenge of the Lack of Education." Working Paper 43, Center for Global Development, Washington, DC.

Pritchett, L., and D. Filmer. 1997. "What Educational Production Functions Really Show: A Positive Theory of Education Spending." Policy Research Working Paper 1795, World Bank, Washington, DC.

Woessmann, L. 2001. "New Evidence on the Missing Resource-Performance Link in Education." Kiel Working Paper 1051, Kiel Institute of World Economics, Kiel, Germany.

———. 2003. "Schooling Resources, Educational Institutions and Student Performance: The International Evidence. *Oxford Bulletin of Economics and Statistics* 65 (2): 117–70.

World Bank. 2005. *World Development Indicators 2004.* Washington, DC: World Bank.

———. 2006. *From Schooling Access to Learning Outcomes: An Unfinished Agenda.* Independent Evaluation Group, Washington, DC.

5

Student Endowments and Behaviors

Research in many countries has shown that what students bring to school when they first enter can affect how well they perform throughout basic education. Household resources, including parental education and income, strongly affect student learning outcomes as well.

What Do Students Bring with Them to School?

Research has found that student-side factors explain most of the variation in learning outcomes (Hanushek and Luque 2003; Pritchett 2004). Some of these endowments, such as age, health, motivation, or innate ability, are inherent characteristics. Others, such as early literacy, health, and early schooling experiences, are more flexible and responsive to the decisions and actions of parents, communities, and governments.

Age of Entry into Primary School

Age of entry into primary school can affect a child's trajectory through and achievement in the education system. Exactly how age of entry and achievement are correlated is a complex matter that has different implications for developed and developing countries.

In the United States, parents sometimes delay their children's entry into primary school in order to increase their chances of success in school. In contrast, in the developing world, delayed entry is usually associated with poverty. Poor parents often keep their children out of school because of stunting, malnutrition, or the opportunity costs associated with educating them. In Latin America lower incomes are associated with later enrollment (McEwan 2006), and many children enroll after the legal minimum age.

In Guatemala, for example, 20 percent of children enroll in primary school after the official age of seven (World Bank 2004).

The age of entry into primary school depends on many factors and creates both costs and benefits to families. Costs of delayed entry may include lower overall educational attainment for students who drop out sooner, having reached the legal age to do so before completing their education (Angrist and Krueger 1991). Late entry may also deprive families of government subsidies associated with enrolling school-age children and deprive students from income, as a result of later entry into the workforce (McEwan 2006).

Benefits to delayed enrollment can include deferment of the costs (both direct and indirect) associated with schooling. Delayed enrollment can also reduce repetition rates and increase student achievement. Evidence from industrial countries points to an increase in student outcomes associated with a small (maximum one-year) delay in enrollment (Bedard and Dhuey 2006; Datar 2006; Elder and Lubotsky 2006). Delayed enrollment may also contribute to higher lifetime wages, stemming from the benefits of a more effective school experience (Glewwe and Jacoby 1995).

Convincing evidence from industrial countries suggests that raising the age of entry into primary school can improve student achievement, reduce grade repetition, and even improve a student's chances of participating in higher education. Bedard and Dhuey (2006) show that in OECD countries, children who enroll at a later age have a long-term advantage, even into adulthood. Using cross-country data, they find that the youngest members of each cohort score 4–12 percentage points lower than the oldest members in grade four and 2–9 percentage points lower in grade eight, depending on the country.

Other evidence yields conflicting results. Lincove and Painter (2006) posit that students from industrial countries gain no advantage from starting school later and that their lifetime capital accumulation may actually be lower than that of students who start school earlier. Data from Canada and the United States indicate that the youngest members of a cohort are less likely to enroll in preuniversity academic-track courses and high-end academic universities, suggesting that the effects of delayed enrollment do not dissipate with age. Datar (2006) and Elder and Lubotsky (2006) find similar results for the United States.

Evidence on the impact of delayed entry in developing countries is scant. One of the few developing-country studies—of child nutrition and learning in the Philippines—finds that much of the learning advantage that well-nourished children have over malnourished children may come from the extra schooling they receive, as stunted children are more likely to delay entry (Glewwe, Jacoby, and King 1999).

The issue of delayed entry is particularly salient for developing countries, where students may not have access to preschool education, schools may have fewer resources to help struggling students, and poor students may start out behind their wealthier peers. Delayed entry may exacerbate Latin America's pronounced socioeconomic inequalities.

Analyzing the consequences of delayed entry for children in developing countries is tricky. If poorer parents are more likely to hold their children back because of lack of physical, emotional, cognitive, or economic readiness—as they seem to do in some countries—higher test scores will be associated with delayed entry.

McEwan and Shapiro (2006) use Chile's strict cutoff date for entry into primary school to identify the impact of delayed enrollment on student outcomes. They compare students' birth dates with the official enrollment cutoff for more than 1 million Chilean first graders. First-grade students born right before the cutoff are almost a year younger than those born just after, thereby creating a natural experiment. Drawing on these data, as well as on data on first-grade repetition, fourth-grade test scores, and eighth-grade TIMSS scores, the authors look for effects of enrollment age on repetition and achievement. They find that the positive impacts of delayed enrollment on educational performance and repetition found for industrial countries hold for Chile as well. Requiring children to enroll after age 6.67 rather than after age 5.67 decreases the probability of repeating first grade by 2 percentage points, from an overall average rate of 3 percent—a decrease of 66 percent from the baseline level. It also increases fourth- and eighth-grade achievement test scores by 0.3–0.5 standard deviations. The authors suggest that reduced repetition could have a positive impact on achievement through the eighth grade and beyond, as shown by test scores.

This new evidence from Chile points to the importance of preparing unready—usually underprivileged—children for school. Children from different backgrounds may require different types of interventions. It is important to keep all of these factors in mind when designing policies on minimum age requirements for primary school and determining how best to prepare underprivileged children for school.

Preparation before Entering Primary School

The preparation a child receives before entering primary school has a strong effect on later learning. Early literacy and reading in the home can have important impacts on a child's readiness for school, as well as on future academic performance and educational attainment. Using parental reporting of a child's literacy skills at the beginning of primary school as a measure of early literacy, Woessmann (2005) finds significant differences in performance between children with moderate-to-high levels of early literacy and children with low levels of early literacy upon entering primary school, particularly in. Argentina and Colombia.[1]

Access to Preprimary Schooling

Access to preprimary schooling can greatly improve student learning outcomes and reduce inequalities in primary and secondary education. Recent evidence suggests that the achievement gap between children from different socioeconomic backgrounds first opens during preprimary school. Studies conducted in countries of varying income levels consistently show that children who do not attend high-quality preschool programs are behind even before they begin primary school. Moreover, international evidence suggests that early childhood education programs can be more cost-effective than other interventions in reducing the achievement gap in schools (Carneiro and Heckman 2003; Cunha and others 2005).

Recent research provides evidence of the positive effects of early childhood education programs in Latin America. Berlinski, Galiani, and Gertler (2006) took advantage of Argentina's massive preschool construction program to study the effects of early childhood education on primary-school achievement. Using data from the school construction program and the country's national education assessment, they find that preschool attendance at ages three to five increases performance in language and math by 4.5–6.0 points (0.23–0.33 standard deviations), with similar gains for boys and girls. Moreover, the effect on third-grade test scores of having attended preschool is twice as large for students from poor backgrounds as for students from nonpoor backgrounds

Berlinski, Galiani, and Manacorda (2006) examine the impact of the expansion of preschool education on primary-school trajectories in Uruguay. Using data from the Uruguayan Household Survey for 2001–05, they analyze students' paths through primary school.[2] They find that preschool attendance has a positive effect on completed years of education, repetition rates, and age-grade distortion (overage). By age 10, children who had attended preschool had an advantage of almost a third of a year of education over children who had not attended preschool. From age 13 onward, these students had a significantly lower chance of dropping out than those who had not. By age 16, they had accumulated 1.1 more years of compulsory education than students who had not attended preschool and were 27 percent more likely to be in school.

Health

Health and educational achievement are strongly correlated (Behrman 1996): malnourished children perform poorly in school. Although the mechanisms by which malnutrition affects learning are not known, deficiencies in proteins, calories, and micronutrients are believed to impair cognitive development.

Because malnourished children generally come from more-disadvantaged families, factors other than the biological effects of malnutrition may also be influencing their poor performance in school. The advantage that well-nourished children have may stem from a longer school career (as a result of on-time school entry) and more-productive learning time (Glewwe, Jacoby, and King 1999).

Language and Ethnicity

Both native language and ethnicity are related to a student's success in the classroom. The population of Latin America and the Caribbean includes an extremely heterogeneous group of about 22–34 million indigenous people (Hall and Patrinos 2006).

As a whole, indigenous students are less likely than their nonindigenous classmates to finish primary school and more likely to repeat a grade (Shapiro and Moreno-Trevino 2004; Hall and Patrinos 2006). Indigenous students and Afro-Brazilian students also perform considerably worse on national assessments (DeFerranti and others 2003; McEwan 2004; Hernandez-Zavala and others 2006; McEwan and Trowbridge 2007).

Achievement of indigenous students appears to be tied closely to societal factors. Indigenous students tend to be poorer than nonindigenous students. They also appear to have less access to good-quality schools. Researchers are studying how much of the test-score gap between indigenous and nonindigenous students is a result of student-side factors (such as coming from poor or rural backgrounds, speaking a nondominant language, or having access to few instructional materials in the home) and how much comes from school-side factors (such as the greater likelihood of attending lower-quality schools, encountering discrimination in the classroom, or receiving instruction in languages they have not mastered).

How Do Parents and Families Support Education?

Household factors and the support children receive at home have traditionally been viewed as having the greatest effect on success in school. Since the Coleman Report was released, in 1966, studies have consistently found that students' socioeconomic status and family background have greater effects on student performance than any other factor. Socioeconomic status, or income, has traditionally been used as a proxy for household factors. Other proxies often used to represent a child's background include a mother's years of schooling, parents' occupation, and educational resources in the home.

These variables alone cannot account for unobservable household dynamics, however, and they often mask what is really going on in the home, such as parents' involvement in, actions regarding, and motivations for supporting their child's education. It is important not to underestimate the influence of what parents do at home on their children's learning.

Whether parents tutor their children, enroll them in school on time, and similar factors may affect how a child's path in school unfolds.

Parents' Socioeconomic Status

Socioeconomic status matters for learning outcomes; all studies measuring socioeconomic status find it a significant variable. Hanushek and Luque (2003) find that family background strongly influences performance and that students from disadvantaged families systematically underperform students from middle- and high-income families. Analyses using PISA 2003 data indicate that an index of economic, social, and cultural status has significant effects on student outcomes (OECD 2004).[3] Woessmann (2005) reports that performance in primary school in Argentina and Colombia is strongly related to various features of students' family backgrounds.

Research shows that parents' education and occupation are strongly related to their children's learning in the classroom (Casassus and others 2000; OECD 2001a; Willms and Somers 2001; Fertig and Schmidt 2002; Hanushek and Luque 2003; Woessman 2003, 2004, 2005; and Fuchs and Woessman 2004). In fact, variables such as a mother's years of education or a father's occupation are often used as proxies for socioeconomic status. Fuchs and Woessmann (2004) find that parental education and occupation have more substantial effects on reading than on math test scores. Such effects can vary according to context. Using PIRLS results, Woessmann (2005) shows that this effect is stronger in Argentina than in Colombia. Fertig and Schmidt (2002) find that mother's education has a greater effect on child's learning overall but that father's education becomes more important when they have attained tertiary levels. Parental occupation and having at least one parent with a full-time job also have important effects on student outcomes (Fuchs and Woessmann 2004). These findings are consistent with research drawing on international assessments.[4]

Books in the Home

Books in the home have a consistently strong and positive affect on student performance across international assessments and subjects (Casassus and others 2000; Kirsch and others 2002; Woessmann 2003, 2004). Using PIRLS, Woessmann (2005) finds a particularly large effect of books in the home in Argentina and a relatively small effect in Colombia (in contrast to England, Germany, Greece, Italy, FYR Macedonia, and Turkey). According to the OECD (2001a), an increase of one standard deviation on the PISA index of home educational resources and cultural possessions is associated with an average increase of 12 points in reading (equivalent to about a third of a school year).[5]

Studies examining student and household factors all point to the same conclusion: in general, socioeconomic background and family background have the largest effects on student performance. This finding calls for policy interventions that mitigate the effects of disadvantageous family background on educational performance.

Policies Affecting Children's Endowments and Behaviors

Student-side factors, especially socioeconomic background, can have a huge effect on classroom success (table 5.1). Developing policies to address these factors is difficult, however, because many of these factors fall within the realm of the home. Nevertheless, policy makers do have a number of policy options for addressing student-side factors (figure 5.1).

Preparation for Primary School

Children's preparedness upon entering primary school can affect their school careers and life outcomes. Most countries require children to enroll by a particular age. Enrollment is delayed in many instances, however, either voluntarily (because parents perceive it advantageous for their children to start primary school at an older age), or involuntarily (because of income constraints).

It is difficult to know how to interpret the results on age of entry and their policy implications. If students who benefit from delayed entry do so because of improved behavioral, cognitive, and linguistic readiness gained with time, then policies aimed at improving children's readiness, such as early childhood education and nutritional interventions, can help prepare disadvantaged children for school. Poor families may also benefit from cash transfers, which reduce the opportunity costs of sending children to school. Such transfers may also induce some families to send children to school before they are cognitively ready, however, in order to benefit from the subsidy.

Because the issues surrounding enrollment delays are complex and policies may have a variety of impacts, it is important to understand the causes and consequences of delays to design good, targeted policies for young children and their families. Some conditional cash transfer programs—in which families receive cash grants conditional on certain behaviors, such as enrolling their children in school or taking their children to health centers—serve a dual purpose, providing money to alleviate income constraints and early childhood interventions to address health and cognitive readiness.

Early Childhood Education

The regional and international evidence suggests that early childhood education may be one of the most effective interventions for improving student

Table 5.1 Student-Factors Affecting Learning and Related Outcomes

Factor	Learning outcomes	Related outcomes	Country	Type of study	Study
Preparation for primary school					
Age upon entry	Students in cohort who are 11 months older outperform youngest students on TIMSS by 4–12 percentage points in fourth grade and 2–9 percentage points in eighth grade.		OECD countries	Econometric	Bedard and Dhuey (2006)
	Delayed enrollment by one year is associated with increase in fourth- and eighth-grade test scores of 0.3–0.4 standard deviations.	Probability of first-grade repetition is 2 percentage points lower (66 percent from baseline) for students who delay enrollment by one year.	Chile		McEwan and Shapiro (2006)
		Youngest members of each cohort are less likely to attend university.	Canada and United States		Bedard and Dhuey (2006)

(continued)

Table 5.1 Student-Factors Affecting Learning and Related Outcomes *(continued)*

Factor	Learning outcomes	Related outcomes	Country	Type of study	Study
Preparation for primary school					
Early literacy	Raises fourth-grade reading performance on PIRLS by 17.69 achievement points (0.18 standard deviations, significant at the 1 percent level) in Argentina and by 15.93 achievement points (0.20 standard deviations, significant at the 1 percent level) in Colombia.		Argentina and Colombia	Education production function	Woessmann (2005)
Access to preprimary schooling	Raises performance in language and math on third-, sixth-, and seventh-grade test scores, with similar gains for girls and boys.		Argentina	Natural experiment, ordinary least squares	Berlinski, Galiani, and Gertler (2006)

(continued)

Table 5.1 Student-Factors Affecting Learning and Related Outcomes *(continued)*

Factor	Learning outcomes	Related outcomes	Country	Type of study	Study
Preparation for primary school					
	Preschool attendance at ages three to five raises language and mathematic performance by 4.5–6.0 points (0.23–0.33 standard deviations), with the effect on third-grade test scores twice as large for poor students as for nonpoor students				
Preschool attendance		Increases educational attainment for students 13 and older. By age 16, those who attended preschool are 27 percent more likely to be in school than those who did not.	Uruguay	Quasi-experiment exploiting differences in preschool attendance among children in the same household	Berlinski, Galiani, and Manacorda (2006)

(continued)

Table 5.1 Student-Factors Affecting Learning and Related Outcomes (*continued*)

Factor	Learning outcomes	Related outcomes	Country	Type of study	Study
Preparation for primary school					
		Reduces repetition and dropout rates. By age 16, children who attended preschool have accumulated 1.1 more years of education than those who did not.			
Early childhood education		By age 40, adults who participated in early childhood education at ages 3 and 4 are 15 percent less likely than those who did not to have been arrested five times, 20 percent more likely to earn at least $20,000 per year, and 20 percent more likely to have graduated from a regular high school.	United States	Controlled experiment that allowed a cost-benefit analysis of the Perry preschool program	Schweinhart (2005)

(continued)

Table 5.1 Student-Factors Affecting Learning and Related Outcomes (*continued*)

Factor	Learning outcomes	Related outcomes	Country	Type of study	Study
Malnutrition					
Malnutrition at 18–24 months	Cognitive ability (as measured by IQ scores) is lower at age eight.		Philippines	Two-stage least squares	Glewwe and King (2001)
Nutrition at 12–24 months	Cognitive ability is 9–10 points (0.72–0.80 standard deviations) higher at age eight.				
Family resources and background					
Number of books in home (more than 200)	Raises fourth-grade reading performance on PIRLS by 53.4 points (0.56 standard deviations, significant at the 1 percent level) in Argentina and by 14.4 achievement points (0.18 standard deviations, significant at the 5 percent level) in Colombia		Argentina and Colombia	Education production function	Woessmann (2005)

(continued)

Table 5.1 Student-Factors Affecting Learning and Related Outcomes (*continued*)

Factor	Learning outcomes	Related outcomes	Country	Type of study	Study
Family resources and background					
Home educational resources (increase of one standard deviation on the PISA index of home educational resources and cultural possessions)	Raises PISA reading score 12 points (equivalent to about a third of a school year).		OECD countries participating in PISA 2000	Education production function	OECD (2001a)
Parent with university degree	Raises fourth-grade reading performance on PIRLS by 39.27 achievement points (0.41 standard deviations, significant at the 1 percent level) in Argentina and by 14.96 achievement points (0.19 standard deviations, significant at the 10 percent level) in Colombia.		Argentina and Colombia	Clustering-robust linear regressions	Woessmann (2005)

(*continued*)

Table 5.1 Student-Factors Affecting Learning and Related Outcomes *(continued)*

Factor	Learning outcomes	Related outcomes	Country	Type of study	Study
Family resources and background					
Parents' occupational status	Raises reading performance by about 28 points per standard deviation of occupational status (equivalent to about two-thirds of a school-year's learning).		OECD countries participating in PISA 2000	Education production function	OECD (2001a)
Social programs					
Conditional cash transfers to families (Progresa/ Oportunidades)	Lowers failure rates by 4 percent, repetition rates by 6 percent, and intrayear dropout rates by about 10 percent.		Mexico	Difference-in-difference estimates	Gertler, Patrinos, and Rubio-Codina (2006a)

Source: Author compilation.

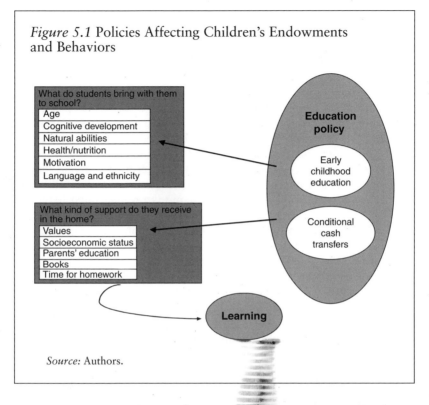

Figure 5.1 Policies Affecting Children's Endowments and Behaviors

Source: Authors.

learning and reducing repetition while mitigating the inequality of opportunity that disadvantaged students face, allowing them to take full advantage of their further schooling. Countries in Latin America and the Caribbean differ in terms of coverage of preschool-age students. Cuba has achieved universal preprimary education for all of its children. Ecuador has high early childhood gross enrollment rates. Mexico has enacted legislation making preschool a mandatory part of basic compulsory education. Uruguay has achieved universal preschool coverage for five-year-olds and is on the verge of achieving universal coverage for four-year-olds (ANEP-CODICEN 2004). For these countries, the principal challenge is ensuring the quality of existing preschool programs. Other countries, including those in Central America, have much lower levels of preschool enrollments, and some are still struggling with getting children through primary school.

Early childhood education programs consistently show higher returns for low-income children than for other children. Countries with nascent early childhood education programs should therefore prioritize children from disadvantaged backgrounds.

Evidence of the impacts of early childhood education on student learning outcomes in Latin America is consistent with strong evidence from the

United States and countries in Europe and Africa. Early childhood education improves children's readiness for primary education, resulting in better learning outcomes in primary school and in some cases secondary school. However, the impact of these programs varies considerably according to their quality, the type of intervention or interventions, and the populations they serve. Minimum quality standards must be achieved for these programs to have an effect (Currie 2001).

Early childhood education is also associated with numerous social benefits. The positive results of participation in early childhood education go far beyond test scores. Research in the United States indicates that early childhood education is associated with lower rates of repetition and enrollment in special education; improved health, nutrition, and emotional well-being; reduced criminal activity; and an increase in tax revenue and a reduction on social security programs (Schweinhart and others 2005). Research from Latin America shows pronounced regional effects of day care attendance on reducing repetition rates (Willms and Somers 2001). Expansion of early childhood education programs also appears to be cost-effective.

A single template for quality does not exist for preschool programs. An approximation that is often used defines quality according to two dimensions: a static dimension, related to the structural characteristics of a program, such as infrastructure or inputs, and a dynamic dimension, related to the processes and experiences that take place within a given environment (Love, Schochet, and Meckstroth 1996; Kamerman 2001; Myers 2004; Engle and others 2006). Structural characteristics can include class or group size, the adult-to-child ratio, the education and training of teachers or caregivers, the materials, and the curriculum. Processes refer to the type of experiences the child has, the activities he or she takes part in, learning opportunities, and the use of available materials. Other dimensions that go beyond what happens in the classroom, such as financing and program administration, also appear to be related to quality (Love, Schochet, and Meckstroth 1996; Myers 2004).

Evaluations of early childhood education programs in the United States suggest that structural characteristics, such as the size of the group and the training of the teacher or caregiver, are associated with better quality; they also contribute to the quality of dynamic processes, such as the interaction between adults and children (Love, Schochet, and Meckstroth 1996; Vandell and Wolfe 2000). Most research indicates that adults respond better to the needs of children and can provide more individualized attention and more educational activities in early childhood education programs in which the size of the group is small and the adult-to-child ratio low (Vandell and Wolfe 2000; Barnett, Schulman, and Shore 2004; Karoly, Kilburn, and Cannon 2005). Evaluations also show that higher teacher-student ratios and stronger teacher preparation are related to the quality of educational processes that take place in the classroom and to better cognitive and social development of the child (Blau 2001; Currie 2001; NICHD 2002).

The status or position of preschool teachers in society also affects learning outcomes (OECD 2001b). The work of preschool teachers and caregivers is generally not recognized professionally or monetarily. Within the teaching profession, preschool teachers often receive the lowest salaries, reducing the ability to attract, retain, and motivate qualified professionals.[6] It is not surprising, therefore, to see high levels of turnover among preschool teachers in many countries. Higher salaries are associated with lower absentee rates among caregivers and higher-quality service (Phillips and others 2000; Schweinhart 2005; Galinsky 2006).

A close relationship between preschool teachers and children is associated with better social skills among children through primary school (Peisner-Feinberg and others 1999; Currie 2001; Loeb and others 2004. The type of adult-child interaction is a central determining factor of the quality of a program (Love, Schochet, and Meckstroth 1996). Children exhibit more intense negative feelings toward teachers or caregivers who do not attend to their needs, for example, and more affection to those who respond positively (Howes, Phillips, and Whitebook 1992; Howes and Smith 1995).

Conditional Cash Transfers

Reducing the cost of school is one of the simplest ways to increase participation, but little is known about its effects on student learning. Conditional cash transfer programs have been successful in increasing educational enrollments across Latin America. Bolsa Escola/Bolsa Familia in Brazil and Progresa/Oportunidades in Mexico are the best known of these programs; Nicaragua has also increased school enrollments through conditional cash transfers.[7]

Although conditional cash transfers are often lauded for their positive impacts on education and health, evidence of the effect of conditional cash transfers on cognitive achievement and student learning is scarce.[8] Gertler, Patrinos, and Rubio-Codina (2006a) find that Mexico's conditional cash transfer program, Progresa/Oportunidades, helped reduce failure, repetition, and dropout rates. The authors suggest that the positive results may reflect the program's nutritional and health components or the fact that the program does not allow students to repeat the same grade more than twice (Gertler, Patrinos, and Rubio-Codina 2006a).

Notes

1. *Early literacy* is defined here as the ability to recognize most of the alphabet, read some words and sentences, and write some letters or words.
2. Analyzing students' progression through primary school is difficult, because preschool attendance is related to unobservable household factors that can influence their progression. Having parents who are concerned about the education of their children is difficult for researchers to observe or quantify, but it

likely has a strong effect on preschool attendance. The apparent positive effect of preschool attendance on school progression may thus simply reflect support in the home. To overcome these limitations, Berlinski, Galiani, and Manacorda (2006) use retrospective information on the number of years of preschool attended by children in the same household to identify the impact of preschool attendance on school progression. It is reasonable to assume that members of the same family are exposed to the same unobservable household variables. Consequently, the impact of preschool attendance on student progression through school can be evaluated by examining outcomes by siblings with different numbers of years of preschool attendance. In Uruguay, where expansion of access to preschool (and state financing for compulsory education for five-year-olds) is relatively recent, most families with observed differences in preschool attendance among siblings tend to come from disadvantaged and highly disadvantaged backgrounds.

3. The PISA index includes the highest International Socioeconomic Index of Occupational Status of parents, the highest parental education level converted into education years, and an index of educational resources in the home.

4. OECD (2001a) finds that a one standard deviation increase in parental occupational status is associated with an increase of about 28 points in the child's performance in reading (equivalent to about two-thirds of a year's learning). Woessmann (2005) finds that substantially higher percentages of high-achieving than low-achieving students had at least one parent with a university degree at home and a professional occupation. These percentages are smaller in Argentina and Colombia than in most other countries, although the differences across groups are still significant.

5. In addition to the classical measures of family wealth, PISA included measures of "cultural" wealth. The survey asked students whether they have classical literature, books of poetry, and works of art in their homes. The responses were then combined in an index of cultural possessions (mean of zero and standard deviation of one for all countries) (OECD 2001a).

6. In the Perry preschool program in the United States, teachers receive a salary equal to that of primary school teachers, something that has also occurred in various OECD countries (Schweinhart 2005).

7. Handa and Davis (2006) review conditional cash transfers in Latin America. Rawlings and Rubio (2004) review programs around the world. See also Schultz (2004); Gertler, Patrinos, and Rubio-Codina (2006a); Kremer (2006); and Schady and Araujo (2006).

8. According to Handa and Davis (2006), only Progresa has been evaluated for impacts on school achievement. Behrman, Sengupta, and Todd (2000) find no significant effects of Progresa on student achievement in the first year of the program.

References

ANEP–CODICEN (Administración Nacional de la Educación Pública y Consejo Directivo Central). 2004. *Panorama de la educación en Uruguay. Una década de transformaciones 2004.* Programa de Evaluación de la Gestión Educativa, Gerencia de Investigación y Evaluación, Gerencia General de Planeamiento y Gestión Educativa, Montevideo.

Angrist, J. D., and A. B. Krueger. 1991. "Does Compulsory Schooling Attendance Affect Schooling and Earnings?" *Quarterly Journal of Economics* 106 (4).

Barnett, S., K. Schulman, and R. Shore. 2004. "Class Size: What's the Best Fit?" *Preschool Policy Matters* 9 (December). National Institute for Early Education Research, New Brunswick, NJ.

Bedard, K., and E. Dhuey 2006. "The Persistence of Early Childhood Maturity: International Evidence of Long-Run Age Effects." *Quarterly Journal of Economics* 121 (4).

Behrman, J. 1996. "The Impact of Health and Nutrition on Education." *World Bank Research Observer* 11: 23–37.

Berlinski, S., S. Galiani, and P. Gertler. 2006. "The Effect of Pre-primary Education on Primary-School Performance." IFS Working Papers W06/04, Institute for Fiscal Studies, London.

Behrman, J., P. Sengupta, and P. Todd. 2000. *The Impact of Progresa on Achievement Test Scores in the First Year*. Final Report. International Food Policy Research Institute, Washington, DC.

Berlinski, S., S. Galiani, and M. Manacorda. 2006. "Giving Children a Better Start: Preschool Attendance and School-Age Profiles." Background paper prepared for this report. World Bank, Washington, DC.

Blau, D. 2001. *Child Care Policy: An Economic Analysis*. Russell Sage Foundation, New York.

Carneiro, P., and J. Heckman. 2003. "Human Capital Policy." In *Inequality in America: What Role for Human Capital Policies?* ed. J. Heckman and A. Krueger. Cambridge, MA: MIT Press.

Casassus, J., S. Cusato, J. E. Froemel, and J. C. Palafox. 2000. *First International Comparative Study of Language, Mathematics, and Associated Factors for Students in the Third and Fourth Years of Primary School*. Second Report, Latin American Laboratory for Assessment of Quality in Education, UNESCO Regional Office for Latin America and the Caribbean, Santiago.

Coleman, J. S. 1966. *Equality of Educational Opportunity*. U.S. Department of Health, Education, and Welfare, Office of Education/National Center for Education Statistics, Washington, DC.

Cunha, F., J. Heckman, L. Lochner, and D. Masterov. 2005. "Interpreting the Evidence on Life Cycle Skill Formation." NBER Working Papers 11331, National Bureau of Economic Research, Inc., Cambridge, MA.

Currie J. 2001. "Early Childhood Intervention Programs: What Do We Know?" *Journal of Economic Perspectives* 15 (2): 213–38.

Datar, A. 2006. "Does Delaying Kindergarten Entrance Give Children a Head Start?" *Economics of Education Review* 25: 43–62.

DeFerranti, D., G. E. Perry, I. Gill, J. L. Guasch, W. F. Maloney, C. Sánchez-Páramo, and N. Schady. 2003. *Closing the Gap in Education and the Technology*. Washington, DC: World Bank.

Elder, T. E., and D. H. Lubotsky. 2006. "Kindergarten Entrance Age and Children's Achievement: Impacts of State Policies, Family Background, and Peers." University of Illinois at Urbana-Champaign and Institute of Labor and Industrial Relations.

Engle, P., M. Black, J. Behrman, M. Cabral de Mello, P. Gertler, L. Kapirini, R. Martorell, and M. Young. 2006. "Strategies to Avoid the Loss of Developmental Potential among 200 Million Children in the Developing World." *Lancet Child Development in Developing Countries* 3 (369): 229–42.

Fertig, M., and M. C. Schmidt. 2002. "The Role of Background Factors for Reading Literacy: Straight National Scores in the PISA 2000 Study." Discussion Paper 545, Institute for the Study of Labor (IZA), Bonn.

Fuchs, T., and L. Woessmann. 2004. "What Accounts for International Differences in Student Performance? A Re-examination using PISA Data." Working Paper 1235, Category 4: Labour Markets, CESifo, Munich.

Galinsky, E. 2006. "Economic Benefits of High-Quality Early Childhood Programs: What Makes the Difference?" Committee for Economic Development, Washington, DC. http://www.ced.org/docs/report/report_prek_galinsky.pdf.

Gertler, P., H. Patrinos, and M. Rubio-Codina. 2006a. "Do Supply-Side-Oriented and Demand-Side-Oriented Education Programs Generate Synergies? Evidence from Rural Mexico." World Bank, Washington, DC.

———. 2006b. "Empowering Parents to Improve Education: Evidence from Rural Mexico." Policy Research Working Paper 3935, World Bank, Washington, DC.

Glewwe, P., and H. G. Jacoby. 1995. "An Economic Analysis of Delayed Primary School Enrollment in a Low-Income Country: The Role of Early Childhood Nutrition." *Review of Economics and Statistics* 77 (1): 156–69.

Glewwe, P., H. G. Jacoby, and E. M. King. 1999. "Early Childhood Nutrition and Academic Achievement: A Longitudinal Analysis." *Journal of Public Economics* 81: 345–68.

Glewwe, P., and E. M. King. 2001. "The Impact of Early Childhood Nutritional Status on Cognitive Development: Does the Timing of Malnutrition Matter?" *World Bank Economic Review* 15 (1): 81–113.

Hall, G., and H. Patrinos. 2006. *Indigenous Peoples, Poverty and Human Development in Latin America: 1994–2004.* New York: Palgrave.

Handa, S., and B. Davis. 2006. "The Experience of Conditional Cash Transfers in Latin America and the Caribbean." *Development Policy Review* 24 (5): 513–36.

Hanushek, E. A., and J. A. Luque. 2003. "Efficiency and Equity in Schools around the World." *Economics of Education Review* 22: 481–502.

Hernandez-Zavala, M., H. Patrinos, C. Sakellariou, and J. Shapiro. 2006. "Quality of Schooling and Quality of Schools for Indigenous Students in Guatemala, Mexico, and Peru." World Bank Policy Research Working Paper 3982, Washington, DC.

Howes, C., and E. W. Smith. 1995. "Relations among Child Care Quality, Teacher Behavior, Children's Play Activities, Emotional Security, and Cognitive Activity in Child Care." *Early Childhood Research Quarterly* 10 (4): 381–404.

Howes, C., D. A. Phillips, and M. Whitebook. 1992. "Thresholds of Quality: Implications for the Social Development of Children in Center-Based Child Care." *Child Development* 63 (2): 449–60.

Kamerman, S. 2001. "Early Childhood Education and Care: International Perspectives." Testimony prepared for the U.S. Senate Committee on Health, Education, Labor and Pensions, March 27, 2001.

Karoly, L., R. Kilburn, and J. Cannon. 2005. *Early Childhood Interventions: Proven Results, Future Promise.* RAND Labor and Population Division, Santa Monica, CA.

Kirsch, I., J. de Jong, D. Lafontaine, J. McQueen, J. Mendelovits, and C. Monseur. 2002. *Reading for Change: Performance and Engagement Across Countries— Publications 2000.* Paris: Organisation for Economic Co-operation and Development.

Kremer, M. 2006. "Randomized Evaluations of Education Programs in Developing Countries: Some Lessons." Paper presented at the World Bank's Human Development Week, Washington, DC, October.

Lincove, J. A., and G. Painter. 2006. "Does the Age that Children Start Kindergarten Matter? Evidence of Long-Term Educational and Social Outcomes." *Educational Evaluation and Policy Analysis* 28 (2): 153–179.

Loeb, S., B. Fuller, S. L. Kagan, and B. Carrol. 2004. "Child Care in Poor Communities: Early Learning Effects of Type, Quality, and Stability." *Child Development* 75 (1): 47–65.

Love, J., P. Schochet, and A. Meckstroth. 1996. "Are They in Real Danger? What Research Does and Doesn't Tell Us about Child Care Quality and Children's Wellbeing." Child Care Research and Policy Paper, Mathematica Policy, Inc. Princeton, NJ.

McEwan, P. 2004. "The Indigenous Test Score Gap in Bolivia and Chile." *Economic Development and Cultural Change* 53 (1): 157–90.

———. 2006. "Delayed Primary School Enrollment in Latin America." Inter-American Development Bank, Washington, DC.

McEwan, P., and J. Shapiro. 2006. "Delayed Enrollment and School Readiness in a Developing Country." World Bank, Washington, DC.

McEwan, P., and M. Trowbridge. 2007. "The Achievement of Indigenous Students in Guatemalan Primary Schools." *International Journal of Educational Development* 27 (1): 61–76.

Myers, R. 2004. "In Search of Quality Programmes of Early Childhood Care and Education (ECCE)." Paper prepared for the 2005 *EFA Global Monitoring Report*.

NICHD (National Institute for Child and Human Development) Early Child Care Research Network. 2002. "Study of Early Child Care." *American Educational Research Journal* 39 (1): 133–64.

OECD (Organisation for Economic Co-operation and Development). 2001a. *School Factors Related to Quality and Equity. Results from PISA 2000.* Paris: OECD.

———. 2001b. *Starting Strong: Early Childhood Education and Care.* Paris: OECD.

———. 2004. *Learning for Tomorrow's World: First Results from PISA 2003.* Paris: OECD.

Peisner-Feinberg, E. S., M. R. Burchinal, R. M. Clifford, M. L. Culkin, C. Howes, S. L. Kagan, N. Yazejian, P. Byler, J. Rustici, and J. Zelazo. 1999. *The Children of the Cost, Quality, and Outcomes Study Go to School.* Frank Porter Graham Child Development Center, University of North Carolina, Chapel Hill.

Phillips, D., D. Mekos, S. Scarr, K. McCartney, and M. Abbott-Shim. 2000. "Within and beyond the Classroom Door: Assessing Quality in Child Care Centers." *Early Childhood Research Quarterly* 15 (4): 475–96.

Pritchett, L. 2004. "Towards a New Consensus for Addressing the Global Challenge of the Lack of Education." Working Paper 43, Center for Global Development, Washington, DC.

Rawlings, L., and G. Rubio. 2004. "Evaluating the Impact of Conditional Cash Transfer Programs." *World Bank Research Observer* 20 (1): 29–55.

Schady, N., and C. Araujo. 2006. "Cash Transfers, Conditions, School Enrollment, and Child Work: Evidence from a Randomized Experiment in Ecuador." Policy Research Working Paper 3930, World Bank, Washington, DC.

Schultz, T. 2004. "School Subsidies for the Poor: Evaluating the Mexican Progresa Poverty Program." *Journal of Development Economics* 74: 199–250.

Schweinhart, L. J. 2005. *The High/Scope Perry Preschool Study through Age 40: Summary, Conclusions, and Frequently Asked Questions.* Ypsilanti, MI: High/Scope Press.

Schweinhart, L. J., J. Montie, Z. Xiang, W. S. Barnett, C. R. Belfield, and M. Nores. 2005. "Lifetime Effects: The High/Scope Perry Preschool Study through Age 40." Monograph 14, High/Scope Educational Research Foundation.

Shapiro, J., and J. Moreno-Trevino. 2004. "Compensatory Education for Disadvantaged Mexican Students: An Impact Evaluation using Propensity Score Matching." Policy Research Working Paper 3334, World Bank, Washington, DC.

Vandell, D., and B. Wolfe. 2000. "Child Care Quality: Does it Matter and Does it Need to Be Improved?" Report 78, Institute for Research on Poverty, University of Wisconsin, Madison.

Willms, J. D., and M. Somers. 2001. "Family, Classroom, and School Effects on Children's Educational Outcomes in Latin America." *School Effectiveness and School Improvement* 12 (4): 409–45.

Woessmann, L. 2003. "Schooling Resources, Educational Institutions and Student Performance: The International Evidence." *Oxford Bulletin of Economics and Statistics* 65 (2): 117–70.

———. 2004. "The Effect Heterogeneity of Central Exams: Evidence from TIMSS, TIMSS-Repeat and PISA." Working Paper 1330, Category 4: Labour Markets, CESifo, Munich.

———. 2005. "Families, Schools, and Primary-School Learning: Evidence for Argentina and Colombia in an International Perspective." Policy Research Paper 3537, World Bank, Washington, DC.

World Bank. 2004. *Poverty in Guatemala.* Washington, DC: World Bank.

6

School Endowments and Behaviors

The endowments and behaviors of schools, especially teachers, can substantially affect how students learn (Woessmann 2003). Researchers and policy makers have tried to understand just how school-side factors affect student achievement by examining differences across classrooms, schools, municipalities, and countries. This chapter focuses on two categories of factors that can influence how schools affect student learning: school characteristics (such as class size, materials, and time spent in school) and teacher characteristics (such as teacher behavior, knowledge, and teaching methodologies) (figure 6.1).

Which Factors and Policies Affect Teacher Effectiveness?

A growing body of evidence supports the intuitive notion that teachers play a key role in what, how, and how much students learn.[1] Attracting qualified individuals into the teaching profession, retaining qualified teachers, providing them with the necessary skills and knowledge, and motivating them to do the best job they can is arguably the key challenge in education.

The characteristics and behaviors of school staff, especially teachers, have a huge impact on student learning. A teacher's impact on student learning outcomes is cumulative and long lasting. An ineffective teacher potentially reduces a student's performance for years; several ineffective teachers in a row may compound such an effect (Sanders and Rivers 1996).

Less clear is the nature of the characteristics and behaviors of effective teachers.[2] Because of the paucity of information on teacher effectiveness,

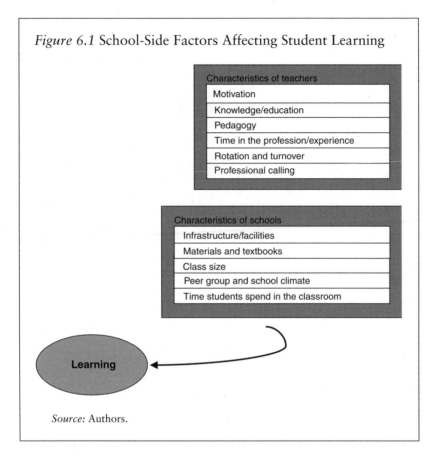

Figure 6.1 School-Side Factors Affecting Student Learning

Characteristics of teachers

| Motivation |
| Knowledge/education |
| Pedagogy |
| Time in the profession/experience |
| Rotation and turnover |
| Professional calling |

Characteristics of schools

| Infrastructure/facilities |
| Materials and textbooks |
| Class size |
| Peer group and school climate |
| Time students spend in the classroom |

Learning

Source: Authors.

especially in developing countries, much of what is known about teacher characteristics and how they affect learning has been gleaned from experiences with teacher policies and school reform—by observing what works and what does not. These policies generally fall into two categories: (a) policies that improve teachers' skills and knowledge through training and capacity building and (b) incentives that attract, motivate, and retain high-quality teachers (Navarro 2002; Vegas 2005).

Brazil's experience with the Fund for the Maintenance and Development of Basic Education and Teacher Appreciation (FUNDEF) provides insights into the role of teachers (box 6.1). Although it is not possible to separate out which aspects of the reform contributed to narrowing the learning gap, the fact that the majority of spending went toward teachers underscores the critical role that teachers play in improving student learning.

Box 6.1 Does Investment in Teachers Affect Student
Learning? Evidence from Brazil

Implemented in 1998, the Fundo de Manutenção e Desenvolvimento
do Ensino Fundamental e de Valorização do Magistério (FUNDEF) is
a national finance equalization reform for primary education in which
each state and municipal government in Brazil pools funds at the state
level that are then redistributed equally, on a per student basis, to each
governmental education authority (state and municipal). Although
the FUNDEF accounts do not pool all educational funding, they do
ensure that spending on primary education is more equitable across
state and municipal governments, addressing long-standing inequality
in education finance. As part of the reform, the federal government
provides additional funds for any pooled account in which per-student
funds fall below set spending floors. These "top-ups" have benefited
the poorer states of Brazil, located primarily in the northeast. This
mechanism is a first step toward addressing interstate inequalities in
educational spending.

FUNDEF has had a strong effect on teachers' working conditions.
Sixty percent of FUNDEF funds are earmarked for teachers. These
funds are used to hire new teachers, train underqualified teachers, and
increase teacher salaries. The increases in mandated per pupil spending lowered average teacher-pupil ratios, prompting the hiring of new
teachers. A survey carried out by the Brazilian ministry of education
shows that salaries increased 13 percent in the first year of FUNDEF
alone. Salaries increased most in municipally run schools, where they
rose 18.4 percent, and in the poor northeastern states, where they rose
49.6 percent. There was also a dramatic decrease in the percentage of
teachers who had completed only primary education, particularly in
the poorer regions of Brazil and in the earlier primary school grades,
where higher proportions of teachers had been underqualified before
the reform. The reform, however, was introduced at about the same
time as new legislation that required teachers to have at least a secondary education degree; the funds received from FUNDEF were not
significantly associated with the steep decline in underqualified teachers, although some of the FUNDEF revenue was used to train and
educate teachers.

The FUNDEF reform and the changes it created in educational
inputs have produced changes in student outcomes. More students
in the poorer states of Brazil are now attending school, particularly
at the higher grades of basic education. Having teachers with higher
education levels is related to lower levels of overage students in the
classroom, suggesting that better-qualified teachers helps students stay

(continued)

Box 6.1 Does Investment in Teachers Affect Student
Learning? Evidence from Brazil *(continued)*

on track in school, repeat less, drop out and reenter less, and perhaps also
enter first grade on time. As low-performing students suffer most from
inequalities in per-student spending, finance equalization reforms that decrease these inequalities may also decrease the performance gap between
low- and high-performing students and between whites and nonwhites.

Source: Gordon and Vegas 2005.

Experience

Evidence of the impact of teachers' observable characteristics on student
learning is scant and often inconclusive. While research has established that
teachers have a strong effect on student learning, the teacher characteristics
that lead to improved learning outcomes have not been well documented.
One exception is the finding that the least-experienced teachers are the least
effective, especially during the first three years of their careers (Darling-
Hammond 2000). More effective and longer-term training can make up
for the novice teacher effect, however (Denton and Peters 1988; Andrew
and Schwab 1995). Collaborative and continuous learning can help experienced teachers maintain and improve their skills (Rosenholtz 1989). A
recent study drawing on 10 years of data on students and teachers in North
Carolina supports the notion that teacher experience, teachers' test scores,
and regular licensure increase students' achievement in math (Clotfelter,
Ladd, and Vigdor 2007).

Salary Level and Structure

How teachers are paid—both in absolute terms and relative to comparable professionals—can affect teaching quality. Both teacher pay and
active and prospective teachers' attitudes about prospects for advancement can affect who enters and remains in the profession (Glewwe, Ilias,
and Kremer 2003; Corcoran, Evans, and Schwab 2004a, 2004b; Hoxby
and Leigh 2004; Lavy 2004). Salary level and structure are particularly
important in Latin America and the Caribbean, where few other remuneration mechanisms are in place and those that do exist increase the wage
level only modestly.[3]

In Latin America, as in other parts of the world, there is a widely held
belief that teachers are not well paid and generally earn less than professionals in comparable fields. In the past decade, however, teacher salaries
have risen considerably in much of the region. A study of teacher salaries
in 17 Latin American countries reveals that the difference between teacher

and nonteacher earnings varies considerably from country to country, depending on which professions constitute the comparator group and how the comparisons are made (Hernani-Limarino 2005).[4] While individuals' decision to become a teacher and remain in the profession will more likely depend on their perceptions of relative teacher salaries than on actual differences, the empirical evidence indicates that, with a few exceptions, teachers are generally not severely underpaid and that their salaries should not create any major disincentive for entering the profession.[5] Furthermore, despite substantial increases in enrollment in primary and secondary education in many Latin American countries, none of the countries in the region has experienced severe teacher shortages in recent years, suggesting that teacher salaries are not so low as to discourage professionals from choosing a teaching career.[6] This may partly reflect recent increases in average teacher salaries in several countries in the region.

Some concerns do exist regarding the qualifications of people who become teachers. In the few instances where teachers earn salaries substantially less than comparable workers in other occupations, many of the best-qualified individuals are likely to choose professions other than teaching. Indeed, recent studies suggest that teacher salaries influence who enters the field and how long they remain in teaching (Loeb and Page 2000).

Other working conditions and regulations can reduce or amplify the effect of salaries on teachers.[7] In Chile, for example, changes in salary levels over a 20-year period were accompanied by changes in the number and quality of applicants to the teaching profession (Mizala and Romaguera 2005). In the 1980s, teachers experienced a 32 percent decline in real salaries as a result of government budget cuts. Over this period, the number of students entering education programs dropped 43 percent.

Both trends reversed in the 1990s, as real teacher salaries rose 156 percent between 1990 and 2002. During this time, the government launched a publicity campaign to encourage students to become teachers, and it created a scholarship program for outstanding students to study teaching. It also allocated substantial additional resources to schools, thereby improving working conditions for teachers. While the individual effect of each of these variables on the influx of education students remains unclear, the number of education students increased 39 percent and the average score for applicants to education programs rose 16 percent.[8] These patterns suggest that changes in salary levels can affect an individual's choice to become a teacher.

A different picture emerges in República Bolivariana de Venezuela, where neither wage premiums (relative teacher salaries) nor wage dispersion appears to affect the quality of the applicant pool of students planning to major in education (Ortega 2006).[9] If anything, wage premiums have the effect of attracting more students from the bottom quintile of the test-score distribution—a trend that could reduce teacher quality.[10] Additional evidence from República Bolivariana de Venezuela shows that the majority of first-year students in education-related majors report having chosen teaching careers for personal and vocational reasons rather than economic ones (Bruni-Celli, González, and Ramos 2002).

The inconsistency between the results from República Bolivariana de Venezuela and those from Chile suggests that the influence of teachers' salaries on indicators such as student dropout rates, completion rates, and test scores may stem from how salaries act as an incentive for teachers already in the field rather than for those considering whether or not to become teachers. Salaries may act as morale boosters or motivators for teachers already in the classroom or increase teacher effectiveness through increased social recognition.

The structure of salaries also affects teachers. Salary structures of public school teachers in most countries in Latin America and the Caribbean are set and implemented nationally (Argentina and Brazil are important exceptions). In most countries, salary scales are different at the preprimary, primary, and secondary levels; they are rarely, if ever, different for teachers of different subject matters. A recent study of 17 Latin American countries shows that the teacher wage structure is flatter and begins at a higher level than the salary structure of nonteachers (Hernani-Limarino 2005). Teachers throughout the region receive higher base salaries (the part of their salary that is unrelated to any characteristic) than do comparable workers in other occupations. However, although differences in years of education, training, and experience are the most important determinants of differences in teacher pay, the differences accruing to these characteristics are smaller than in other professions. In practice, then, teachers at the lower end of the wage distribution earn higher salaries than they would in other comparable professions, while teachers with more education and experience earn the same as or less than they would in other comparable professions (Vegas and Umansky 2005).[11]

In Chile, for example, the teachers' earnings profile begins at a higher level than that of nonteachers (all nonagricultural workers 15 years or older), reflecting the more than doubling of average teacher salaries between 1990 and 2005. The structure of teacher salaries is flatter than that of nonteacher salaries, however. Teachers with more experience and education earn higher salaries, but the returns on experience and education are lower for teachers than for nonteachers. Moreover, while teachers' salaries are pegged almost exclusively to seniority and education, nonteachers' salaries tend to vary based on evaluations of on-the-job performance.

Within Bolivia's pay structure, which is similar to that of most countries in the region, the largest part of a teachers' salary depends on experience and education (figure 6.2). In contrast, Chile has tried to increase the share of teacher pay that is related to performance. Even in Chile, however, more than 60 percent of pay continues to depend on characteristics that are unrelated to performance, such as years of service and education. These

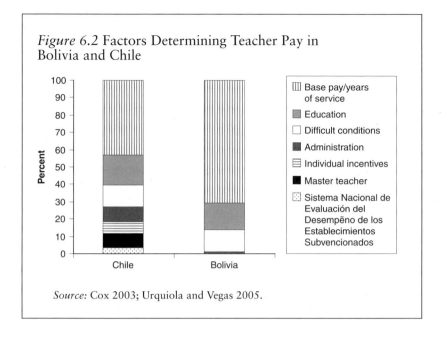

Figure 6.2 Factors Determining Teacher Pay in
Bolivia and Chile

Legend:
- ▦ Base pay/years of service
- ▨ Education
- ☐ Difficult conditions
- ■ Administration
- ☰ Individual incentives
- ■ Master teacher
- ⸬ Sistema Nacional de Evaluación del Desempeño de los Establecimientos Subvencionados

Source: Cox 2003; Urquiola and Vegas 2005.

pay scales allow for little, if any, differentiation based on teachers' activities or effectiveness in the classroom and school.

The incentives created by such a salary structure can be detrimental to the goal of attracting and retaining highly qualified individuals. Research in Latin America and the United States finds that people who become teachers are often not strong students, are not interested in teaching as a career, do not have the appropriate characteristics to succeed as teachers, and are not qualified for the job (Hanushek and Pace 1995; Villegas-Reimers 1998; Vegas, Murnane, and Willett 2001).

Performance-Based Pay

Paying teachers for what they know and do may improve student learning outcomes. The effect of performance-based pay appears to depend critically on how the programs are designed and linked to teacher performance. In Chile's Sistema Nacional de Evaluación del Desempeño de los Establecimientos Subvencionados (SNED), top-performing schools within predetermined groups earn a financial bonus for student performance, which is distributed among the teachers in the winning schools. The scheme initially had no evident effects on student performance. Average student test scores increased slightly in schools with some likelihood of receiving the prize in each of the three years during which the program was implemented (Mizala and Romaguera 2005).

Mexico's Carrera Magisterial program, instituted in 1993, allows teachers to move up consecutive pay levels based on year-long assessments of their professional development and education, years of experience, a peer review, and their students' performance. The awards are substantial—representing 25–200 percent of the teacher's annual salary—and once awarded last throughout a teacher's career, just as a salary increase does. Since 1993 more than 600,000 teachers have received the lowest-level award. The Carrera Magisterial reform resembles an across-the-board wage increase for "good" teachers and may thus be expected to have increased the quality of entering cohorts of teachers.

To assess the effectiveness of the Carrera Magisterial incentives in improving students' test scores, McEwan and Santibáñez (2005) compared two groups. The first group consisted of teacher whose characteristics put them far above or below the threshold for qualifying for a bonus. The second group consisted of teachers who were close to the threshold. This is the group of teachers for whom the policy created incentives to improve student test scores, because they were close to—but not assured of—receiving an award. Mean test scores of students of teachers in this "incentivized" group rose about 0.15–0.20 points—less than 0.1 standard deviations—relative to teachers in the first group. The effect was robust to a variety of alternative specifications and subsamples.

Although Chile's SNED and Mexico's Carrera Magisterial are both nationwide programs involving most teachers, only a minority of teachers has any real likelihood of receiving a bonus (in the case of SNED) or a promotion (in the case of Carrera Magisterial). Most teachers who apply thus have no real incentive to improve performance.

Nonmonetary Incentives

A recent teacher incentive program in India reduced teacher absenteeism and improved student test scores (Duflo and Hanna 2005). A nongovernmental organization (NGO) project in India used a simple financial incentive program to reduce teacher absenteeism and stimulate more teaching and better learning. The NGO initiated the program in 60 informal one-teacher schools in rural India, randomly chosen from a sample of 120 such schools. The remaining 60 schools served as comparison schools. Teachers were given a camera with a tamper-proof date and time function. Children were instructed to photograph the teacher and other students at the beginning and end of the school day; the time and date stamps on the photographs were used to track teacher attendance. Salary was a direct function of teacher attendance.

The effort immediately reduced teacher absenteeism: the absentee rate, measured using unannounced visits in all 120 schools, averaged 43 percent in the comparison schools and 24 percent in the schools under study. The program also improved student achievement: one year after the program's start, test scores in the schools participating in the incentive program were 0.17 standard deviations higher than those in the comparison schools, and children were 43 percent more likely to be admitted into regular schools (from informal schools).

Teacher Assignment

Evidence from Uruguay shows that the country's system of teacher assignment may be contributing to inequality, with less-experienced teachers ending up in the least-desirable schools, as more-experienced teachers chose schools with more-desirable working environments, more resources, and students from higher socioeconomic backgrounds (Vegas, Urquiola, and Cerdán-Infantes 2006). Teachers in Uruguay are assigned a score based on their teacher level and years of service. Every two years, they are allowed to request the schools in which they would like to teach, in order of preference. Postings are made based on the scores they receive. As a result, experienced teachers with more education have a much higher chance of being assigned to their first choice, and new, inexperienced teachers end up being assigned to the least-desirable schools, which in most cases are schools serving disadvantaged populations. The level of teacher qualification greatly influences the probability of switching schools, with less-qualified teachers switching schools and abandoning the school system more often than better-qualified ones.

A system in which teachers select schools based on their professional level (or grade) can act as an incentive to remain in the profession. As teachers acquire higher "status" within the profession, they increase their probability of being assigned to their school of choice. This system can have negative results for students, however, especially the neediest students. The consequences of these patterns for educational equity and quality should not be underestimated. When experienced teachers are concentrated in schools with more-favorable working conditions, disadvantaged students are exposed, year after year, to teachers with the least experience, limiting their possibilities for receiving a good-quality education. A challenge for policy makers is therefore to ensure that all schools, especially those serving students from disadvantaged backgrounds, have at least a core group of experienced, effective teachers.

Teacher Education and Professional Development

Latin America lags behind OECD countries in the quality of its initial teacher education and ongoing professional development, according to a qualitative study carried out by the World Bank and the International Institute for Educational Planning (IIEP) (Duthilleul 2005). While countries such as Chile and Uruguay have made efforts to attract talented students to teaching through scholarship programs, many of Latin America's teacher-education programs lack the flexibility to attract professionals from other fields or candidates interested in a midcareer change. In contrast, most OECD countries allow for multiple entry points into the teaching profession. In addition, many countries in the region have begun to professionalize teacher education, gradually increasing the length of study from two or three years to four or five years and shifting teacher education from normal schools to higher education (table 6.1). Only Guatemala, Honduras, Nicaragua, and Panama continue to offer initial primary-teacher education at the secondary school level. Heterogeneity continues to exist, however, with multiple types of teacher-education institutions often operating simultaneously, creating teacher-education systems that are fragmented and unsystematic.

In theory, making teacher education part of higher education should confer higher status to the profession and recognize a higher level of competencies that teachers must gain through their training. In practice, many reforms have failed to increase teacher quality.

The region has nevertheless seen some innovative reforms. Peru's Ministry of Education has partnered with indigenous communities to implement the Programa de Formación de Maestros Bilingües de la Amazonia Peruana (FORMABIAP). Established in 1988, the program has been recognized through several awards. Uruguay created five regional teacher-education centers in an effort to improve the quality of secondary school teachers. These centers include a new curriculum, an increase in the number of credit hours, and dedicated faculty who commit half their time to mentoring and monitoring students. While these programs look promising, very few have been properly evaluated, making it difficult to assess their impact on teacher quality and student learning.

In-service professional development, which is funded by ministries of education or regional authorities and therefore not linked to school development, appears fragmented and divorced from the reality of schools (Duthilleul 2005). In none of the participating countries in the region were schools responsible for organizing or financing professional development. In contrast, about three-quarters of OECD countries link teacher professional development to school development, and principals and local authorities participate in planning capacity-building programs for teachers. In Latin America, professional development opportunities tend to finance special projects rather than provide systematic initiatives for professional advancement.

Very little research assesses the impact of teacher-education programs. In Argentina, for example, no official evaluation has been conducted of a massive in-service training program carried out in the 1990s, although the sense is that the results have not met expectations. Neither Colombia nor Ecuador nor Nicaragua has carried out official evaluations of their programs; evaluations are underway in Chile and Peru.

In sum, the qualitative evidence collected by the World Bank/IIEP survey suggests that teacher-education policies have not received the focus

Table 6.1 Teacher Requirements in Selected Countries in Latin America and the Caribbean, 2006

Country	Education level required to become a primary, lower-secondary, or upper-secondary school teacher			Entrance exam			Length of program (years)		
	Primary	Lower secondary	Upper secondary	Primary	Lower secondary	Upper secondary	Primary	Lower secondary	Upper secondary
Argentina	Upper secondary	Upper secondary	Upper secondary	No[a]	No	No	3	4	4
Bolivia	Upper secondary	Upper secondary	Upper secondary	Yes[b]			3[c]	3–4	3–4
Brazil	Upper secondary	Upper secondary	Upper secondary	Yes	Yes	Yes	2[d]	3	
Chile	Upper secondary	Upper secondary	Upper secondary	Yes[e]	Yes	Yes	4–5	4–5	4–5
Colombia	Upper secondary	Upper secondary	Upper secondary	No[f]			5[g]	5	5
Ecuador	Upper secondary	Upper secondary	Upper secondary	Yes[h]	Yes	Yes	3	3–4	3–4
El Salvador	Upper secondary	Upper secondary	Upper secondary	Yes			3	3	
Guatemala	Lower secondary		Upper secondary	No	No	No	3–4	4	4

(continued)

Table 6.1 Teacher Requirements in Selected Countries in Latin America and the Caribbean, 2006 *(continued)*

Country	Education level required to become a primary, lower-secondary, or upper-secondary school teacher			Entrance exam			Length of program (years)		
	Primary	*Lower secondary*	*Upper secondary*	*Primary*	*Lower secondary*	*Upper secondary*	*Primary*	*Lower secondary*	*Upper secondary*
Honduras	Lower secondary	Upper secondary	Upper secondary	Yes	Yes	No	2–3		3
Mexico	Upper secondary	Upper secondary	Upper secondary	Yes[i]			4	4	4
Nicaragua	Upper secondary[j]	Upper secondary	Upper secondary	No	No	No	2–3[k]	4	4
Panama	Lower secondary	Upper secondary	Upper secondary	Yes[l]	Yes	Yes	3+1	4–5	4–5
Paraguay	Upper secondary	Upper secondary	Upper secondary	Yes	Yes	Yes	4	4	4
Peru	Upper secondary	Upper secondary	Upper secondary	Yes	Yes	Yes	5	5	5
Uruguay	Upper secondary	Upper secondary	Upper secondary	No	No	No	4	4	4

(continued)

Table 6.1 Teacher Requirements in Selected Countries in Latin America and the Caribbean, 2006 (*continued*)

Country	Education level required to become a primary, lower-secondary, or upper-secondary school teacher			Entrance exam			Length of program (years)		
	Primary	*Lower secondary*	*Upper secondary*	*Primary*	*Lower secondary*	*Upper secondary*	*Primary*	*Lower secondary*	*Upper secondary*
Venezuela, R. B. de	Upper secondary	Upper secondary	Upper secondary				5		

Source: Duthilleul 2005.

a. Some provinces are beginning to introduce entrance exams; the situation varies by province and institution. Physical education, language, and art teachers are usually required to take entrance exams.

b. Includes an exam, a psychological assessment, and an interview; for teachers of bilingual education, a language exam is also required.

c. Extension to four years for all levels is planned.

d. Two years for preschool teachers and teachers of primary grades 1–4.

e. Like all other university programs, Prueba de Selección Universitaria, required at all universities, is financed by the state.

f. A minimum passing score on the final upper-secondary exam is required.

g. In normal schools, the program for preschool and primary teachers is two years.

h. Institutes currently have their own entrance exams; a standardized entrance exam is being developed.

i. Varies by state.

j. Most candidates enter normal schools after completing ninth grade and complete a teaching degree during secondary education. Completion of upper-secondary school is obligatory.

k. Some students entered training with six years of primary school and nine years of basic education. According to the previous existing regulations, they would complete secondary education and have one more additional year before becoming primary teachers.

l. An average of 3.8 is required for candidates 19-years-old, plus a psychological assessment and written test. To enter university, candidates must take an entrance exam and pass a psychological test.

they deserve in the region, especially given the singular role they play in improving student learning. Student learning may be suffering as a result and may continue to do so unless teacher education is given focused and sustained attention.

Lessons from Policies Addressing Teachers and Teaching

Education policies may affect a variety of teacher characteristics (figure 6.3) Evaluations of policies yield several lessons.

Design Teacher Incentives to Affect Most Teachers

A first lesson from the impact evaluations of teacher incentive policies is the importance of crafting incentives that affect most, if not all, teachers. Only when the majority of teachers are eligible to receive the benefits of hard work and improved outcomes will the incentive mechanism itself have the potential to improve outcomes in a majority of students. This is not to say that most or all teachers should receive the incentive reward. Indeed, if teachers have a high likelihood of receiving the reward without any behavioral change, the mechanism no longer provides an incentive to improve teaching and learning. Instead, as many

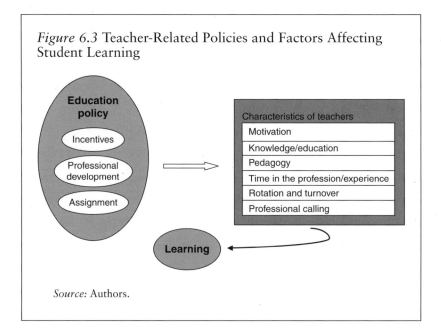

Figure 6.3 Teacher-Related Policies and Factors Affecting Student Learning

Source: Authors.

teachers as possible should feel that they have a chance of receiving the reward if they put in the effort to bring about the desired changes in student learning.

Incentive programs should generate incentives for the highest proportion of teachers possible, particularly for teachers whose performance is lower than average. In Mexico this could mean awarding more points to components that teachers can directly influence, such as their students' performance and their own performance on exams.

It could also mean setting up homogenous groups, so that teachers compete only with teachers who work with similar populations. In Chile this could mean reconfiguring the "homogenous groups," supporting low-performing schools in order to increase their possibility of obtaining the award. This combination of support to improve performance along with incentives to motivate performance may be a promising combination.

A different option that Chile is currently pursuing is to reward a larger proportion of schools. In the next round of the SNED, Chile is planning to reward schools serving 35 percent rather than 25 percent of national enrollment, a change that will motivate a larger number of teachers. Without policies to support teachers in their work, however, it is unlikely that the SNED will yield the desired improvements in student learning outcomes in the lowest-performing schools.

Link Incentives to Desired Outcomes

Although all teachers should be eligible to receive recognition for hard work and good results, for an incentive scheme to work effectively, it must recognize only teachers who achieve the desired performance and results. Weak links between desired performance and, for example, extra pay, result in misallocation of rewards. In the first years of Carrera Magisterial, nearly all teachers who participated in evaluations received promotions. In contrast, the program in India maintained a very tight link between the desired behavior (teacher attendance) and rewards.

Make Incentives Large Enough to Affect Teacher Behavior

Incentives should be large enough to merit extra effort. Often, the base salary accounts for a large share of total compensation; incentives for specific behaviors (working in rural schools, serving children with special needs) account for only a small proportion of total pay. In these cases, the compensation may be strongly linked to the desired outcome or behavior, but the reward may be too small for teachers to be induced to adopt the desired behavior.

In Chile, for example, the SNED bonus amounts to 5–7 percent of a teacher's total compensation. This small pay increase may not be enough to motivate teachers to improve their teaching practice and ensure that their students learn more and perform better on the national exam. For this reason, the next round of SNED will double the size of the rewards.

Faced with pressures from teachers' unions to increase salaries for all teachers, as well as with countervailing pressures to improve the efficiency of education spending and to improve incentives for teacher performance, education policy makers run the risk of doling out numerous bonuses for various behaviors and characteristics (working in rural areas, attendance, time for preparing classes). A typical Peruvian teacher, for example, receives compensation for about 15 different "behaviors," which are not monitored or awarded to all teachers (Vegas and Umansky 2005). Each bonus is small and accrues to most or all teachers; together these "bonuses" amount to increases in pay without any strong association with teacher performance or clear messages to teachers regarding specific behaviors.

In sum, it is important to design incentives that effectively compensate teachers for desired behaviors. The reward size should be large enough to merit the additional effort that the incentive hopes to promote. Incentives may be more effective if they are limited in number, clearly communicated to teachers, and carefully monitored.

Ensure That All Schools Have Effective Teachers

Many kinds of incentives exist, both monetary and nonmonetary. These include, among others, adequate school infrastructure and educational materials, the internal motivation to improve children's lives, the opportunity to grow professionally, and nonsalary benefits such as pensions, job stability, and working conditions. Indeed, in most countries, teachers cite working conditions as one of the critical factors affecting their performance.

The method of teacher selection and assignment can affect the quality of teaching and student learning. A mechanism of teacher assignment designed to meet specific objectives will not necessarily be resisted by teachers if it is accompanied by a policy that compensates teachers who choose to teach in disadvantaged schools. Such compensation could include not only salary bonuses but also support programs that improve working conditions in schools (reducing overcrowding, improving infrastructure, providing monetary resources to be administered by the school for maintenance and teaching materials, and so forth).

Once schools have at least a core group of teachers with an adequate level of experience, achieving improvements in quality and equity will require that teachers work with school directors to design strategies for every child. To be able to do so, teachers will need technical and administrative support from school administrators, as well as regular updating of their professional skills. School administrators have an important role to play in ensuring quality and equity in their schools: they need to work with teachers on their professional development plans, support them in updating their subject matter knowledge, and encourage them to work as a team to improve their students' learning. School administrators must allow teachers time for professional development and collaboration during the school day and year. If administrators do not provide pedagogical leadership and opportunities for professional development, teachers cannot acquire new skills, improve their own learning, or generate communities of professional development needed to improve students' learning.

Improve and Evaluate Teacher-Education Programs

Teacher education and professional development need to be improved, systematized, and transformed to address new priorities.[12] If teachers are to receive the support and training they need to help students learn, teacher-education policies in the region need to be approached systematically and with a focus on quality.

Quality is a tricky concept to pin down. However, several shifts in the vision of teacher education in OECD countries illustrate what quality might mean going forward. These include (a) shifting the focus on individual abilities to communities of practice; (b) shifting the focus from teacher education to development of teacher capacities; (c) recognizing culture as an asset, not an obstacle; (d) linking teacher development with leadership development; and (e) treating teacher education as a career-long process. Many teacher-education policies in OECD countries, described below, reflect these new concepts of quality. These policies can help guide countries in the region as they focus on upgrading initial education, improving in-service opportunities, and collecting information on results.

Create a profile of teacher competencies to guide teachers in their learning and facilitate alignment of teacher education, development, and certification. With the exception of Chile, no country in the region has developed teacher-education policies in this vein. Developing teacher profiles can be time consuming, because it involves the buy-in of a variety of stakeholders, including government, employers, and unions, as well as agreement on what teachers should know and be able to do. However, the process is critical to shifting the focus on teacher education from inputs to outcomes.

Treat teacher education as a career-long process. Within a framework of continuous education, the initial education of teachers is only a first step in a series of important steps allow teachers to grow and develop professionally over time. When such a framework is coupled with a profile of teacher competencies, teachers have guidelines to follow while developing different aspects of their professional competencies. Different institutions, acting in an independent and disjointed manner, often provide initial education and in-service training in Latin America and the Caribbean. These programs need to be integrated to ensure that training leads to better-quality teaching. Curricular reforms should be introduced concurrently with sufficient support for the development of teaching staff.

Understand the value of flexibility. Flexibility in teacher-education programs facilitates career changes, allowing a broader pool of candidates to enter the field. Such flexibility, which is common in OECD countries, can also help offset teacher shortages.

Recognize that new teachers need special support. New teachers are often the most likely to drop out of the profession, as research from Uruguay shows (Vegas, Urquiola, and Cerdán-Infantes 2006), and teachers are often least effective during their first three years in the profession (Darling-Hammond 2000). However, new teachers also bring enthusiasm and energy that veteran teachers may lack. OECD countries have prioritized the support of new teachers through induction programs. In contrast, countries in Latin America and the Caribbean tend to focus on upgrading unqualified or underqualified teachers. Better understanding of the types of programs that support new teachers is an important area for future research.

Integrate teacher education with school development. As this volume shows, many in-service teacher-education programs in the region have thin ties to the schools they supposedly serve. Incorporating professional development into the school context would help simultaneously meet the needs of teachers and schools.

Promote professional learning communities. Most in-service teacher education comes in the form of short workshops or programs that provide courses required for certification, upgrading, or promotion. Recent efforts have been made to promote the development of learning communities, which help teachers support one another in the development of their technical skills, as well as in the moral, intellectual, and emotional aspects of teaching (Hargreaves and Fink forthcoming).

Evaluate programs in a systematic manner. Very little is known about the impact of in-service teacher-education activities on student learning outcomes. While most countries in the region have data on initial teacher education, very few follow up by collecting data on teaching practices and in-service training programs. Lack of data and systematic evaluation are hindering understanding of which policies are most effectively train effective teachers.

Which School Characteristics Affect Student Learning?

Research on the relation between investment in school resources and student learning indicates a tenuous relation at best. It appears that the efficient allocation of resources in a manner that is appropriate to the political and educational context is more important than the volume of resources (Pritchett and Filmer 1997).

Textbooks and Facilities

Textbooks are one of the few inputs that have consistently been shown to have a strong impact on student learning (Jamison and others 1981; Heyneman, Jamison, and Montenegro 1984; Lockheed and Verspoor 1991; Harbison and Hanushek 1992).[13] School facilities are also important for creating positive learning environments and increasing educational attainment, especially in areas that may lack the basic infrastructure necessary to promote positive learning environments (Harbison and Hanushek 1992; Duflo 2001). In contrast, evidence of the significance of infrastructure expansion for improving student performance is weak (Pritchett 2004).

Information and Communication Technologies

Information and communication technologies (ICTs) have the potential to improve student learning. The promise that ICTs can expand access to education and improve teaching and learning processes has contributed to their rising profile in education among developing and developed countries alike (Linden, Banerjee, and Duflo 2003; World Bank 2006). Furthermore, as ICTs become increasingly pervasive in life and work, computer literacy is becoming a basic requirement for many jobs, making computer-skills training vital. Investment in ICTs in education is viewed as a primary way to prepare people for the new demands of the labor market and to allow underserved populations to develop the competencies necessary to have equal access to employment opportunities (Hepp and others 2004). Despite the surge in the use of ICTs in education, systematic, rigorous evaluation of their impact on student learning is scarce and yields mixed results.

The use of ICTs in education falls under two main categories: learning how to use computers and using computers for learning. This section focuses on using computers for learning.

Two evaluations show that the potential of ICTs for student learning may depend on how they are used and the types of activities they may be replacing. Evidence from India supports the notion that computer-assisted learning program may be beneficial for students in developing countries (Linden, Banerjee, and Duflo 2003). An NGO–implemented program provided children from the urban slums of Vadodara (one of the largest cities in western India) in grade four with two hours of shared computer time to play educational games that reinforce math skills ranging from the standard one to the standard three levels. The results on student learning were positive, with an average increase in math scores of 0.37 standard deviations. The program effect was slightly higher at the bottom of the distribution, but it covered the entire distribution, with comparable results for both girls and boys.

In contrast, an Israeli program that provided computers to elementary and middle schools for computer-assisted instruction appeared to have little effect on Hebrew or math test scores; some children receiving computer-assisted instruction actually performed worse than those who did not receive such instruction (Angrist and Lavy 2002). This finding may reflect that computers replaced time spent in well-equipped classrooms with well-trained teachers. In developing countries with fewer resources and teachers with less training, computer-assisted learning may be beneficial. Moreover, the transition to computer-assisted instruction takes time; the one-year average use of computer-assisted instruction in the study may not have been long enough for the program to take effect.

Evidence from international assessments is also mixed and seldom draws on the experience of developing countries. Many researchers and practitioners contend that effective use of technology tools in education can help build learning environments and improve student learning (see, among others, Van Dusen and Worthen 1995; Honey 2001; and Earle 2002), and some studies have shown important educational outcomes related to ICTs. A 2006 OECD study using PISA 2003 data reports that 15-year-olds who had access to computers over an extended period of time (more than five years) scored well above the OECD average in math, suggesting that consistent exposure over a long period of time is an important factor in learning. Students with limited experience with computers tend to score below the average, in most countries even after controlling for socioeconomic background. In addition, computers in the home generally have a greater positive effect than computers at school after controlling for socioeconomic status. Surprisingly, students who used computers a "moderate" amount (once a week to once a month) scored better than those who used computers frequently or not at all (OECD 2006).

In an analysis of PISA 2000 data in 31 countries, including Mexico and Brazil but no other developing countries, Fuchs and Woessmann (2004) find that the use of computers at school has no effect on student performance. Computer use at home, however, particularly Internet access, e-mail, and educational software, is associated with better test performance. These types of mixed, even negative results regarding the impact of computer and Internet use on student learning may be attributable to several factors, including inappropriate implementation of computer-based programs and short-term evaluations of processes that yield only long-term results (World Bank 2005).

As investment in ICTs continues to grow, it will be important to uncover how effective ICTs are in promoting student learning. According to a 2001 study by the U.K. Department for International Development (DFID), there has been "no systematic research in developing countries that compares the effect of [providing computer access to students] against the alternative use of resources such as textbooks, basic furniture, teacher education or nutritional supplements, which may also improve educational attainment" (Cawthera 2001: 10). Even in developed countries, the outcomes of huge investments in ICTs for education have been "disappointing," according to the OECD (2004). The effective integration of ICT into educational systems is a complex, multifaceted process that involves massive investments not only in hardware and software but also in curriculum and pedagogy, institutional readiness, teacher and principal competencies, long-term financing, and other areas (World Bank 2006).

Time Spent in School and How It Is Used

The number of days students attend school each year, the number of hours they spend in school each day, and the amount of time students are engaged in instructional activities at school can affect student learning. Most countries set the number of hours students are required to be in school. In almost all countries, governments mandate that children attend a certain number of years of school-based instruction. The number of years of compulsory education in Latin America and the Caribbean ranges from 6 to 12 (figure 6.4).

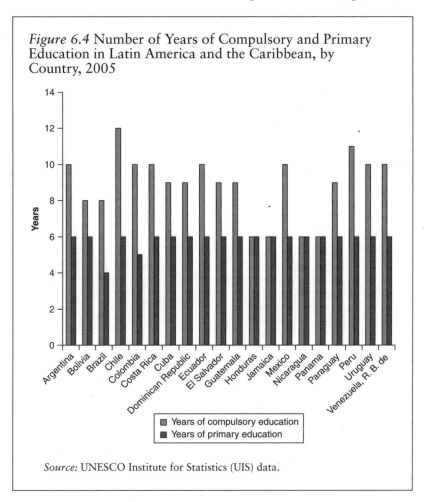

Figure 6.4 Number of Years of Compulsory and Primary Education in Latin America and the Caribbean, by Country, 2005

■ Years of compulsory education
■ Years of primary education

Source: UNESCO Institute for Statistics (UIS) data.

Benavot (2004) provides a comprehensive survey of instructional time patterns across the world. He finds that in 2000, annual instructional time in first grade averaged 722 hours, increasing gradually to a mean of 907 hours in eighth grade. While augmenting the number of intended hours of instruction is no guarantee of more learning, it is generally accepted that an increase in engaged learning time is beneficial. With the exception of Chile, most countries in the region provide fewer hours of intended instructional time in basic education than do countries in East or South Asia (figure 6.5).

Studies show that wastage of instructional time is a serious impediment to student learning (Stallings 1976). Time can be lost as a result of a variety of factors, including student absenteeism; teacher absenteeism; and school closures as a result of strikes, holidays, agricultural seasons, and lack of facilities.[14] In addition, schools in many countries operate in two or even three shifts, which requires shortening the class day to accommodate more students.

How time is used also affects learning. Recent evidence from the field of cognitive neuroscience examines the importance of how time is used in the classroom (Abadzi 2006). Increasing instructional time—time spent in the classroom on task—is an important part of improving learning. In an "efficient" classroom, as much as 90 percent of class time is spent on learning. In lower-income countries, this figure is about 25 percent (Abadzi 2006).

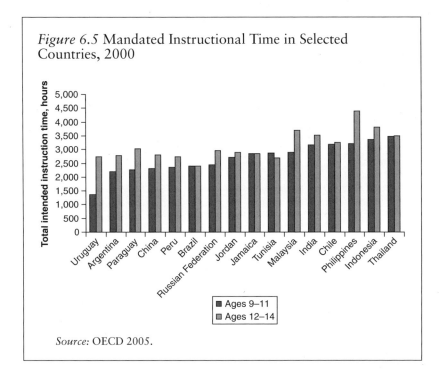

Figure 6.5 Mandated Instructional Time in Selected Countries, 2000

Source: OECD 2005.

Time on task and student attendance are mutually reinforcing: students who see an opportunity to learn are more likely to attend class than those who are bored or whose teachers are absent.

In Uruguay, and to a lesser extent, Chile, full-time schools appear to have improved student test scores, especially for the most disadvantaged students (Bellei 2005; Valenzuela 2005; Cerdán-Infantes and Vermeersch 2006). Empirical evidence on the impact of such programs is scarce, however, though generally positive.

Studies of other countries show very little correlation between time spent in school and learning (Martinic 1998; OECD 2005), largely because of data limitations. Impact evaluations conducted in the United States generally show positive results (Walston and West 2004), but they suffer from methodological restrictions that do not allow for definitive proof of impact.

Two programs that do show positive correlations between time spent in school and learning outcomes are Chile's Full School Day (FSD) program and Uruguay's Full-Time School (FTS) reform. Chile's program shows a small but positive impact on learning outcomes, with greater gains in language than in math (Bellei 2005; Valenzuela 2005). The program was implemented in response to the country's curriculum reform, which established new, more-demanding learning objectives, and in reaction to evidence that Chilean students spent less time in the classroom than their peers in other countries (Cox 2006). It increased annual time spent in the classroom and made the corresponding infrastructure investments to meet the needs of a single shift. It did not involve any specific interventions to improve teaching during the additional school hours, but it was instituted concurrently with other reforms focusing on teacher professional development and compensation for poor schools, among others.

Evaluation of Uruguay's FTS program (Cerdán-Infantes and Vermeersch 2006) shows an even greater impact than Chile's FSD, possibly attributable to the multifaceted nature of the program. The program extends the school day in regular schools from four hours to seven, uses a pedagogic approach designed to compensate for household-level differences, encourages community participation, and provides substantial teacher professional development in pedagogic practices tailored to the model. In a subset of FTS schools, a bilingual (English-Spanish or Portuguese-Spanish) immersion education program has also been implemented.

The program appears to have contributed to improving learning outcomes of participating schools, particularly in the most-disadvantaged schools, reducing some of the inequities in Uruguay's education system. At schools serving disadvantaged populations with below-average infrastructure before joining FTS, math scores rose 0.30 points (out of 24) per year of participation and language scores rose 0.20 points. A cycle of six years of primary education could thus be expected to increase math scores by 1.8 points and language scores by 1.2 points. In this subset of schools, where the average score is about 12 and almost 60 percent of students do not pass, an increase of almost 2 points would raise the number of passing students by about 10–15 percent.

In sum, Uruguay's FTS program, and to a lesser extent Chile's FSD, appear to have improved learning outcomes, particularly at schools that serve the lowest-income segments of the population. Expansion of those programs in such schools would improve the equity of the education system.

Class Size and Student-Teacher Ratios

Class size and student-teacher ratios have been at the center of discussions of whether resources in education matter. Class size has been among the most-frequently measured school-level factors in education production functions in within-country and international analyses (Hanushek 1995, 2003; Pritchett and Filmer 1997; Hanushek and Kimko 2000; Woessmann 2001; and Pritchett 2004).

Evidence on the effects of class size and student-teacher ratios on student learning is inconclusive. Most assessments find inconsistent results, showing weak, or sometimes negative, correlations between class size and student performance (Hanushek 1986, 1998; Woessmann 2001; Krueger 2002). Lazear (2001) posits that discipline and class size are substitutes, which explains why Catholic schools, with large classes, outperform public schools. In his model, the optimal class size is larger for well-behaved students, so that the observed relation between student learning outcomes and class size is small or possibly positive.

Cross-country studies also provide inconclusive results. Willms and Somers (2001) find weak albeit significant negative effects of student-teacher ratios on achievement and repetition, and these effects become even weaker for higher student-teacher ratios. OECD (2001) finds that as the student-teaching ratio rises above 25, there is a continuous decline in school performance in all PISA subjects. In contrast, a study by the OECD, UNESCO, and IIS (2003) does not find a performance advantage (or a statistically significant relation) of smaller student–teaching staff ratios. These results indicate that, on average, differences in student-teacher ratios do not explain differences in attainment.

The research on the effects of class size is extensive (see, for example, Fertig and Schmidt 2002; Woessmann and West 2002, 2006; Hanushek and Luque 2003; and Woessmann 2003, 2005).[15] Most research does not address the key policy question of whether smaller class sizes lead to higher student learning outcomes. The few studies that do confirm what previous literature has extensively shown: class size and student-teacher ratios appear to have a small (if any) association with student outcomes.

Research also indicates important cross-country (and age) differences. Angrist and Lavy (1999), for instance, show a nonlinear but significant relation between class size and student achievement in Israel. They find that reducing class size raises test results for fourth and fifth grades but not for third graders.

The Role of Schools in the Indigenous/Nonindigenous Achievement Gap

Much of the difference in achievement between indigenous and non-indigenous students can be explained by school-level factors. Analyzing the test scores of indigenous students on national assessments, McEwan (2004) finds that 50–70 of the gap can be explained by poor schools, even in countries such as Bolivia and Chile that have made efforts in recent years to more equitably redistribute educational resources and, in the case of Bolivia, to focus reforms on indigenous students. About 20–40 percent of the achievement gap can be explained by family variables. A small share of the gap is unexplained, possibly attributable to unobserved household variables, teacher bias, and curriculum and resources that are linguistically and culturally inadequate. In sum, indigenous students in Bolivia and Chile not only come from disadvantaged backgrounds, they also appear to attend lower-quality schools than their nonindigenous peers.

McEwan and Trowbridge (2007) try to disentangle the effects that create barriers to learning among rural indigenous students in Guatemala. Bolivia and Guatemala have the highest indigenous populations and prevalences of indigenous language use in the region. Guatemala has extremely poor educational indicators, with rural indigenous students achieving far below their urban and nonindigenous peers. Using data from the national PRONERE exam from more for than 500 rural Guatemala schools, McEwan and Trowbridge find that family background explains an even smaller portion of the achievement gap than in Chile and Bolivia, leaving schools responsible for a large part of the difference. As in Chile and Bolivia, differences across schools explains about 50–70 percent of the achievement gap between indigenous and nonindigenous students, implying that the schools to which indigenous students have access are of lower quality. In Guatemala a larger proportion of the achievement gap is "unexplainable" (attributable neither to students' background nor their schools). This suggests that the difference lies within schools, meaning that indigenous and nonindigenous students in the same school may perform differently. The authors believe that this "unexplained" portion of the gap could reflect unobserved family characteristics, discrimination within the school, low teacher expectations, or lack of appropriate materials and pedagogy, such as bilingual instruction and culturally appropriate curriculum.

Both McEwan (2004) and McEwan and Trowbridge (2007) emphasize that while school-side factors are largely responsible for the poor test-score performance of indigenous students, which school-side factors are responsible is not clear.[16] Because school-side factors are responsible for such a large part of the achievement gap, distinguishing which of these factors play important roles in student achievement is critical to developing policy alternatives.

Summary

Research shows that school-side factors are responsible for a smaller variation in student learning outcomes than student-side factors. However, certain school characteristics, such as teachers, have been shown to have a significant impact on student learning (table 6.2). The characteristics of effective teachers are not clear, although years of experience, credentials, and teacher test scores seem to make a difference. More attention needs to focus on developing good teacher-education programs and evaluating teacher education with an eye toward understanding how to educate teachers to be most effective.

Schools may be able to make up for some of the disadvantages faced by certain students, including indigenous students and students from low socioeconomic backgrounds (table 6.3). But poor-quality schools may (negatively) affect such students more than they affect students from more-privileged backgrounds. Redistributing resources and technical support to struggling schools through school-based compensatory programs or extending the length of the school day are two ways to offset those inequalities.

Lessons from Policies Addressing School Characteristics

Policies can affect the endowments and behaviors of education authorities, school administrators, and teachers, influencing what students experience in school (figure 6.6). Policies addressing school characteristics must ensure that children have adequate time and resources to learn in schools. This section focuses on three types of school-side interventions that have been shown to improve student learning: ensuring that all schools are adequately equipped to foster learning, guaranteeing that all children have adequate time and resources to learn in schools, and targeting compensatory programs effectively to those most in need. It also addresses the needs of multigrade schools, although strong empirical evidence is lacking in this area.

Ensure That All Schools Are Adequately Equipped to Foster Learning

Students need adequate learning environments. Although programs focusing on broad resource-based initiatives appear to have little effect on student

Table 6.2 Research Findings on Effects of Teachers on Learning and Other Outcomes

Factor	Student learning outcomes	Other outcomes	Site of study	Type of study	Source
Teacher experience and credentials					
Years of experience, completion of competitive undergraduate program, possession of teacher's license, average test score, graduate degree	Lower math and, to a lesser degree, reading scores associated with inexperienced teachers with below-average credentials. Reductions in math test scores of about 0.150–0.206 standard deviations; effect is larger than effect of class size, similar to that of having a parent without a college degree.		North Carolina, United States	Education production function	Clotfelter, Ladd, and Vigdor (2007)
Finance equalization					
Fundo de Manutenção e Desenvolvimento do Ensino Fundamental e de Valorização do Magistério (FUNDEF)	Gap between high- and low-performing students within states fell	Class size declined, number of overage children in primary and secondary schools fell.	Brazil	Instrumental variables estimation, quantile regression analysis	Gordon and Vegas (2005)

(continued)

Table 6.2 Research Findings on Effects of Teachers on Learning and Other Outcomes *(continued)*

Factor	Student learning outcomes	Other outcomes	Site of study	Type of study	Source
Salaries and incentives					
Increased teacher wages over 20-year period		Salary increase of 156 percent associated with 39 percent increase in number of teacher-education applicants and 16 percent increase in average test scores applicants. Similar test-score increase not observed among applicants to other university programs.	Chile	Descriptive statistics	Mizala and Romaguera (2005)
Increase in relative wages and wage dispersion		Teacher wage premiums did not attract more qualified candidates into teaching; may have attracted more from bottom quintile.	Venezuela, R. B. de	Estimates of teacher wage premiums 1975–2003 (coefficients on teacher dummy variables in Mincer-type regressions); quantile regression analysis to estimate impact of changes in wage premiums on distribution of applicants' test scores	Ortega (2006)

(continued)

Table 6.2 Research Findings on Effects of Teachers on Learning and Other Outcomes *(continued)*

Factor	Student learning outcomes	Other outcomes	Site of study	Type of study	Source
Salaries and incentives					
School-based performance bonus (SNED) for teachers	Mean score on national assessment of schools that participated in all three applications rose slightly.		Chile	Generalized least squares	Mizala and Romaguera (2005)
Performance-based promotion for teachers (Carrera Magisterial)	Student test scores did not improve as a result of performance-based pay reform.		Mexico	Regression discontinuity	McEwan and Santibáñez (2005)
Salary linked to teacher attendance, tracked by student-taken photos	After one year of participation in the program, test scores were 0.17 standard deviations higher than those of students from comparator schools.	Teacher absenteeism fell (23 percent in test group, 43 percent in comparator group), and students were more likely to be admitted into formal schools.	India	Controlled experiment	Duflo and Hanna (2005)

(continued)

Table 6.2 Research Findings on Effects of Teachers on Learning and Other Outcomes *(continued)*

Factor	Student learning outcomes	Other outcomes	Site of study	Type of study	Source
Teacher assignment					
Teacher mobility and retention		Experienced teachers choose "better" schools, forcing inexperienced teachers to teach in poorer schools.	Uruguay	Linear probability regressions with school fixed effects	Vegas, Urquiola, and Cerdán-Infantes (2006)

Source: Author compilation.

Table 6.3 Research Findings on Effects of Schools on Learning and Other Outcomes

Factor	Student learning outcomes	Other outcomes	Site of study	Type of study	Source
Textbooks					
	Test scores rose 0.06, 0.30, 0.34, and 0.36 standard deviations in different countries.		Developing countries	Literature review of four studies	Lockheed and Hanushek (1988)
	Test scores rose one-third of a standard deviation after one year.	Gap between rural and urban students narrowed.	Nicaragua	Controlled experiment	Jamison and others (1981)
	Giving 1 textbook per 2 students and 1 textbook per student (compared with control group of 1 textbook per 10 students) improved test scores. Effect was greatest among students from poor families, whose scores rose by one-third of a standard deviation in grade 1 language and grades 1 and 2 math and by half a standard deviation in grades 1 and 2 science. Little difference between 1:2 and 1:1 textbook-to-student ratio.		Philippines	Differences-in-differences estimation	Heyneman, Jamison, and Montenegro (1983)

(continued)

Table 6.3 Research Findings on Effects of Schools on Learning and Other Outcomes *(continued)*

Factor	Student learning outcomes	Other outcomes	Site of study	Type of study	Source
Textbooks					
	Test scores rose only for top performance quintile.		Kenya	Controlled experiment	Glewwe, Kremer, and Moulin (2007)
Information and communication technologies					
Computer-assisted instruction	Effect was mostly negative and only marginally significant.	Computer use among teachers rose.	Israel	Exploited a natural experiment—random assignment of computers to school by lottery—to identify impact of computers using two-stage least squares and instrumental variables estimation.	Angrist and Lavy (2002)

(continued)

Table 6.3 Research Findings on Effects of Schools on Learning and Other Outcomes *(continued)*

Factor	Student learning outcomes	Other outcomes	Site of study	Type of study	Source
	Math scores for children in standards 4 rose 0.37 standard deviations. Effect was slightly stronger at the bottom of the distribution, same for girls and boys.		India	Controlled experiment	Linden, Banerjee, and Duflo (2003)
Long-term access to computers (over five years)	PISA math scores rose.		OECD and other countries participating in PISA 2003	Education production function	OECD (2006)
Moderate use (once a week to once a month)	PISA math and reading scores on rose.				
Time in school/time on task					
Full school day (number of hours increased from 955 or 1,043 to 1,216)	Scores on the Sistema de Medición de la Calidad de la Educación (SIMCE) rose 0.2 standard deviations in language and remained unchanged in math in public schools that participated in the program. Among voucher-recipient schools, test scores rose 0.3–0.5 standard deviations in language and about 0.3 in math.		Chile	Differences-in-differences estimation and propensity-score matching techniques	Valenzuela (2005)

(continued)

Table 6.3 Research Findings on Effects of Schools on Learning and Other Outcomes *(continued)*

Factor	Student learning outcomes	Other outcomes	Site of study	Type of study	Source
	SIMCE scores in math and language rose.		Chile	Differences-in-differences estimation	Bellei (2005)
Full school day (number of hours increased from four to seven)	Test scores rose 0.30 points (out of 24) per year of participation in math and 0.20 in language, with greatest effects in most-disadvantaged schools.		Uruguay	Differences-in-differences estimation and propensity-score matching techniques	Cerdán-Infantes and Vermeersch (2006)
School-based compensatory programs					
Consejo Nacional de Fomento Educativo (CONAFE)	Math scores of indigenous students rose 6.5 points over non–CONAFE nonindigenous students and 5 points over comparable CONAFE nonindigenous students. No effect on language scores.	Improved intermediate quality indicators, such as repetition and failure rates.	Mexico	Differences-in-differences estimation and propensity-score matching techniques	Shapiro and Moreno-Trevino (2004)

(continued)

Table 6.3 Research Findings on Effects of Schools on Learning and Other Outcomes *(continued)*

Factor	Student learning outcomes	Other outcomes	Site of study	Type of study	Source
Telesecundaria	Test scores of less-disadvantaged group rose 1.4 points in math and 3.4 points in Spanish.	Reduced gap between students who participated and those who did not by 24 percent in math and 33 percent in language.	Mexico	Differences-in-differences estimation and propensity-score matching techniques	Shapiro and Moreno-Trevino (2004)
P-900 and Full School Day		Reduced gap between indigenous and nonindigenous students' test scores by 0.2 standard deviations in Spanish and 0.1 standard deviations in math.	Chile	Oaxaca decomposition to identify determinants of reduction in indigenous-nonindigenous test-score gap.	McEwan (2006a)

Source: Author compilation.

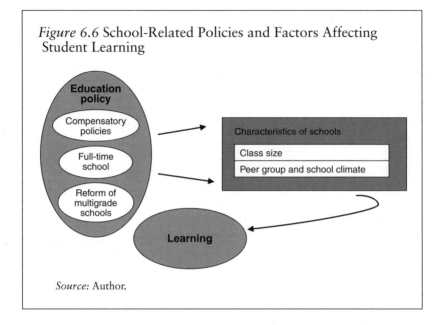

Figure 6.6 School-Related Policies and Factors Affecting Student Learning

Source: Author.

achievement, schools need an adequate level of equipment (buildings, textbooks, supplies, library materials, heating, and so forth) to be able to function properly. Where facilities and equipment are inadequate, compensatory programs that target needy schools are needed.

A school's resources can also affect the type of teachers it attracts. As evidence from Uruguay shows, among the most important variables for a teacher when choosing a school are access to adequate teaching materials and infrastructure (Vegas, Urquiola, and Cerdán-Infantes 2006). Given teachers' inclination to choose schools with better working conditions, it is important to try to even out these conditions across schools.

Guarantee That All Children Have Time and Resources to Learn in Schools

Children need adequate time and resources to learn in schools. For students who attend schools in shifts or who have shorter school days, expanding the time spent in school, with concurrent curricular and pedagogical support, can improve learning. Doing so also has important equity implications. Uruguay's Full-Time School program has shown that disadvantaged children benefit disproportionately from a longer school day (Cerdán-Infantes and Vermeersch 2006). Initially focusing a full-time program on the neediest children is likely to yield the greatest benefit while beginning to close the achievement gap between rich and poor students.

Target Compensatory Programs Effectively to the Neediest Students and Schools

Providing extra resources to schools enrolling disadvantaged students can help compensate for students' early disadvantages. In the United States, Chapter 1 (formerly Title 1) and Head Start provide resources to disadvantaged students early in their careers. Title 1 yields immediate improvement in student test scores, but the effects last only a year (Slavin 1989). Head Start students show improvement in test scores, dropout rates, and repetition rates, but the effects dissipate by the third grade, and Head Start students are no more likely than other students to complete high school (Currie and Thomas 2000). These findings suggest that compensatory programs such as Head Start may need to stay in place longer to produce long-term effects (Shapiro and Moreno-Trevino 2004).

Evidence from Latin America indicates that compensatory programs and extended school days can improve student learning and reduce failure, repetition, and dropout rates, especially among indigenous students. In Latin America the poor generally have access to lower-quality schools. When this trend is coupled with the often meager financial, cultural, and social capital of poor families, disadvantaged students face extremely high barriers to learning. Compensatory programs provide targeted resources, such as didactic materials, funds, or special support to teachers, to poor or struggling schools in an attempt to redistribute resources and redress such inequality (Reimers 2000). Mexico's Consejo Nacional de Fomento Educativo (CONAFE) program and Chile's school reform (P-900 and Full School Day) both appear to have had positive effects on indigenous student learning (box 6.2). Because schools appear

---

Box 6.2 Compensatory Programs for Indigenous Students in Chile and Mexico

A recent study of the Chilean school reform of the 1990s draws on data from the eighth-grade Sistema de Medición de la Calidad de la Educación (SIMCE) tests from 1997 and 2000 in Spanish and math to examine the reform's impact on indigenous student achievement (McEwan 2006a). The study shows that the gap between indigenous and nonindigenous students' test scores diminished by 0.2 standard deviations in Spanish and 0.1 standard deviations in math within a relatively short period.[a] The author attributes this convergence in test scores to two elements of the reform: P-900 and the Full School Day (FSD), both of which were more likely to target indigenous students. P-900 focuses on low-achieving students, providing tutoring to students in grades 1–4. Although the selection criteria for this component of the program are not clear, if inclusion

(continued)

Box 6.2 Compensatory Programs for Indigenous Students in Chile and Mexico *(continued)*

was based on socioeconomic status or achievement, indigenous students may have been disproportionately represented. FSD appears to have had a greater impact on indigenous students.[b] McEwan considers, but then rejects, a number of plausible alternative explanations for the convergence in test scores, including the increased socioeconomic well-being of indigenous families and sorting across schools.

Inclusion in Chile's P-900 reform appears to have been based on test scores and socioeconomic factors rather than indigenous status. It nevertheless reached a disproportionate number of indigenous students. Basing recipient schools on test results alone can be problematic, however (see chapter 3) (Chay, McEwan, and Urquiola 2005).

Mexico's CONAFE program provides extra resources to disadvantaged schools and supports rural secondary students in *telesecundaria* (distance learning) education. CONAFE schools include all schools serving indigenous students, as well as some other secondary and rural schools. Schools enrolling indigenous students receive curricular support, didactic materials, and indigenous- and Spanish-language textbooks to aid bilingual education. CONAFE also supports intercultural bilingual education for indigenous students. Rural schools receive up-to-date audiovisual technology, professional development for teachers, and infrastructure improvements, among other interventions. CONAFE also provides audiovisual materials and infrastructure improvements for *telesecundaria* education (Shapiro and Moreno-Trevino 2004).

An impact evaluation shows that CONAFE is most effective in improving learning in primary-school math and secondary-school Spanish. Although indigenous students remained behind their nonindigenous counterparts, indigenous primary-school students improved significantly in math, closing the gap with non–CONAFE nonindigenous students by 6.5 points and closing the gap with comparable CONAFE nonindigenous students by 5.0 points. There was no effect on Spanish learning at the primary level. Spanish scores among *telesecundaria* students did increase, however. CONAFE also improved intermediate quality indicators, such as repetition and failure rates. The authors conclude that CONAFE appears to be well targeted.

CONAFE appears to improve short-term learning results for disadvantaged students. Its effect on long-term results is an area for future research, as is research on which components of the program were responsible for its effectiveness.

a. Reduction in the test-score gap in Spanish and math may have been at the expense of promotion of indigenous languages (McEwan 2006a).

b. A previous quasi-experimental evaluation showed that FSD yields larger test-score gains among schools that enroll disproportionately large numbers of disadvantaged students (Valenzuela 2005).

to play the largest role in the test-score gap between indigenous and nonindigenous children, school-based compensatory programs are likely to help reduce this gap.

How schools are chosen to take part in compensatory programs is important. When students and schools have very different endowments, improving achievement while ensuring that all students achieve acceptable levels of learning can be a challenge. Compensatory programs are a tool for compensating for lower student or school endowments. They can be targeted in many different ways (by targeting poor students, underequipped schools, or underperforming schools, for example).

Three types of information are necessary for the central administration to be able to make efficient allocative decisions: results information, context information, and means information. In many countries in Latin America and the Caribbean, comprehensive school-level information needs development.

Internationally, countries have taken at least two steps to match the needs of schools to educational financing. First, the budget devoted to each school has been more tightly linked to the needs of the school, not only in terms of poverty but also in terms of comprehensive information on the adequacy or deficiency of equipment and infrastructure. Second, schools have been granted greater autonomy in determining how to allocate their budgets. Many countries use local oversight mechanisms (including parents, communities, and teachers) to ensure that school funds are used in optimal ways (figure 6.7). Strengthening these mechanisms in Latin America and the Caribbean could help improve budget-allocation decision making at the school level. Indeed, programs that provide small grants to schools have improved student learning and intermediate quality indicators, such as repetition and dropout rates, in many Latin American countries (Gertler, Patrinos, and Rubio-Codina 2006b). (For a discussion of Mexico's Apoyo a la Gestión Escolar [AGE], program, see chapter 9.)

Provide Special Support to Multigrade Schools

Many students from rural areas attend multigrade schools, which enroll students of varying ages and abilities in the same class, enabling greater access to schooling in remote areas and reducing costs. Multigrade schools are generally staffed by a single teacher, who receives no special training or materials to effectively manage such a diverse classroom. Many of those schools do not offer a full course of primary education. As a result, students often delay enrollment, repeat grades, drop out, or do not enroll at all. The needs of multigrade schools are so great that traditional cash transfer programs or community management programs cannot offset the disadvantages that students in these schools face.

Reforms of multigrade schools, which have their roots in Colombia's Escuela Nueva program, have been adopted in various countries, including

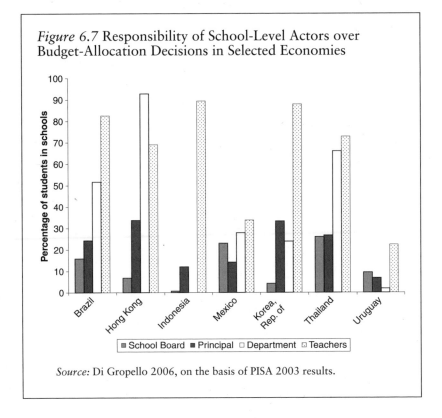

Figure 6.7 Responsibility of School-Level Actors over Budget-Allocation Decisions in Selected Economies

Source: Di Gropello 2006, on the basis of PISA 2003 results.

Chile (the MECE-Rural program) and Guatemala (Nueva Escuela Unitaria). These three programs share a number of characteristics. First, the reforms emphasize adequate training for teachers to teach more effectively in a multigrade setting. Second, they provide both teachers and students with appropriate materials and textbooks. Third, they provide additional opportunities for potentially isolated teachers to interact with colleagues, in an attempt to motivate teachers to find bottom-up solutions to challenges they face in the classroom. Fourth, they encourage students to participate actively in their own learning and to work independently and creatively (McEwan 2006b).

A review of multigrade school reforms in Chile, Colombia, and Guatemala (McEwan 2006b) finds that in many cases schools have not fully integrated the reforms, perhaps because the programs did not adopt the bottom-up process favored by the initial proponents of Escuela Nueva. In the worst cases, schools do not even receive the prescribed materials.

Most evaluations of these schools and their impact on student learning are plagued by selection bias and other threats to internal validity. The most-compelling evaluations come from Colombia (McEwan 1998;

Psacharopolous, Rojas, and Velez 1993). They show consistently positive effects on academic achievement in the early primary grades, but the effects on student achievement are less apparent in the upper primary grades and for nonacademic outcomes. The most credible evidence, from Chile and Guatemala, also show gains in treated schools (Universidad Austral and Universidad de Playa Ancha 1998; Juarez and Associates 2003). The implication is that multigrade school reforms have the potential to overcome rural/urban inequities if they are properly implemented. Future evaluations could be facilitated by selection procedures such as randomized assignment.

Notes

1. For evidence that teacher quality has a strong impact on student achievement, see Rivkin, Hanushek, and Kain (1998) and Rockoff (2004). Ehrenberg and Brewer (1995) and Ferguson and Ladd (1996) provide evidence that teachers' math and language skills are strongly related to student outcomes.
2. For a review of what is known about teacher characteristics, see Darling-Hammond (2000).
3. This section draws heavily on Vegas and Umansky (2005).
4. This chapter compares hourly wages of teachers and nonteachers. The advantage of using hourly wages, rather than monthly or annual salaries, is that they take into account differences in the number of hours worked. This is particularly important when analyzing teacher salaries, as teachers often work fewer hours per week and fewer weeks per year than comparable workers in other occupations.
5. Hernani-Limarino (2005) looks at hourly rather than annual salaries. Because teachers typically work fewer hours than people in other professions, their monthly salaries may be lower, discouraging some from entering or remaining in the field.
6. Latin America now faces the daunting task of massively expanding secondary education from the 2000 net enrollment rate of 64 percent (World Bank 2003). Secondary school teachers require more specialized and advanced subject-specific knowledge than do primary school teachers. Although to date acute teacher shortages have not developed in Latin America, the challenges of recruiting and retaining sufficient numbers of qualified and talented secondary school teachers may require higher salaries.
7. Murnane and others (1991), Loeb and Page (2000), and Kingdon and Teal (2002) suggest that salary levels are critical to teacher recruitment, retention, and quality. Others—including Hoxby (1996); Ballou and Podgursky (1997); Rivkin, Hanushek, and Kain (2001); and Bennell (2004)—counter that other working conditions and considerations may be more important than salary levels.
8. The quality of applicants did not rise in all degree programs; in as engineering, for example, the average entrance exam score remained more or less constant.
9. Because Venezuela's university system is rigid and students rarely change majors after enrolling, a students' declared major is a good proxy for his or her future career.
10. These results imply that wage premiums and wage dispersion do not affect teacher performance or educational quality by drawing more-talented candidates into teaching. They may, however, affect teacher performance and educational quality in other ways.

11. This volume does not address pensions and other nonsalary benefits. Teachers' pensions, however, are widely believed to be higher than those of nonteachers, earned at an earlier age, and fiscally secure. High, early, and secure pensions may be a strong incentive for teachers to enter and remain in the field.

12. This section draws heavily on Duthilleul (2005) and Hargreaves and Fink (2002).

13. A notable exception is Glewwe, Kremer, and Moulin (2000), who find that textbook provision improved only the scores of the top quintile in Kenya, albeit by a significant 0.22 standard deviations.

14. According to the government of Honduras, in 2006 the average number of school days over the previous three years was 72. It hopes to increase this figure to 200 in 2006 (presentation by the government of Honduras, August 25, 2006).

15. None of these studies attempts to measure the cost-effectiveness of reducing class size versus alternative policy-related interventions.

16. In Guatemala, for instance, primary schools are highly segregated. The interaction of peers within such schools could also be affecting students' performance.

References

Abadzi, H. 2006. *Efficient Learning for the Poor: Insights from the Frontier of Cognitive Neuroscience.* Washington, DC: World Bank.

Andrew, M., and R. L. Schwab. 1995. "Has Reform in Teacher Education Influenced Teacher Performance? An Outcome Assessment of Graduates of Eleven Teacher Education Programs." *Action in Teacher Education* 17: 43–53.

Angrist, J. D., and V. Lavy. 1999. "Using Maimonides' Rule to Estimate the Effect of Class Size on Scholastic Achievement." *Quarterly Journal of Economics* 114 (2): 533–75.

———. 2002. "New Evidence on Classroom Computers and Pupil Learning." *Economic Journal* 112 (October): 735–65.

Ballou, D., and M. Podgursky. 1997. *Teacher Pay and Teacher Quality.* W. E. Upjohn Institute of Employment Research, Kalamazoo, MI.

Bellei, C. 2005. "Does the Length of the School Day Have an Impact on the Students' Academic Achievement?" Harvard Graduate School of Education, Cambridge, MA.

Bennell, P. 2004. "Teacher Motivation and Incentives in Sub-Saharan Africa and Asia." Knowledge and Skills for Development, Brighton. http://www.eldis.org/fulltext/dfidtea.pdf

Benavot, A. 2004. "Studies on Instructional Time." Background paper for *EFA Global Monitoring Report 2005.* United Nations Educational, Scientific, and Cultural Organization (UNESCO), International Bureau of Education, Geneva.

Bruni-Celli, J., M. González, and O. Ramos. 2002. "Venezuela: La importancia del ámbito institucional para el desempeño." In *¿Quiénes son los maestros? Carreras e incentivos docentes en América Latina,* ed. J. C. Navarro. Washington, DC: Inter-American Development Bank.

Cawthera, A. 2001. "Computers in Secondary Schools in Developing Countries: Costs and Other Issues." Serial 43, Department for International Development, World Links, and World Bank, Washington, DC.

Cerdán-Infantes, P., and C. Vermeersch. 2006. "More Time Is Better: An Evaluation of the Full-Time School Program in Uruguay." Background paper prepared for this report. World Bank, Washington, DC.

Chay, K. Y., P. J. McEwan, and M. S. Urquiola. 2005. "The Central Role of Noise in Evaluating Interventions That Use Test Scores to Rank Schools." *American Economic Review* 95 (4): 1237–58.

Clotfelter, C., H. F. Ladd, and J. L. Vigdor. 2007. "How and Why Do Teacher Credentials Matter for Student Achievement?" NBER Working Paper 12828, National Bureau of Economic Research, Cambridge, MA.

Corcoran, S., W. Evans, and R. Schwab. 2004a. "Changing Labor-Market Opportunities for Women and the Quality of Teachers, 1995–2000." *American Economic Review* 94 (2): 230–35.

———. 2004b. "Women, the Labor Market, and the Declining Relative Quality of Teachers." *Journal of Policy Analysis and Management* 23 (3): 449–70.

Cox, C. 2003. "Las políticas educacionales de Chile en las últimas dos décadas del siglo XX." *In Políticas educacionales en el cambio de siglo: La reforma del sistema escolar en Chile*, ed. C. Cox. Santiago: Editorial Universitaria.

———. 2006. "Policy Formation and Implementation in Secondary Education Reform: The Case of Chile at the Turn of the Century." Education Working Paper Series 3, World Bank, Washington, DC.

Currie, J., and D. Thomas. 2000. "School Quality and the Longer-term Effects of Head Start." *Journal of Human Resources* 35 (4): 755–74.

Darling-Hammond, L. 2000. "Teacher Quality and Student Achievement: A Review of State Policy Evidence." *Education Analysis Policy Archives* 8 (1).

Denton, J. J., and W. H. Peters. 1988. "Program Assessment Report: Curriculum Evaluation of a Nontraditional Program for Certifying Teachers." Texas A & M University, College Station, TX.

Di Gropello, E., ed. 2006. *Meeting the Challenges of Secondary Education in Latin America and East Asia*. Washington, DC: World Bank.

Duflo, E. 2001. "School and Labor Market Consequences of School Construction in Indonesia: Evidence from an Unusual Policy Experiment." *American Economic Review* 91 (4): 795–813.

Duflo, E., and R. Hanna. 2005. "Monitoring Works: Getting Teachers to Come to School." NBER Working Paper 11880, National Bureau of Economic Research, Cambridge, MA.

Duthilleul, Y. 2005. "Teacher Education, Professional Development and Certification Policies in Latin America: The Missing Link to Improving Education Quality in the Region." Background paper prepared for this report. World Bank, Washington, DC.

Earle, R. 2002. "The Integration of Instructional Technology into Public Education: Promises and Challenges." *Education Technology Magazine* 42 (1): 5–13.

Ehrenberg, R., and D. Brewer. 1995. "Did Teachers' Verbal Ability and Race Matter in the 1960s? Coleman Revisited." *Economics of Education Review* 14 (1): 1–21.

Ferguson, R., and H. Ladd. 1996. "How and Why Money Matters: An Analysis of Alabama Schools." In *Holding Schools Accountable: Performance-Based Reform in Education*, ed. H. F. Ladd, 265–98. Washington, DC: Brookings Institution.

Fertig, M., and M. C. Schmidt. 2002. "The Role of Background Factors for Reading Literacy: Straight National Scores in the PISA 2000 Study." Discussion Paper 545, Institute for the Study of Labor (IZA), Bonn.

Fuchs, T., and L. Woessmann. 2004. "Computers and Student Learning: Bivariate and Multivariate Evidence on the Availability and Use of Computers at Home and at School." CESifo Working Paper 1321, Munich.

Gertler, P., H. Patrinos, and M. Rubio-Codina. 2006a. "Do Supply-Side-Oriented and Demand-Side-Oriented Education Programs Generate Synergies? Evidence from Rural Mexico." World Bank, Washington, DC.

———. 2006b. "Empowering Parents to Improve Education: Evidence from Rural Mexico." Policy Research Working Paper 3935, World Bank, Washington, DC.

Glewwe, P., N. Ilias, and M. Kremer. 2003. "Teacher Incentives." NBER Working Paper 9671, National Bureau of Economic Research, Cambridge, MA.

Glewwe, P., M. Kremer, and S. Moulin. 2007. "Many Children Left Behind? Textbooks and Test Scores in Kenya." Harvard University, Center for International Development Working Paper 149, Cambridge, MA.

Gordon, N., and E. Vegas. 2005. "Education Finance Equalization, Spending, Teacher Quality, and Student Outcomes." In *Incentives to Improve Teaching*, ed. Emiliana Vegas. Washington, DC: World Bank.

Hanushek, E. A. 1986. "The Economics of Schooling: Production and Efficiency in Public Schools." *Journal of Economic Literature* 49 (3): 1141–77.

———.1995. "Interpreting Recent Research on Schooling in Developing Countries." *World Bank Research Observer Research Observer* 10 (2): 1141–77.

———. 1998. *"Conclusions and Controversies about the Effectiveness of School Resources,"* FRBNY *Economic Policy Review* 4 (1): 11–28.

———. 2003. "The Failure of Input-Based Schooling Policies." *Economic Journal* 113 (February): F64–F98.

Hanushek, E. A., and D. D. Kimko. 2000. "Schooling, Labor-Force Quality, and the Growth of Nations." *American Economic Review* 90 (5): 1184–1208.

Hanushek, E. A., and J. A. Luque. 2003. "Efficiency and Equity in Schools around the World." *Economics of Education Review* 22 (5): 481–502.

Hanushek, Eric A., and R. Pace. 1995. "Who Chooses to Teach (and Why)?" *Economics of Education Review* 14 (2): 101–17.

Harbison, R. W., and E. A. Hanushek. 1992. *Educational Performance of the Poor: Lessons from Rural Northeast Brazil.* New York: Oxford University Press for the World Bank.

Hargreaves, A., and D. Fink. 2006. "Redistributed Leadership for Sustainable Professional Learning Communities." *Journal of School Leadership* 16(5).

Hepp, P. K., E. Hinostoza, E. Laval, and L. Rehbein. 2004. "Technology in Schools: Education, ICT, and the Knowledge Society." Human Development Network, World Bank, Washington, DC.

Hernani-Limarino, W. 2005. "Are Teachers Well Paid in Latin America and the Caribbean? Relative Wage and Structure of Returns of Teachers in Latin America and the Caribbean." In *Incentives to Improve Teaching. Lessons from Latin America*, ed. E. Vegas. Washington, DC: World Bank.

Heyneman, S., D. Jamison, and X. Montenegro. 1984. "Textbooks in the Philippines: Evaluation of the Pedagogical Impact of a Nationwide Investment." *Educational Evaluation and Policy Analysis* 6 (2): 139–50.

Honey, M. 2001. "Technology's Effectiveness as a Teaching and Learning Tool." Testimony presented before the Labor, Health and Human Services Subcommittee of the U.S. Senate. Education Development Center, Newton MA.

Hoxby, C. 1996. "How Teachers' Unions Affect Education Production." *Quarterly Journal of Economics* 111 (3): 671–718.

Hoxby, C., and A. Leigh. 2004. "Pulled Away or Pushed Out? Explaining the Decline of Teacher Aptitude in the United States." *American Economic Review* 94 (2): 236–46.

Jamison, D., B. Searle, K. Galda, and S. Heyneman. 1981. "Improving Elementary Mathematics Education in Nicaragua: An Experimental Study of the Impact of Textbooks and Radio on Achievement." *Journal of Educational Psychology* 73 (4): 556–67.

Juarez and Associates, Inc. 2003. *The Effects of Active Learning Programs in Multi-grade Schools on Girls' Persistence in and Completion of Primary School in Developing Countries.* Report prepared for the U.S. Agency for International Development (USAID). Los Angeles.

Kingdon, G., and F. Teal. 2002. "Does Performance-Related Pay for Teachers Improve Student Performance? Some Evidence from India." Working Paper 165, Center for the Study of African Economies, Oxford University, United Kingdom.

Krueger, A. B. 2002. "Economic Considerations and Class Size." NBER Working Paper 8875, National Bureau of Economic Research, Cambridge, MA.

Lavy, V. 2004. "Performance Pay and Teachers' Effort, Productivity, and Grading Ethics." NBER Working Paper 10622, National Bureau of Economic Research, Cambridge, MA.

Lazear, E. P. 2001. "Educational Production." *Quarterly Journal of Economics* 116 (3): 777–803.

———. 2003. "Teacher Incentives." *Swedish Economic Policy Review* 10 (3): 179–214.

Linden, L., A. Banerjee, and E. Duflo. 2003. "Computer-Assisted Learning: Evidence from a Randomized Experiment." Poverty Action Lab Paper 5, Massachusetts Institute of Technology, Cambridge, MA.

Lockheed M. E., and A. M. Verspoor. 1991. *Improving Primary Education in Developing Countries.* New York: Oxford University Press.

Loeb, S., and M. Page. 2000. "Examining the Link between Teacher Wages and Student Outcomes: The Importance of Alternative Labor Market Opportunities and Nonpecuniary Variation." *Review of Economics and Statistics* 82(3): 393–408.

Martinic, S. 1998. "Tiempo y aprendizaje." LCSHD Working Paper Series, World Bank, Washington, DC.

McEwan, P. 1998. "The Effectiveness of Multigrade Schools in Colombia." *International Journal of Educational Development* 18 (6): 435–52.

———. 2004. "The Indigenous Test Score Gap in Bolivia and Chile." *Economic Development and Cultural Change* 53 (1): 157–90.

———. 2006a. "Can Schools Reduce the Test Score Disadvantage of Ethnic Minorities? Evidence from Chile." Background paper prepared for this report. World Bank, Washington, DC.

————. 2006b. "Multigrade School Reform in Latin America: What We (Don't) Know." Background paper prepared for this report. World Bank, Washington, DC.

McEwan, P., and L. Santibáñez. 2005. "Teacher and Principal Incentives in Mexico." In *Incentives to Improve Teaching*, ed. E. Vegas. Washington, DC: World Bank.

McEwan, P., and M. Trowbridge. 2007. "The Achievement of Indigenous Students in Guatemalan Primary Schools." *International Journal of Educational Development* 27 (1): 61–76.

Mizala, A., and P. Romaguera. 2005. "Teachers' Salary Structure and Incentives in Chile." In *Incentives to Improve Teaching*, ed. E. Vegas. Washington DC: World Bank.

Murnane, R., J. Singer, J. Willet, J. Kenple, and R. Olsen. 1991. *Who Will Teach? Policies That Matter*. Cambridge, MA: Harvard University Press.

Navarro, J. C., ed. 2002. *¿Quienes son los maestros? Carreras e incentivos docentes en América Latina*. Inter-American Development Bank, Washington, DC.

OECD (Organisation for Economic Co-operation and Development). 2001. Knowledge and Skills for Life: *First Results from PISA 2000: Publications 2000*. Paris: OECD.

————. 2004. *Learning for Tomorrow's World. First Results from PISA 2003*. Paris: OECD.

————. 2005. *Education at a Glance*. Paris: OECD.

————. 2006. *Are Students Ready for a Technology-Rich World? What PISA Studies Tell Us*. Paris: OECD.

OECD, UNESCO (United Nations Educational, Scientific, and Cultural Organization), and IIS (Institute for Statistics). 2003. *Literacy Skills for the World of Tomorrow: Further Results from PISA 2000: Publications 2000*. Paris: OECD/UNESCO–UIS.

Ortega, D. 2006. "The Effect of Wage Compression and Alternative Labor Market Opportunities on Teacher Quality in Venezuela." Background paper prepared for this report. World Bank, Washington, DC.

Pritchett, L. 2004. "Towards a New Consensus for Addressing the Global Challenge of the Lack of Education." Working Paper 43, Center for Global Development, Washington, DC.

Pritchett, L., and D. Filmer. 1997. "What Educational Production Functions Really Show: A Positive Theory of Education Spending." Policy Research Working Paper 1795, World Bank, Washington, DC.

Psacharopolous, G., C. Rojas, and E. Velez. 1992. "Achievement Evaluation of Colombia's Escuela Nueva: Is Multigrade the Answer?" Policy Research Working Paper Series 896, World Bank, Washington, DC.

Reimers, F. 2000. "Educational Opportunity and Policy in Latin America." In *Unequal Schools, Unequal Chances*, ed. F. Reimers. Cambridge, MA: Harvard University Press.

Rivkin, S., E. Hanushek, and J. Kain. 1998. "Teachers, Schools and Academic Achievement." NBER Working Paper w6691, National Bureau of Economic Research, Cambridge, MA.

————. 2001. "Teachers, Schools, and Academic Achievement." Working Paper 6691, Cambridge, MA.

Rockoff, J. 2004. "The Impact of Individual Teachers on Student Achievement: Evidence from Panel Data." *American Economic Review* 94 (2): 247–57.

Rosenholtz, S. 1989. *Teacher's Workplace: The Social Organization of Schools.* New York: Longman.

Sanders, W., and J. Rivers. 1996. *Cumulative and Residual Effects of Teachers on Future Student Academic Achievement.* University of Tennessee, Value-Added Research and Assessment Center, Knoxville, TN. http://www.heartland. org/pdf/21803.

Schweinhart, L. J., J. Montie, Z. Xiang., W. S. Barnett, C. R. Belfield, M. Nores. 2005. "Lifetime Effects: The High/Scope Perry Preschool Study through Age 40." Monograph 14, High/Scope Educational Research Foundation, Ypsilanti, MI.

Shapiro, J., and Jorge Moreno-Trevino. 2004. "Compensatory Education for Disadvantaged Mexican Students: An Impact Evaluation using Propensity Score Matching." Policy Research Working Paper 3334, World Bank, Washington, DC.

Stallings, J. A. 1976. "How Instructional Processes Relate to Child Outcomes in a National Study of Follow Through." *Journal of Teacher Education* 27 (1): 43–47.

UNESCO Institute for Education Statistics. Data. *http://www.uis.unesco.org.*

Universidad Austral, and Universidad de Playa Ancha. 1998. *Estudio de evaluación de la línea de educación rural del Programa* MECE. Valdivia and Valparaíso, Chile.

Urquiola, M., and E. Vegas. 2005. "Arbitrary Variation in Teacher Salaries." In *Incentives to Improve Teaching: Lessons from Latin America*, ed. E. Vegas. Washington, DC: World Bank.

Valenzuela, J. P. 2005. "Partial Evaluation of a Big Reform in the Chilean Education System: From Half Day to Full Day Schooling." University of Michigan, Ann Arbor.

Van Dusen, L. M., and B. Worthen. 1995. "Can Integrated Instructional Technology Transform the Classroom?" *Educational Leadership* 53 (2): 28–33.

Vegas, E., ed. 2005. *Incentives to Improve Teaching: Lessons from Latin America.* Washington, DC: World Bank.

Vegas, E., R. J. Murnane, and J. B. Willett. 2001. "From High School to Teaching: Many Steps, Who Makes It?" *Teachers College Record* 103 (3): 427–49.

Vegas, E., and I. Umansky. 2005. *Improving Teaching and Learning through Effective Incentives.* Washington, DC: World Bank.

Vegas, E., M. Urquiola, and P. Cerdán-Infantes. 2006. "Teacher Assignment, Mobility and Their Impact on Equity and Quality of Education in Uruguay." Background paper prepared for this report. World Bank, Washington, DC.

Villegas-Reimers, E. 1998. *The Preparation of Teachers in Latin America: Challenges and Trends.* World Bank, Washington, DC.

Walston, J. T., and J. West. 2004. *Full-Day and Half-Day Kindergarten in the United States: Findings from the Early Childhood Longitudinal Study, Kindergarten Class of 1998–99.* NCES 2004–078, U.S. Department of Education, National Center for Education Statistics. Washington, DC: U.S. Government Printing Office.

Willms, J. D., and M. Somers. 2001. "Family, Classroom, and School Effects on Children's Educational Outcomes in Latin America." *School Effectiveness and School Improvement* 12 (4): 409–45.

Woessmann, L. 2001. "New Evidence on the Missing Resource-Performance Link in Education." Kiel Working Paper 1051, Kiel Institute of World Economics, Kiel, Germany.

———. 2003. "Schooling Resources, Educational Institutions and Student Performance: The International Evidence." *Oxford Bulletin of Economics and Statistics* 65 (2): 117–70.

———. 2005. "Families, Schools, and Primary-School Learning: Evidence for Argentina and Colombia in an International Perspective." Policy Research Paper 3537, World Bank, Washington, DC.

Woessmann, L., and M. R. West. 2002. "Class-Size Effects in School Systems around the World: Evidence from between-Grade Variation in TIMSS." Institute for the Study of Labor (IZA), Bonn.

Woessmann, L., and M. R. West. 2006. "Class-Size Effects in School Systems around the World: Evidence from Between-Grade Variation in TIMSS." *European Economic Review* 50 (3): 695–736.

World Bank. 2003. *World Development Report 2004: Making Services Work for Poor People*. Washington, DC: World Bank.

———. 2005. *Expanding Opportunities and Building Competencies for Young People*: A New Agenda for Secondary Education. Washington, DC: World Bank.

———. 2006. *A Review of ICT Components in World Bank Education Projects (2001–2004)*. InfoDev, Washington, DC.

7

Organizational Factors and Policies

A country's education system can be organized, managed, and governed in a number of ways. The organizational structure of the system plays a key role in student learning. Responsibility for decision making regarding financing, spending, teacher hiring and firing, pedagogical decisions and curriculum—all of which may affect student learning outcomes—can lie at a number of levels.

Organizational Factors Affecting Student Learning

A growing body of research uses international assessments to examine the effect on cross-country differences in student scores of various organizational factors. This research suggests that organizational factors may explain up to 25 percent of variations in test scores across countries (Fuchs and Woessmann 2004b). Cross-country comparisons suggest that student achievement, as measured by test scores, is positively correlated with the following features:

- Centralized control of curricular and budgetary affairs
- Administration of schools at the intermediate (rather than the central) level.
- School autonomy over process and personnel decisions
- Incentives for individual teachers
- Teacher-selected teaching methods
- Limited influence of teacher unions
- National assessments
- Parental involvement

Level of Decision-Making Authority

Differences in the level at which the authority over decision-making rests can affect student learning. Since the 1990s, many Latin American countries have devolved administrative—and to a certain extent financial—control to the subnational (regional, state, or municipal) level. This is especially true in geographically large countries, such as Argentina, Bolivia, Brazil, Chile, Colombia, and Mexico. Over the past 10–20 years, these countries have decentralized their education systems, often in reaction to expansive and complex systems that had become too cumbersome to manage centrally (Navarro 2005). Other countries in the region have experimented with school-based management and school autonomy, placing responsibility for some functions in the hands of community- and school-level actors, such as principals, teachers, parents, and community members. Central American countries have been especially active in such initiatives, which are premised on the idea that devolving some responsibilities to the most local level improves accountability and promotes more efficient use of resources according to school needs and context.

Cross-country evidence shows that greater school autonomy over personnel management and process decisions (hiring of teachers, textbook choice, budget allocations within schools) appears to be correlated with better student performance. (Fuchs and Woessmann 2004b). Centralized decision making in areas with a larger scope for opportunistic behavior, such as formulating overall school budgets, is also associated with better student performance (Fuchs and Woessmann 2004b).

Single-country evidence shows that the impacts of decentralization may vary depending on which actors or institutions have control over which types of decisions. In their study of three education reforms in Brazil, Pães de Barros and Mendonça (1998) show that two reforms—increased financial autonomy for schools and the creation of school councils—had a statistically significant but small impact on a number of intermediate quality indicators, such as failure rates and age-grade distortion. The third intervention—local control of selection of school principals—had a (very slight) impact only on student achievement. In their study of Nicaragua's autonomous school reform, King and Ozler (2000) provide evidence that greater school autonomy over teacher staffing and the monitoring and evaluation of teachers may raise student performance. Filmer and Eskeland (2002) find that autonomy of primary schools in Argentina is associated with better student performance.

Decentralization can also increase inequality within countries. An analysis of the impact of education decentralization on student outcomes in Argentina finds that while decentralization had, on average, a positive and significant impact on student performance, disaggregated results show increased inequality. In poor municipalities that had had weak institutional capacity before the decentralization reform, student test scores dropped as much as 15 percent after the reform (Galiani, Gertler, and Schargrodsky 2005).

Decentralization has also been associated with increased inequality in Brazil, one of the most decentralized countries in the region. State and municipal governments in Brazil have managed education systems for many decades. This high degree of decentralization resulted in enormous inequality in the resources available for education systems in states and municipalities. In an effort to remedy those inequities, in 1998 the federal government mandated reform that introduced a per pupil spending floor across states and equal per pupil spending in primary education within states.[1] The Fundo de Manutenção e Desenvolvimento do Ensino Fundamental e de Valorização do Magistério (FUNDEF) reform resulted in smaller class sizes, fewer overage children in primary and secondary schools, and a smaller gap between high- and low-performing students. Because low-performing students suffer most from inequalities in per pupil spending, finance equalization reforms that decrease spending inequalities may also decrease the performance gap between high- and low-performing students and between white and nonwhite students.

Three studies from Central America show some evidence of the positive impact on student learning of school-based management, which is particularly popular there. While local control over resources may improve efficiency, a key question is the extent to which school- or community-based management can improve student test scores or other intermediate quality indicators, such as repetition, dropout, or completion rates. Recent evidence suggests that such reforms can help raise quality indicators, but the context, design, and implementation of reforms affect their success.

El Salvador, Honduras, and Nicaragua have instituted reforms that devolve some powers to the community or school levels. These reforms have wide-ranging goals, based on the idea that schools will meet the needs of students and communities better if they are accountable directly to local stakeholders. Education goals frequently include higher quality, greater relevance, expanded access, and increased efficiency. Community- and school-based management has proven promising in many of these areas, but like other decentralization policies, these policies can increase educational inequality between communities of differing income levels and management capacities (Arnove 1994; McGinn and Welsh 1999; Gunnarsson and others (2004).

The Programa de Educación de la Comunidad (EDUCO) program in El Salvador grew out of the country's civil war, during which rural communities that found themselves cut off from services established and ran their own local schools. After the war, the government expanded the program, recognizing its success in effectively reaching areas the government could not reach. Through the EDUCO program, the government provides block grants to community associations for managing schools.

An early evaluation of EDUCO found lower student absenteeism as a result of a reduction in teacher absences. The authors speculated that this reduction might eventually improve achievement (Jimenez and Sawada 1999). A more recent study shows that their instincts were correct. After controlling for background factors (EDUCO students tend to be poorer than traditional students), Sawada and Ragatz (2005) find that EDUCO students performed better in Spanish, and at least as well in math and science, than students at traditional schools.

Like EDUCO, the Proyecto Hondureño de Educación Comunitaria (PROHECO) focuses on expanding and improving community-run schools in rural areas. Achievement among PROHECO students is even more promising than that of EDUCO students, with students scoring higher on math, science, and Spanish exams than students in similar non–PROHECO schools (Di Gropello and Marshall 2005).

In contrast to the school-based management programs in El Salvador and Honduras, Nicaragua's Autonomía Escolar reform targeted urban schools with above-average resources, focusing on changing the status of existing schools rather than setting up new schools. By 2002, 63 percent of Nicaraguan students attended autonomous schools (Parker 2005).

King and Ozler (2000) suggest that there is a positive relation between school autonomy over teacher issues and student performance. Using a longer panel of data, Parker (2005) concludes that the changes in teacher incentive structures that come with autonomous school reform have not contributed to increased student learning. She finds that by the sixth grade, students in autonomous schools perform worse than their peers in traditional schools.

What explains these results? In the case of EDUCO, it is difficult to know which factors of the decentralization program may have contributed to improved student outcomes. Although school associations felt that they had greater influence in administering schools, many administrative processes had not been devolved to the local level. Hiring and firing decisions were under the control of local actors, however. If this aspect of the program indeed contributed to EDUCO's success, it would be consistent with findings based on international comparisons that indicate that local control over the hiring and firing of teachers is associated with higher student learning outcomes (Woessmann 2003; Fuchs and Woessmann 2004b). It makes sense that a school with autonomy to hire its own teachers might be able to match local needs with teacher capacities better than a centrally controlled teacher assignment system (Vegas and Umansky 2005). EDUCO may also have increased teacher motivation, as suggested by the reduction in absenteeism and the increase in time dedicated to teaching and meeting with parents (Sawada and Ragatz 2005).

Some of PROHECO's success stems from the fact that teachers in PROHECO schools worked longer hours than teachers in poor rural non-PROHECO schools. In PROHECO schools, the more a teacher worked per week, the higher student achievement was in all three subjects. The frequency of homework, which was also higher in PROHECO schools, was associated with higher achievement in Spanish and math (Vegas and Umansky 2005). PROHECO teachers did not appear to be more motivated than traditional teachers and were more likely to use conventional teaching methods than non–PROHECO teachers (Di Gropello and Marshall 2005).

A number of possible explanations may account for the disappointing results in Nicaragua. First, while in El Salvador and Honduras much of the decision-making power was placed in the hands of local communities and school boards, in Nicaragua it was concentrated in the hands of the school principal. Second, the reform focused more on the administrative decentralization of power and less on devolving curricular or pedagogical decisions (Vegas and Umansky 2005). Fully identifying the aspects of Nicaragua's autonomous schools that may contribute to or detract from student achievement is a subject for future research.

Parental Participation

Evidence from Mexico shows that parental participation in education management can be both effective and cost-efficient. In 1992 the Mexican government began decentralizing educational services from the federal to the state level. As part of these reforms, in 1996 it introduced the Apoyo a la Gestión Escolar (AGE) program, which provides monetary support and training to parent associations. These associations can spend AGE funds on small school infrastructure and improvement projects. Despite its limited size, the program represents a significant advance for the Mexican education system, where parent associations have tended to play a minor role in school decision making. A recent impact evaluation finds a positive effect of the AGE program on intermediate quality indicators, such as repetition and dropout rates in rural primary schools, even after controlling for other compensatory programs that were introduced simultaneously (Gertler, Patrinos, and Rubio-Codina 2006).

It is unclear exactly how the AGE program improves schooling outcomes. The institutionalization of parental participation appears to have given parents a strong voice in the school community and provided them with official channels through which to communicate with teachers and administrators. This formal participation of parents improves relations between schools and parents as well as the overall school climate. The program may reduce teacher absenteeism as well, although data on absenteeism are not available.

School Choice/Vouchers

Latin America has a long history of private provision of schooling, especially for preschool, secondary, and higher education, and the private sector plays an important role in educating Latin Americans.[2] How effective public versus private administration of schools, school-choice programs, and vouchers are in raising educational quality remains a hotly debated issue among education economists worldwide.

A school-choice system works by providing a publicly funded subsidy to a student (or directly to the school on a per-student basis), which can then be applied toward school expenses, including tuition at private institutions. School-choice systems may be designed in various ways, but they are almost always based on the theory of promoting internal competition within a school system.

Proponents of school choice advocate for allowing nongovernmental groups to provide schooling with funding partially or totally provided by government. They argue that private schools are more efficient and effective than public schools. According to them, opening up all schools to competition by providing vouchers and increasing parental choice improves learning in both public and private schools (Hoxby 2003). School-choice proponents also argue that private schools are more successful in retaining the best new teachers and in developing the skills of existing teachers; as a result, they tend to generate better student outcomes. Some of the reasons given for these successes include private schools' greater supervision and mentoring of new teachers, their ability to require that teachers have higher-quality education, their tendency to attract teachers who exert more effort and independence, and their freedom to dismiss teachers for poor performance (Ballou and Podgursky 1998; Hoxby 2000).

Opponents argue that while school choice may be an effective means of improving student achievement among some groups, voucher schemes lead to increased sorting, with richer students choosing "better" schools, leaving the poor to languish in increasingly neglected institutions (Hsieh and Urquiola 2003; González, Mizala, and Romaguera 2004). They assert that because private schools can select students while public schools cannot, privatization leads to increased sorting by racial/ethnic, socioeconomic, and cultural background, leaving the public sector with the difficult task of serving the most-disadvantaged children with fewer resources than would have been available in a fully public system (Fuller and Elmore 1996).

Chile. Established in 1980, Chile's school-choice system is the longest-standing program of its type in Latin America. Unlike most programs in the United States, it is nationwide and unrestricted, providing all students, regardless of socioeconomic status, with access to subsidies for use at public and private schools. Since school choice was introduced in Chile, private school enrollment has increased 20 percent.

What effect has the program had on student performance? Hsieh and Urquiola (2003) claim that the voucher system has not only failed to improve average academic performance among students, it has also contributed to sorting, through a process of middle-class flight to private subsidized schools.[3] In parts of the country where private-school enrollment increased significantly, repetition and age-for-grade indicators actually worsened.

González, Mizala, and Romaguera (2004) argue that while the effects of sorting are less severe than Hsieh and Urquiola claim, the voucher system has increased social inequality. Mizala, Romaguera, and Ostoic (2004) show that students from the lowest socioeconomic quintiles attending private subsidized schools perform worse than their public school counterparts. These inequalities are attributed to the unrestricted nature of Chile's system. Both studies suggest reforming the voucher program so that it ties the amount of the voucher to students' socioeconomic status through a means-tested voucher (paired with the unrestricted voucher) to make up for the greater challenge—and hence higher cost—of educating low-income students.

Colombia. Colombia is the only Latin American country other than Chile to institute a significant voucher program. Its Programa de Ampliación de Cobertura de la Educación Secundaria (PACES) program, established in 1991, has raised graduation rates and learning outcomes of voucher recipients over the long term.

The program differs from Chile's program in a number of ways. First, it is restricted, targeting secondary school students from urban, low-income neighborhoods. Second, vouchers cover only about half of average private-school tuition. Third, renewal of vouchers depends on satisfactory academic performance.[4] Fourth, because the demand for vouchers was greater than the number available, students were awarded vouchers through a lottery system, thereby creating a natural control group (those who did not win the vouchers) that researchers could compare with the treatment group.

Two successive evaluations show positive short- and long-term effects of the PACES program on intermediate quality indicators and student learning. Three years after the start of the program, voucher recipients were 10 percent more likely to complete eighth grade than nonrecipients, as a result of a reduction in repetition rates (the program allows students to repeat only a certain number of times). Recipients also scored 0.2 standard deviations higher than nonrecipients on achievement tests (Angrist and Lavy 2002). A follow-up study seven years after the program began suggests that these results persist into graduation. Recipients were 5–7 percent more likely to graduate from secondary school than nonrecipients, and they scored higher than nonrecipients on the Instituto Colombiano para el Fomento de la Educación Superior (ICFES) college entrance exam (Angrist, Bettinger, and Kremer 2006).

The United States. Evidence of the effectiveness of school choice in the United States is inconclusive. Milwaukee's Parental Choice Program has inspired fans, foes, and pragmatists. The program provides vouchers to poor students (from families earning 175 percent of the federal poverty level or below), which can be used at private schools.

Evaluations of the program have led to disparate conclusions of its effectiveness, partly as a result of the difficulty in constructing comparison groups. Results have demonstrated everything from stagnating test scores to improvements in both math and reading (Witte, Sterr, and Thorn 1995; Greene, Peterson, and Du 1997; Rouse 1998; Hoxby 2003). Rouse (1998) finds that some particularly successful public schools outpace many private voucher schools and that school choice in Milwaukee has been most beneficial to some subsets of students, such as Latino students.

Curriculum, Standards, and National Assessment

The design and implementation of curriculum and standards can have important consequences for what and how students learn. However, large-scale curricular reforms are rarely accompanied by evaluations. Little is therefore known about how changes and variations in curricula affect student learning.

Curriculum is frequently considered the core of schooling. Other major aspects of education, such as pedagogy and educational structure, are of critical importance but tend to be less visible. Curriculum defines objectives for what students should know, do, and believe, making it both a powerful and a contested feature of education (Astiz, Wiseman, and Baker 2002).

During the 1990s a new wave of curricular reform swept Latin America (table 7.1). Reforms included the partial decentralization of curricular decision-making power from national to regional or local control; the development of national standards; the shift toward competencies rather than discrete knowledge as the primary learning goal; and the emergence of national assessment systems.

One of the most important ways in which the new curricula established in the 1990s differed from earlier curricula was the effort to decentralize curricular control. In general, the new model gives the central government the responsibility to set curricula broadly, through standards, guidelines, minimum contents, or goals. It then allows for adaptation of the broad curricular framework and setting of more specific curricula at the regional and local levels. Under this model, localized actors take the central government's guidelines and adapt them to respond to the needs, expectations, and realities of their jurisdictions. In theory, the model provides a guarantee of basic quality and equity in education while allowing for greater efficiency, autonomy, and diversification (Astiz, Wiseman, and Baker 2002; Gvirtz 2002).

The level of curricular autonomy may affect student learning. Analysis of international assessments indicates that centralized curriculum standards coupled with local flexibility in curricular implementation are associated with higher test scores (Woessmann 2003). School responsibility for course selection is associated with higher PISA scores (Schleicher 2006).

Table 7.1 Curricular Reforms in Selected Countries in Latin America and the Caribbean

Country	Year new curriculum introduced	Legal basis	Focus	Standards	Degree of flexibility	Pedagogy	Implementation methods
Argentina	1995	Ley Federal de Educación (1993)	Competencies	Basic Common Contents	National standards with adaptation at provincial, school, and classroom levels	Constructivist and cognitivist	Teacher education, new materials
Bolivia	1994	Ley de la Reforma Educativa (1994)	Intercultural and participatory learning	None	Low	Constructivist (in primary schools)	New materials distributed (in primary schools). Adoption of intercultural bilingual education. Reform of teacher pay scale and education structure

(continued)

Table 7.1 Curricular Reforms in Selected Countries in Latin America and the Caribbean *(continued)*

Country	Year new curriculum introduced	Legal basis	Focus	Standards	Degree of flexibility	Pedagogy	Implementation methods
Brazil	1996 and 1997	Lei de Diretrizes e Bases da Educacao Nacional (1996)	Competencies and skills	National Curricular Parameters (1997); some states have set learning expectations	Adaptation of national base at regional and local levels	Constructivist and conceptual	—
Chile	1996, updated in 2003	Ley Organica Constitucional de la Enseñanza (1990)	Competencies and skills	Fundamental Objectives and Obligatory Minimum Contents (1996 primary; 1998 secondary)	Significant adaptation designed to occur at school level	Active	Voluntary plans and programs, Textbooks, Teacher in-service training and incentives
Colombia	1998 and 2002	Constitution (1991), Ley General de Educación 115 (1994)	Competencies	Curricular Standards (2002 and 2003)	Significant adaptation designed to occur at school level	—	Teacher education and supplementary materials

(continued)

Table 7.1 Curricular Reforms in Selected Countries in Latin America and the Caribbean *(continued)*

Country	Year new curriculum introduced	Legal basis	Focus	Standards	Degree of flexibility	Pedagogy	Implementation methods
Costa Rica	1998, 2002, and 2006	Política Educativa Hacia el Siglo XXI (1994)	Competencies, values, and attitudes	Project for the Establishment of Primary Education Standards for Central America	Low	Constructivist, humanist, and rationalist	—
El Salvador	1999	Ley General de Educación (1990), Education Plan (1995)	Competencies	Dominios Curriculares Básicos (1999); Project for the Establishment of Primary Education Standards for Central America	Low	Constructivist	—

(continued)

Table 7.1 Curricular Reforms in Selected Countries in Latin America and the Caribbean *(continued)*

Country	Year new curriculum introduced	Legal basis	Focus	Standards	Degree of flexibility	Pedagogy	Implementation methods
Honduras	1993	No major legislation	Competencies	Standards developed for basic education, being developed for secondary education	Low	Constructivist	New textbooks, national standards documentation, in-service teacher education
Mexico	1992, updated in 1999 and 2000	Changes to Mexican Constitution (1992), Ley General de Educación (1993), Acuerdo Nacional para la Modernización de la Educación Básica (ANMEB) (1992)	Conceptual learning	Some states have established learning expectations	States can submit to center suggestions for regional curricular contents; beyond this, little flexibility at state or school level	Interactive and conceptual	Free national textbooks and teacher guides distributed. System of teacher incentives introduced and teacher education reformed.

(continued)

Table 7.1 Curricular Reforms in Selected Countries in Latin America and the Caribbean *(continued)*

Country	Year new curriculum introduced	Legal basis	Focus	Standards	Degree of flexibility	Pedagogy	Implementation methods
Nicaragua	1996	Constitutional reform (2001)	Competencies	National Education Standards (2001); Project for the Establishment of Primary Education Standards for Central America	Low	Constructivist	—
Peru	1998	Ley General de Educación (2003)	Competencies	Standards being developed	National curriculum with adaptation at regional, school, and classroom levels	Constructivist	Teacher education, new materials

(continued)

Table 7.1 Curricular Reforms in Selected Countries in Latin America and the Caribbean *(continued)*

Country	Year new curriculum introduced	Legal basis	Focus	Standards	Degree of flexibility	Pedagogy	Implementation methods
Uruguay	1999	No major legislation	Curricular organization by areas instead of subjects	None	Low (open curricular space in secondary school)	—	Lengthening of school day, reform of preservice teacher education, new textbooks and teacher guides.
Venezuela, R. B. de	1997	Education plans 1994 and 1995	—	Standards being defined for end of each school cycle	—	—	—

Source: National education plans and programs; Braslavsky 1999; Ferrer 2000, 2004; Galindo 2002; Dussel 2004; Soares 2004; UNESCO 2005.
Note: For information on assessments, see table 3.1.
— Not available.

In practice, curricular decentralization in Latin America has been problematic. Distinguishing and coordinating between the roles of the central and local governments has proven difficult in many countries. Problems have included poor planning, timing, or implementation of reforms; weak capacity and inadequate support for curricular adaptation at the local level; and resistance to changing engrained practices of curricular centralization (Ferrer 2004).

In Chile, for example, the national curricular framework was designed to be adapted at the school level. The government developed the more traditional Plans and Programs (specific curricular content) to support schools that chose not to develop their own specific curricula. By 2001, 80–87 percent of schools were using the national Plans and Programs (Ferrer 2004).

In Peru there is evidence of only weak adaptation of national guidelines at the regional and school levels. As a result, most teachers rely on broad and vague guidelines that were not intended to be curricular plans. The extent to which teachers may adapt the curriculum at the classroom level depends on teachers' skills and knowledge rather than a well-planned and designed curricular adaptation to local needs and interests (Ferrer 2004).

Standards are another recent development in Latin America. In the context of greater decentralization of curricular control, standards allow central governments to enforce minimum requirements for educational quality and equity of educational outcomes. While the curriculum defines what should be taught in the classroom, standards identify minimum learning outcomes. Until the reforms of the 1990s, educational standards were virtually nonexistent in the region. Curricula guided teaching content and influenced learning, but there was no definition or establishment of what constituted adequate, inferior, or superior learning levels. The reforms of the 1990s indicate a growing emphasis on setting these standards.

Several countries are moving toward fully implementing comprehensive national standards in education. Argentina and Chile have established or are in the process of establishing minimum standards and defining acceptable and unacceptable levels of learning. Colombia has established both content standards and minimum conditions. Central American countries have established common subregional standards, but they are not being used in all countries. Honduras has set and distributed math and language standards for primary education and is developing standards for secondary (PREAL 2005).

Nearly all the curricular reforms in Latin America embodied, at least officially, a move toward competencies and skills as the primary learning goal. This focus lays out both a new role for students and teachers and a new definition of learning and what a graduate should know and be able to do. The focus on competencies emerged as a reaction to the outdated and encyclopedic content that was being taught in most classrooms through traditional pedagogies such as rote memorization and copying.

The shift in focus prioritizes students' learning of problem solving, creativity, critical thinking, flexibility, and other competencies. The goal is for students to leave school as engaged, productive citizens (Braslavsky 1999; Gvirtz 2002; Ferrer 2004).

Beyond this broad understanding, however, there are multiple definitions of competencies and multiple interpretations of how to teach them. In Argentina standards are first based on competencies and then divided into curricular areas. In contrast, Chile views competencies as transversal veins that run through all curricular areas.

In addition to curricular decentralization, establishment of standards, and the curricular shift toward competencies and skills, national assessment systems have also been implemented in almost all countries in the region to varying degrees. (For a discussion of assessment, see chapter 3.)

The curricular reforms of the 1990s continue to face a number of challenges. In addition to the difficulties accompanying decentralization, these challenges include the weak alignment between curricular changes and changes in textbooks, exams, teacher education, and pedagogy; the absence of hospitable environments for curricular reform, including broad political consensus, appropriate educational context, and accompanying educational reforms alignment; and the incomplete implementation of many reforms.

Major changes in curriculum require changes in many aspects of an education system, ranging from teaching methods to exams, textbooks, linkages between different grades and education cycles, and teacher education and professional development. These curricular areas often end up misaligned, because of limited resources, problems in planning or timing, interests of multiple stakeholders, or weak political consensus. Teacher education and professional development is frequently the weakest area of alignment with new curricula (Braslavsky 1999; Ferrer 2004). Standardized assessment poses another challenge to effective alignment in new curricular reforms. While over time countries have increasingly aligned standardized exams to new curricula, this process is still far from complete. Even in countries in which national curricular guidelines and exams are aligned, there are often serious disconnects between exams and the actual curricula implemented in the classroom (Esquivel 2000).

Another critical challenge in implementing curricular reforms is the need to ensure an adequate policy environment that fosters general consensus and support for reform. Deep reforms that redefine the goals of education in addition to what and how students learn require a strong and supportive context. This context involves both the educational system and the political and social context. Curricular reforms require a broad-based consensus among stakeholders, including parents, regional governments, and teacher unions, and political consensus across incoming administrations (Montero-Sieburth 1992). There is ample evidence that in countries in which this context is weak, it is more difficult to succeed in reform implementation.

The (scant) evidence on the degree of actual classroom implementation of the 1990s curricular reforms in Latin America suggests that implementation has been partial and incomplete. Although 87 percent of Peruvian teachers report using the new curriculum in their classrooms, only 51 percent report covering all of the new curriculum (Galindo 2002). In Chile 62 percent of schools use both the new and the old curricula, and primary schools cover only about half of the new curriculum on average (Ferrer 2004). As time passes, schools and teachers may increasingly embrace the new curricula, but without sufficient resources, support, and capacity, it is unlikely that all of the goals of the new reforms will be realized.

Policies Affecting System Organization and Administration

The organization and administration of school systems and educational institutions can affect how much students learn. A number of policies at the institutional level—from simple low-cost interventions that institutionalize parental participation to comprehensive systemwide policies that promote decentralization—address these organizational issues (figure 7.1 and table 7.2).

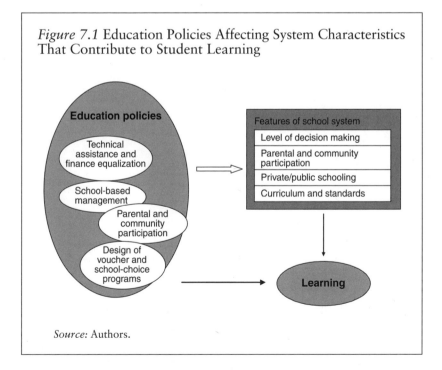

Figure 7.1 Education Policies Affecting System Characteristics That Contribute to Student Learning

Source: Authors.

Table 7.2 Effect of Reforms on Student Learning and Other Outcomes

Factor	Student learning outcomes	Other outcomes	Site of study	Type of study	Source
Level of decision making					
School autonomy over personnel management and process decisions (hiring of teachers, selection of textbooks, allocating budget within school)	PISA 2000 scores rose 0.2 standard deviations in math and 0.3 standard deviations in reading.		OECD and other countries participating in PISA 2000	Education production functions using clustering-robust linear regressions	Fuchs and Woessmann (2004b)
External exit exams	PISA 2000 scores in math, science, and reading rose 0.02–0.04 standard deviations.				
Increased financial autonomy for schools		Repetition rates, age-grade distortion, and number of children out of school fell.	Brazil	Education production functions	Pães de Barros and Mendonça (1998)

(continued)

Table 7.2 Effect of Reforms on Student Learning and Other Outcomes *(continued)*

Factor	Student learning outcomes	Other outcomes	Site of study	Type of study	Source
Creation of school councils		Repetition rates fell slightly.			
Local control over selection of school principals	Student achievement improved, as measured by test scores				
Greater school autonomy over teacher staffing and monitoring and evaluation of teachers	At primary-education level, 1.0 standard deviation increase in decision-making power associated with 6.7 percent increase in math scores. Effect on test scores in math was 2.0 times that of an increase in textbooks, 1.5 times that of an increase in teachers' years of education, and 1.4 times that of a 1.0 standard deviation reduction in class size.		Nicaragua	Education production functions with Heckman selection correction estimates	King and Ozler (2000)

(continued)

Table 7.2 Effect of Reforms on Student Learning and Other Outcomes *(continued)*

Factor	Student learning outcomes	Other outcomes	Site of study	Type of study	Source
	At secondary-education level, language scores rose significantly (effect on math scores was insignificant), and effect was larger than that of increase in number of textbooks or improvement in teacher's education.				
Autonomy and parental participation (joint effect)	Coefficient estimate on interaction of autonomy and participation is 1–5 percent of 1 standard deviation for math, with largest effect among poorest students and schools.		Argentina	Education production functions	Filmer and Eskeland (2002)

(continued)

Table 7.2 Effect of Reforms on Student Learning and Other Outcomes (*continued*)

Factor	Student learning outcomes	Other outcomes	Site of study	Type of study	Source
Decentralization of secondary schools	After five years of decentralization, math scores were 3.8 percent higher and Spanish scores 5.9 percent higher than provincial (state) schools. Test scores in poor municipalities and poorly administered provinces fell 14 percent in math and more than 9 percent in Spanish.	Test-score inequality rose.	Argentina	Quasi-experimental design exploiting expansion of access to preschool, differences-in-differences estimation	Galiani, Gertler, and Schargrodsky (2005)
School-based management (EDUCO program in El Salvador)	Spanish test scores rose 1.5 standard deviations.	Teacher motivation rose: absenteeism fell, teachers spent more time with parents and other school members and more time teaching.	El Salvador	Education production functions with propensity score matching to construct control group	Sawada and Ragatz (2005)

(*continued*)

Table 7.2 Effect of Reforms on Student Learning and Other Outcomes (continued)

Factor	Student learning outcomes	Other outcomes	Site of study	Type of study	Source
School-based management (PROHECO program in Honduras)	Spanish, math, and science scores rose	Teachers worked longer hours, class size declined.	Honduras	Education production functions with two-stage Heckman style and propensity score matching to construct control groups	Di Gropello and Marshall (2005)
Parental participation					
Monetary support and training to parent associations		Repetition and dropout rates fell.	Mexico	Differences-in-differences estimation	Gertler, Patrinos, and Rubio-Codina (2006)
Vouchers					
Targeted vouchers for private secondary school attendance; renewal dependent on satisfactory academic performance	After three years, standardized test scores rose 0.2 standard deviations.	After three years, voucher recipients completed 0.1 more years of school than nonrecipients and were 10 percent more likely to complete eighth grade.	Colombia	Natural experiment based on random assignment of vouchers to applicants by lottery	Angrist and Lavy (2002)

(continued)

Table 7.2 Effect of Reforms on Student Learning and Other Outcomes *(continued)*

Factor	Student learning outcomes	Other outcomes	Site of study	Type of study	Source
	After seven years, standardized test scores were higher; difference depends on how selection bias is controlled for.	After seven years, voucher recipients were 5–7 percent more likely than nonrecipients to graduate from secondary school.	Colombia	Natural experiment based on random assignment of vouchers to applicants by lottery	Kremer, Miguel, and Thornton (2004)
Curriculum and standards					
Curriculum-based central exit exams	TIMSS and PISA scores in countries with exit exams were one grade level higher than those without exit exams.		54 countries participating in both TIMSS and PISA	Clustering-robust linear, weighted least squares regressions, and quantile regressions	Woessmann (2004)
	TIMSS test scores rose an average of 22 points		15 countries	Clustering-robust linear and weighted least squares regressions	Woessmann (2003)

Source: Author compilation.

Technical Assistance and Finance Equalization

Providing additional support to struggling schools in the form of technical assistance can help offset disparities created by decentralization, as can finance equalization reform. Decentralization to the state or provincial level can increase student test scores, but it often comes at the expense of equity. Finance equalization reforms can help even out the disparities caused by decentralization, as can targeted interventions and support to schools in areas with fewer resources or large shares of disadvantaged students.

Decentralization, School-Based Management, and Parental and Community Participation

Devolving some responsibilities to schools, parents, and communities can contribute to student learning, but the design of school-based management programs affects their impact. When discussing programs of school autonomy and decentralization, it is important to examine the extent to which meaningful authority is devolved to the school level, the level and type of authority, and who bears this authority. Understanding the nature of decentralization can contribute to the understanding of how decentralization does or does not contribute improve learning environments.

School-based management experiences in El Salvador, Honduras, and Nicaragua provide some lessons. First, simply devolving authority to the local level does not ensure that schools will be better managed. School councils can suffer from the same—or worse—bureaucratic problems that plague centralized systems if they lack the ability to manage effectively. Similarly, devolving authority does not necessarily empower communities. In some school-based management systems, few responsibilities actually lie in the hands of local stakeholders. Communities and parents must have both the mandate and the capacity to manage schools effectively and make decisions about the use of resources. It is also important to avoid placing too much responsibility in the hands of a single actor, as is the case in Nicaragua (Parker 2005).

Second, while school-based management seems to be changing the behaviors and practices of some teachers (as evident in the case of EDUCO), which can help improve student learning, it does not appear to improve teaching methodologies or professionalization. In fact, in Honduras and Nicaragua, teachers reported having less power in the classroom following adoption of school-based management. Coupling the empowerment of communities with the empowerment of teachers, complemented by skills development and training in teaching methodologies, can make school-based management more successful.

Third, experience from Mexico suggest that less-drastic and less-costly reforms that involve parents in their children's schooling as part of compensatory programs can contribute to reducing grade repetition and failure (Gertler, Patrinos, and Rubio-Codina 2006). Because socioeconomic background is such an important factor in a child's learning, involving parents in schooling may also increase demand for education in families that otherwise may not prioritize education for their children.

Per-Student Financing Programs

Per-student financing programs can have important effects on student enrollments and learning outcomes. The design and implementation of these programs can have important consequences. In Chile, for example, the per-student subsidy is tied to student attendance, not learning outcomes. The program has probably been effective in encouraging all students stay in school throughout the 12 years of compulsory education. The large increases in education coverage in recent years undoubtedly have lowered average test scores, especially in secondary school, as children who would otherwise have been outside the school system (and whose parents had not attended school) enter school. In 2003 the number of students taking the SIMCE tests rose by about 20 percent over the previous year. The Ministry of Education estimates that half of this increase was a result of demographic growth and the other half a result of increases in coverage and retention rates. A concrete achievement of the reform has thus been to increase coverage and retention. The impact on school quality is questionable.

Differences between private and municipal schools. Several differences between subsidized private and municipal schools—including the admission process, teacher contracting, and access to alternative sources of financing—have impeded the creation of an "educational market" that fosters educational efficiency and quality. Chilean public and private schools compete under different conditions, limiting the gains in efficiency and quality that would have been expected from the voucher-type student-based subsidy. As a result, the "quasi-market" for education has not only been unable to raise average student achievement for the system as a whole, it has also fallen short of ensuring a high-quality education for the elites (Eyzaguirre and others 2005).

Private schools (both subsidized and fee-paying) have complete freedom to accept, reject, and dismiss students and to establish their own selection processes. In contrast, municipal schools are required to accept any student who wishes to enroll unless it can be demonstrated that there are no vacancies at the school.

Teachers in municipal schools are governed by special legislation (the Teacher Statute) and subject to a centralized collective-bargaining process. As a result, teacher wages in the public sector are based on uniform pay scales, with bonuses for training, experience, and working under difficult conditions, as well as restrictions on teacher dismissal. Private schools (both subsidized and fee-paying) operate as firms; their teachers come under the same labor code covering other private-sector workers in Chile. These schools can select, hire, and dismiss teachers; in contrast, municipal governments centrally hire and assign teachers to municipal schools. Because these teachers are governed by the Teacher Statute, their dismissal is also much more difficult than that of teachers in private schools.

In 1993 cofinancing was approved (with funds contributed by parents) for private subsidized and secondary municipal schools. Municipal elementary schools are not permitted to charge fees.

The information on quality that is disseminated to parents and the public in general includes only each school's average scores on the SIMCE tests. These averages mask important differences in the distribution of student achievement and the population of students served. School quality is more than simply student performance on national assessments; other information, such as the proportion of students who continue their education, can help inform parents and improve the functioning of the educational market in Chile.

The role of the state. The state has an important role to play in easing constraints in the education market and guaranteeing that all children have access to a good education. This role is especially important in open voucher systems, such as Chile's, which may exacerbate inequality, but it is also important for restricted voucher systems, in which the private sector takes on considerable responsibility for educating children.

The state has the authority to demand accountability for the public resources it allocates to schools. It has a role in developing and enforcing standards, norms, and incentives for the education system in a framework of free school choice with financing through student-based subsidies. It has a responsibility to supervise and support schools in achieving the expected results. In addition, most people would agree that the state has a responsibility to ensure equality of educational opportunity.

The state also has an important role to play in improving the information available to parents and civil society on school quality. Given that the benefits from evaluations of education policies and programs are public goods, the state should support them.

Support for Implementing Curricular Reforms

Wide-reaching restructuring of curriculum should be supported with the necessary resources (financial and otherwise), as well as with support to teachers, schools, and teacher-education institutes and universities in adopting new curricular frameworks and aligning the various actors and institutions to ensure implementation. Consensus building is another important aspect of curriculum reform that can better guarantee its effectiveness. Evaluation designs should accompany curricular reforms, in order to provide policy makers and stakeholders with a better understanding of why and how reforms are or are not effective.

Conclusion

The way in which schools and school systems are organized and administered can have a bearing on how much students learn and on the equitability of student learning opportunities. Many countries in the region have decentralized or experimented with certain aspects of decentralization, such as school autonomy and parental participation. In some cases, decentralization has produced disappointing results, actually reducing student performance in poor or badly managed schools or districts. However, certain aspects of decentralization, such as parental participation and school autonomy over personnel and some financial decisions, appear to be effective in raising test scores and improving other intermediate quality indicators, such as repetition and dropout rates. Much of the success of decentralization hinges on understanding the best way to allocate responsibilities and ensuring that the various levels of decision making have the institutional capacity to effectively carry out their respective responsibilities. The effectiveness of private provision and per-student financing schemes as vehicles for ensuring that all students learn remains questionable. The design of a voucher system is a key variable in its success, however. Finally, curricular reforms need to be accompanied by evaluations in order to assess their effectiveness and the level to which they actually reach classrooms and contribute to student learning.

Notes

1. Gordon and Vegas (2005) analyze the impact of the reform on enrollment, teacher qualifications, and test-score inequality.

2. For a multifaceted look at private education in Latin America, see Wolff, Navarro, and González (2005).

3. Chile has a mixed system of education made up of public municipal schools; private subsidized (non-fee-charging) schools; and private, tuition-charging schools, which are generally reserved for the elite and do not accept vouchers.

4. In this sense, the program shares similarities with successful merit-based interventions, such as girls' scholarships in Kenya, which increased test scores of both boys and girls (Kremer, Miguel, and Thornton 2004).

References

Angrist, J. D., E. Bettinger, and M. Kremer. 2006. "Long-Term Consequences of Colombian School Vouchers." *American Economic Review* 96 (3): 847–62.

Angrist, J. D., and V. Lavy. 2002. "New Evidence on Classroom Computers and Pupil Learning." *Economic Journal* 112 (October): 735–65.

Arnove, R. 1994. *Education as Contested Terrain: Nicaragua, 1979–1993*. Boulder, CO: Westview Press.

Astiz, M. F., A. Wiseman, and D. Baker. 2002. "Slouching towards Decentralization: Consequences of Globalization for Curricular Control in National Education Systems." *Comparative Education Review* 46 (1): 66–88.

Ballou, D., and M. Podgursky. 1997. *Teacher Pay and Teacher Quality*. W. E. Upjohn Institute of Employment Research, Kalamazoo, MI.

Ballou, D., and M. Podgursky. 1998. "Teacher Recruitment and Retention in Public and Private Schools." *Journal of Policy Analysis and Management* 17 (3): 393–417.

Braslavsky, C. 1999. *The Secondary Education Curriculum in Latin America: New Tendencies and Challenges*. Paper presented at an International Bureau of Education conference, Buenos Aires.

Di Gropello, E., and J. Marshall. 2005. "Teacher Effort and Schooling Outcomes in Rural Honduras." In *Incentives to Improve Teaching*, ed. E. Vegas. Washington, DC: World Bank.

Dussel, I. 2004. "Las reformas curriculares en la Argentina, Chile, y Uruguay: Informe comparativo." In *Las reformas educativas en la década de 1990: Un estudio comparado de Argentina, Chile, y Uruguay*, ed. M. Carnoy, G. Cosse, C. Cox, and E. Martínez. Buenos Aires: Inter-American Development Bank; Ministries of Education of Argentina, Chile, and Uruguay; and Advisory Group of Stanford.

Esquivel, J. 2000. "El diseño de la pruebas para medir logro académico: ¿Referencia a normas o a criterios?" In *Los próximos pasos: ¿Hacia dónde y cómo avanzar el la evaluación de aprendizajes en América Latina?* ed. P. Ravela, R. Wolfe, G. Valverde, and J. Esquivel. Lima: Grupo de Análisis para el Desarrollo (GRADE).

Eyzaguirre, N., M. Marcel, J. Rodríguez, and M. Tokman. 2005. "Hacia la economía del conocimiento: El camino para crecer con equidad en el largo plazo." Estudios Públicos 97 (Verano), Centro de Estudios Públicos, Santiago.

Ferrer, G. 2000. *Aspectos del curriculum prescrito en América Latina: Revisión de tendencias contemporáneas en curriculum, indicadores de logro, estándares, y otros instrumentos*. Partnership for Educational Revitalization in the Americas (PREAL) and Grupo de Análisis para el Desarrollo (GRADE), Santiago.

———. 2004. "Las reformas curriculares de Perú, Colombia, Chile y Argentina: ¿Quién responde pos los resultados?" Working Paper 45, Grupo de Análisis para el Desarrollo (GRADE), Lima.

Filmer, D., and G. A. Eskeland. 2002. "Autonomy, Participation, and Learning in Argentine Schools: Findings and Their Implications for Decentralization." World Bank Policy Research Working Paper 2766, Washington, DC.

Fuchs, T., and L. Woessmann. 2004a. "Computers and Student Learning: Bivariate and Multivariate Evidence on the Availability and Use of Computers at Home and at School." CESifo Working Paper 1321, Munich.

———. 2004b. "What Accounts for International Differences in Student Performance? A Re-examination using PISA Data." Working Paper 1235, Category 4: Labour Markets, CESifo, Munich.

Fuller, B., and R. Elmore. 1996. *Who Chooses Who Loses? Culture, Institutions, and the Unequal Effects of School Choice*. New York: Teachers College Press.

Galiani, S., P. Gertler, and E. Schargrodsky. 2005. "School Decentralization: Helping the Good Get Better, but Leaving the Poor Behind." Universidad de San Andrés, Buenos Aires.

Galindo, C. 2002. "El currículo implementado como indicador del proceso educativo." In *Análisis de los resultados y metodologia de las pruebas CRECER 1998*, ed. J. Rodríguez and S. Vargas. Lima: Ministerio de Educación.

Gertler, P., H. Patrinos, and M. Rubio-Codina. 2006. "Do Supply-Side-Oriented and Demand-Side-Oriented Education Programs Generate Synergies? Evidence from Rural Mexico." Background paper prepared for this report. World Bank, Washington, DC.

González, P., A. Mizala, and P. Romaguera. 2004. "Vouchers, Inequalities and the Chilean Experience." National Center for the Study of Privatisation in Education, New York.

Gordon, N., and E. Vegas. 2005. "Education Finance Equalization, Spending, Teacher Quality, and Student Outcomes." In *Incentives to Improve Teaching*, ed. E. Vegas. Washington, DC: World Bank.

Greene, J. P., P. E. Peterson, and J. Du. 1997. "The Effectiveness of School Choice: The Milwaukee Experiment." Harvard University Education Policy and Governance Occasional Paper 97–1, Cambridge, MA.

Gunnarsson, L. V., P. Orazem, M. Sanchez, and A. Verdisco. 2004. "Does School Decentralization Raise Student Outcomes? Theory and Evidence on the Roles of School Autonomy and Community Participation." Working Paper 04005, Department of Economics, Iowa State University, Ames.

Gvirtz, S. 2002. "Curricular Reforms in Latin America with Special Emphasis on the Argentine Case." *Comparative Education* 38 (4): 453–69.

Hoxby, C. 2000. "Does Competition among Public Schools Benefit Students and Taxpayers?" *American Economic Review* 90 (5): 1209–38.

———. 2003. "School Choice and School Competition: Evidence from the United States." *Swedish Economic Policy Review* 10.

Hsieh, C-T., and M. Urquiola. 2003. "When Schools Compete, How Do they Compete? An Assessment of Chile's Nationwide School Voucher Program." NBER Working Paper 10008, National Bureau of Economic Research, Cambridge, MA.

Jimenez, E., and Y. Sawada. 1999. "Do Community-Managed Schools Work? An Evaluation of El Salvador's EDUCO Program." *World Bank Economic Review* 13 (3): 415–41.

King, E., and B. Ozler. 2000. "What's Decentralization Got to Do with Learning? Endogenous School Quality and Student Performance in Nicaragua." World Bank, Development Research Group, Washington, DC.

Kremer, M., E. Miguel, and R. Thornton. 2004. "Incentives to Learn." NBER Working Paper 10971, National Bureau of Economic Research, Cambridge, MA.

McGinn, N., and T. Welsh. 1999. *Decentralization of Education: Why, When, What and How?* Paris: United Nations Educational, Scientific, and Cultural Organization.

Mizala, A., P. Romaguera, and C. Ostoic. 2004. "Equity and Achievement in the Chilean School Choice Experience: A Multilevel Analysis." Paper presented at the annual meetings of the Latin American Econometric Society.

Montero-Sieburth, M. 1992. "Models and Practice of Curriculum Change in Developing Countries." *Comparative Education Review* 36 (2): 175–93.

Navarro, J. C. 2005. "Las reformas educativas como reformas del estado: América Latina en las dos últimas décadas." Draft. Inter-American Development Bank, Washington, DC.

Pães de Barros, R., and R. Mendonça. 1998. *O impacto de três inovações institucionais na educação brasileira*. Instituto de Pesquisa Econômica Aplicada (IPEA), Rio de Janeiro.

Parker, C. 2005. "Teacher Incentives and Student Achievement in Nicaraguan Autonomous Schools." In *Incentives to Improve Teaching*, ed. E. Vegas. Washington DC: World Bank.

PREAL. 2005. Informe de Progreso Educativo, Honduras, Programa de Promocíon de la Reforma Educativa en América Latina y El Caribe (PREAL), Washington, DC, and Santiago, Chile.

Rouse, C. 1998. "Schools and Student Achievement: More Evidence from the Milwaukee Parental Choice Program." *FRBNY Economic Policy Review*.

Sawada, Y., and A. Ragatz. 2005. "Decentralization of Education, Teacher Behavior, and Outcome: The Case of El Salvador's EDUCO Program." In *Incentives to Improve Teaching. Lessons from Latin America*, ed. E. Vegas. Washington, DC: World Bank.

Schleicher, A. 2006. "Education Policy, Learning Outcomes and Labour Competitiveness." Paper presented to the World Bank Human Development Forum, Washington, DC, October 31.

Soares, S. 2004. *Bolivia: Education Sector Study*. World Bank, Washington, DC.

UNESCO (United Nations Educational, Scientific, and Cultural Organization). 2005. *Segundo estudio regional comparativo y explicativo 2004–2007: Análisis curricular*. Santiago: UNESCO.

Vegas, E., and I. Umansky. 2005. *Improving Teaching and Learning through Effective Incentives*. Washington, DC: World Bank.

Witte, J. F., T. D. Sterr, and C. A. Thorn. 1995. "Fifth-Year Report: Milwaukee Parental Choice Program." University of Wisconsin.

Woessmann, L. 2003. "Schooling Resources, Educational Institutions and Student Performance: The International Evidence." *Oxford Bulletin of Economics and Statistics* 65 (2): 117–70.

———. 2004. "The Effect Heterogeneity of Central Exams: Evidence from TIMSS, TIMSS-Repeat and PISA." Working Paper 1330, Category 4: Labour Markets, CESifo, Munich.

Wolff, L., J. C. Navarro, and P. González, eds. 2005. *Private Education and Public Policy in Latin America*. Partnership for Educational Revitalization in the Americas (PREAL), Washington, DC.

Part III

Quality Assurance and Beyond

Although most education systems in Latin America and the Caribbean have adequate systems in place to provide access to schooling, many lack the necessary institutional structures to ensure that all students learn. The challenge for most countries is to ensure that students not only enroll and stay in school throughout the basic education cycle but that the years they spend in the classroom equip them with knowledge and skills they can apply throughout their lives. Part III reviews evidence from countries that have succeeded in ensuring that all children have access to good-quality education, and closes with a summary of the main conclusions from this book.

8

Instructional Visions and Institutions for Ensuring That All Students Learn

This chapter presents a conceptual framework, derived from recent work by the World Bank for the government of Chile, for analyzing the institutional structures for quality assurance.* It then summarizes the findings from the application of the conceptual framework to the institutional design of education systems in Chile; England, Wales, and Northern Ireland; Finland; New Zealand; the Republic of Korea; Spain; and two school districts in the United States (Boston, Massachusetts, and Houston, Texas). The chapter closes by examining four alternative institutional visions for quality assurance and their implications for the allocation of roles and responsibilities to the various participants in an education system.

Conceptual Framework for Evaluating Quality Assurance Systems

Many individuals and institutions work together to generate and support student learning. They include students, teachers, principals and school administrators; schools; and local, regional, and the national government.

An effective education quality assurance system should have well-defined goals for each of these actors, as well as strategies to measure and hold them accountable for how much students learn. The framework for quality assurance developed by the World Bank for the government of Chile includes eight components that can help ensure that all students learn: performance standards; performance assessments; performance

---

*This chapter draws on a World Bank report prepared with Joseph Olchefske, Erika Molina, and Amy Walter.

reporting; impact evaluation of policies and programs; requirements to operate; adequate and equitable resources; autonomy, intervention, and support; and accountability and consequences.

Performance Standards

Targeted performance levels should be established for each of the actors that interacts to produce education quality. Clearly defined standards for students and teachers should lay out what students should know and be able to do at each grade and level of the education system.

Performance Assessments

Methodologies must be in place with which to assess the extent to which individuals and institutions meet the agreed-upon standards. They include standardized methods for objectively measuring what students know and are able to do and for appraising the performance of teachers and school administrators. Methodologies also include frameworks for analyzing institutional performance, such as the degree to which schools are meeting the learning needs of all students. Such assessments are used to make decisions about the level of autonomy, intervention, and support granted to individuals and institutions, as well as to determine accountability and consequences for varying levels of performance.

Performance Reporting

Processes for disseminating the outcomes of performance assessments are critical. Individual student assessment information can be made available to students themselves, to their parents or guardians, to their teachers, and to administrators. Teacher assessment information can be made available to school administrators, local government officials, and parents. School assessment information can be made available to local and regional governments. Local and regional assessment information can be made available to national government authorities.

Impact Evaluation of Policies and Programs

An effective quality assurance system must regularly evaluate the impact of policies and programs and incorporate this information into existing and new policies and programs. Does the program raise student learning or other student outcomes, such as retention and labor market outcomes? How does the program improve student outcomes? How cost-effective is the program? Answering each of these questions implies a different evaluation strategy. The methodology for evaluating impact should be established before the policies or programs are introduced, as it is much more difficult to construct a credible evaluation strategy after a policy or program is already in place.

Requirements to Operate

An education system should establish norms for entry into and operation in the system for each of the actors that operates in it. These range from age of entry requirements for students to professional requirements for teachers to basic conditions that all schools must meet.

Adequate and Equitable Resources

Education quality assurance systems should have management, financing, and administrative procedures in place to achieve the established standards. These range from school financing mechanisms—such as per-student subsidies or per-school allocations based on established norms—to the processes by which resources are channeled to each of the actors in the system.

Autonomy, Intervention, and Support

Instruments should be in place that assist individuals and institutions in meeting performance standards. These instruments include autonomy in setting policy and managing resources, technical-pedagogic support to teachers and school administrators, and coordination with (government and private) support institutions and networks.

Accountability and Consequences

Mechanisms should be in place to reward or sanction individuals and institutions for meeting or failing to meet agreed-upon requirements and performance standards. Many education systems in Latin America have established direct consequences for students who do not meet standards; indeed, most systems have secondary school–exit examinations or national university entrance examinations. These examinations have direct consequences for students, whose ability to pursue their education depends on their performance on these assessments. In contrast, few education systems in the region have established consequences for teachers or schools that fail to meet performance standards.

Quality Assurance Systems in Selected Countries

Many countries have been successful in establishing quality assurance systems for education (table 8.1). This section reviews the experience in nine of those systems.

Table 8.1 Levels of Control and Administrative Organization in Selected Countries

National system	Subnational level		School level	Comment
	First level	Second level		
England	150 local education authorities		School governing bodies	The Department for Education and Skills (DfES) defines national policies, guidelines, and curricula. Local governments and individual institutions implement and administer national and regional policies and are statutorily responsible for ensuring that education is provided and for exercising discretion over, among others, the school funding formula and staffing of schools
Republic of Korea	16 provincial education authorities or metropolitan offices of education	About 180 school district offices of education	School management committees	Budgetary, administrative, and curricular powers are gradually being delegated to provincial education authorities and metropolitan offices of education.
New Zealand	No significant participation of government entities at the regional or local levels		Boards of trustees	Ministry of Education provides policy advice, allocates resources, develops curriculum, and monitors effectiveness. Boards of trustees (elected by parents) develop school charter of aims and objectives. *(continued)*

Table 8.1 Levels of Control and Administrative Organization in Selected Countries *(continued)*

National system	Subnational level		School level	Comment
	First level	Second level		
Spain	17 autonomous communities	Local authorities, such as municipal school councils	Governing/ coordinating bodies (such as councils of individual schools)	Ministry of Education is responsible for general regulation of system, policies, and guidance. Autonomous communities are responsible for, among other duties, overseeing implementing nationally defined standards, adapting them to local situations, setting up teaching establishments, and administering personnel.
Wales	22 local education authorities		School governing bodies	Responsibility for education provision has been devolved to schools and school governing bodies.

Source: Author compilation.
Note: Except in New Zealand, where the Ministry of Education and the Education Review Office share responsibility for education, the national ministry or department of education is responsible for national education policy.

Chile

Historically, Chile's education system was centralized, with the national government controlling not only curriculum design but also education financing and provision. A decentralization process initiated in the early 1980s transferred the administration of public schools to municipal governments. The reform also opened the way for private sector participation as a provider of publicly financed education by establishing a voucher-type student-based subsidy. Three types of schools were established: municipal schools, financed by the student-based subsidy granted by the state and run by municipalities; private subsidized schools, financed by the state student-based subsidy and run by the private sector; and private fee-paying schools, financed by fees paid by parents and run by the private sector. The size of the subsidy per student is the same for municipal and subsidized private schools. Fee-paying private schools are generally for-profit; subsidized private schools can be nonprofit or for-profit. Nonprofit private schools include church schools and schools that depend on foundations or private corporations, some of which are linked to sectors of industry. For-profit schools operate like firms, generating returns for their owners.

While education provision was decentralized to municipalities and private schools, a number of important policy decisions remained within the purview of the national ministry of education. These include determining public (municipal) school teachers' remuneration system and negotiating their contracts; setting operational requirements for schools, teachers, and administrative staff; setting curricula and student assessment systems; and determining the size of the per-student subsidy. The Superior Education Council is charged with approving curricula and standards developed by the Ministry of Education.

Together with private provision of education, the per-student subsidy (or voucher system) was expected to promote competition among schools by attracting and retaining students, creating an "education market" that would increase efficiency and educational quality through competition. Research remains inconsistent regarding the extent to which competition between private and public schools improved student outcomes or increased inequality across groups of students.[1] Although the reforms have not led to the desired impacts on education quality, coverage and retention have increased (World Bank 2005).

England, Wales, and Northern Ireland

Government responsibility for education in England, Wales, and Northern Ireland was radically altered by the British government's devolution of legislative powers to Scotland, Wales, and Northern Ireland in 1999. The Scottish Parliament and Northern Ireland Assembly gained legislative authority in domestic affairs, including education.[2] The National Assembly for Wales acquired secondary legislative powers; responsibility for primary legislation remained with the British Parliament. For this reason, education regulations in Wales are broadly similar to those in England.

Education in England, Wales, and Northern Ireland is managed and administered at the national and local levels rather than the regional level. The Department for Education and Skills (DfES) in England, the Department for Training and Education (DfTE) in Wales, and the Department for Education (DE) in Northern Ireland are responsible for education at the national level; at the local level, management and administration of education is the responsibility of local authorities in England and Wales and Education and Library Boards in Northern Ireland. Governing bodies of educational institutions have a high degree of autonomy over the management of their institutions.

The central government has powers over and responsibility for providing education services. The education departments in England, Wales, and Northern Ireland determine national education policy and legislation and plan the direction of the system as a whole. They are also responsible for strategic planning and, accordingly, financial and resource allocation.

Education departments receive substantial support from two sets of national agencies: qualifications, curriculum, and assessment authorities and inspection authorities. Qualifications, curriculum, and assessment authorities are nondepartmental public bodies sponsored by and reporting to their respective education departments. Their main statutory function is to advise the government on matters affecting the school curriculum, pupil assessment, and publicly funded qualifications. Inspection authorities are nonministerial government departments responsible for the independent management of school regulation and inspection systems. Their duties include the inspection of educational services provided by local authorities.

Local governments and individual institutions implement and administer national and regional policies. They also have their own statutory powers and responsibilities. Local authorities are statutorily responsible for ensuring that education is provided and for exercising discretion over, among others, the school funding formula and staffing of schools.

The extent of local control over the education system has diminished in recent years, as public educational institutions have been granted more administrative and managerial autonomy.[3] Schools have spending discretion over their budgets and autonomy over admissions policy, teaching methodologies, and the school term. The Department for Education and Skills explains the new relation between local authorities and schools as one in which "good schools manage themselves" and local authorities "only intervene in schools' management in inverse proportion to those schools' success" (DfEE 2000).

"Maintained" schools in England and Wales and grant-aided schools in Northern Ireland refer to schools, private or public, that are publicly funded. Private schools financed by tuition and fees paid by parents also operate in England, Wales, and Northern Ireland. Although they are exempt from most regulations applicable to publicly maintained schools, private schools are still subject to minimum operating requirements set by the state regarding health and safety, reporting, welfare, and education quality standards. Private schools are also subject to external inspections.

Finland

The education system in Finland is not unlike the British systems in terms of its vertical allocation of institutional responsibilities. Decentralization is evident throughout the system, not just at the local level but also at the school level. At the central administration level, education falls within the purview of two national institutions: the Ministry of Education and the Finnish National Board of Education (FNBE). Government authority at the regional level is exercised by provincial state offices. Although these entities are endowed with an education and culture department, education management and administration is not effected primarily at the regional level.[4] Local authorities are responsible for organizing basic education at a local level. The state grants some operating licenses for private schools (which served roughly 3 percent of all compulsory school enrollment in Finland in 2004, but almost all schools providing basic education are maintained by local authorities. Private schools are publicly funded and under public supervision; they follow the national core curricula and the requirements of the competence-based qualifications established by the FNBE.

Regarding the statutory distribution of functions, the Ministry of Education is responsible mainly for preparing educational policy and legislation; working in close cooperation with the ministry, it is the national agency in charge of education development. It elaborates and approves national curricula and qualification requirements, conducts evaluations of learning results, and provides information and support services. Although ministries direct the central boards in general, they do not intervene in their individual decisions. Thus, the FNBE is comparatively independent within its own field and publicly liable for the legality of its actions. The Finnish Education Evaluation Council, which is responsible for planning, developing, and coordinating evaluating of education, provides important support to the Ministry of Education.

The next concentration of education authority lies with municipalities. Local authorities have the statutory duty to ensure the provision of education. They are also responsible for providing student welfare services and ensuring, through direct provision or outsourcing, the delivery of a number of educational services. Municipal governments share responsibility for financing education with the central government. As a result of decentralization, responsibility for developing and implementing the national curriculum has increasingly been transferred to schools. Consequently, educational institutions have become differentiated and the options they provide have multiplied, increasing the need for evaluation.

Republic of Korea

The centralized nature of the education system in the Republic of Korea makes it the most distinct of the countries analyzed. The education administration consists of three layers of authority: the Ministry of Education and Human Resources Development at the national level, the supervisors of education at the metropolitan and provincial level, and the district boards of education at the local level. The Ministry of Education and Human Resources Development drafts, plans, and coordinates national education policies; develops the national curriculum; publishes and approves school textbooks and teaching guides; provides administrative and financial support for schools; supports local educational agencies; and operates the teacher education system. The Ministry of Education delegates some budget-planning processes and administrative decisions to municipal and provincial education authorities or metropolitan and provincial offices of education at the regional level. These authorities in turn delegate certain responsibilities to the local office of education.

Under this structure, the role of individual education institutions is relegated to implementing the policies and regulations defined by the government. Schools are required to adopt nationally mandated subjects, contents, textbooks, time allocation, curriculum organization and implementation guidelines, teaching, assessment and reporting guidelines, and school administration guidelines, as well as provincially determined staffing and operational guidelines. Even private schools, which represent roughly 30 percent of all education institutions (largely pre- and postcompulsory institutions) are subject to state curriculum, student enrollment, and staff regulations.

Korea's education system remains highly centralized, although the government is moving toward some decentralization. Recent curriculum reviews have aimed to introduce some flexibility in the centralized curriculum framework and encourage schools and individual teachers to become actively involved in the decision and planning process for the curriculum (O'Donnell 2004). In 1995 the Presidential Commission on Education Reform recommended that the process of increasing local self-government in education should continue, regional distinctiveness respected, and the autonomy of individual schools expanded. As a result, some schools were required to set up experimental school management committees comprising parents, teachers, principals, community leaders, and education specialists with deliberative, consultative, and decision-making powers. This initiative had limited success, largely because of principals' concerns about the possibility of excessive parental interference in schools' internal affairs.

New Zealand

The institutional structure of the education system in New Zealand since the reform of 1989 is heavily decentralized. Individual schools have considerable responsibility for their own governance and management, working within the framework of requirements, guidelines, and funding set by the central government and administered through its agencies. Within this framework, the allocation of roles and responsibilities for quality assurance is distributed between individual schools and national government agencies, with no significant participation of government entities at the regional or local levels.

At the national level, central government responsibility for education is generally divided between the Ministry of Education and the Education Review Office. The faculties and responsibilities of the ministry include setting the direction of education policy and overseeing the implementation of approved policies; developing curriculum statements; allocating funding and resources to schools; providing and purchasing services for schools and students; collecting and processing education statistics and information; and monitoring the effectiveness of the education system as a whole. The principal remit of the Education Review Office is to evaluate the performance of individual schools and publicly report evaluation results.

A number of national agencies operate in an independent manner, accountable to individual governing boards and not reporting directly to any minister of the crown. Of particular relevance are the Teachers Council and the New Zealand Qualifications Authority. The Teachers Council is responsible for registering teachers, removing their practicing certificates when necessary, and approving teacher education programs that can lead to registration. All practicing teachers, including those in private schools, fall under the remit of this agency. The New Zealand Qualifications Authority sets and reviews standards relating to qualifications, provides awareness about established qualifications, oversees the curriculum, and sets all secondary-school and many tertiary examinations.[5]

Administrative authority for providing most education services has been devolved from the central government to educational institutions. Schools exercise discretion in the spending of their operational budget, teaching, and resource allocations across subject areas. Schools also have autonomy over governance, as exemplified by school charters. The school charter is an integral part of school self-management, because it reflects the mission, aims, objectives, directions, and targets of the board that will give effect to the national education guidelines and the board's priorities. Although there is diversity in the forms of institutions through which education is provided, national policies and quality assurance provide continuity and consistency across the system. The school charter provides a base against which the school's performance can be assessed. In this sense, private schools (which represent roughly 4 percent of all compulsory-school enrollment) are also regulated by the state, as their registration depends on premise, equipment, staffing, and curriculum standards.

Spain

Spain's education system distributes quality assurance roles and responsibilities among the state, autonomous communities, municipal authorities, and education institutions. As stated in the constitution, the state retains the authority to ensure the unity, homogeneity, and equity of the education system. This power is held by the Ministry of Education. The state has exclusive competence over matters relating to the length of compulsory schooling, the levels and cycles of the system, minimum education standards, school operating requirements, staffing qualifications and levels, funding, and inspection. The state also holds executive responsibilities, including responsibility for coordinating and promoting educational research and ensuring compliance with legal requirements.

Autonomous communities assume all regulatory and executive responsibilities not included within the state's exclusive area of competence. These responsibilities include authorizing and setting up educational institutions, administering personnel, expanding and developing education programs, counseling students, and providing grants and loans.

Although town councils do not have education authority status, autonomous communities can delegate powers to these municipal entities. Town councils are usually responsible for providing land for building public institutions, maintaining and renovating schools, developing programs for extracurricular and complementary activities, and supervising attendance at compulsory schools.

Educational institutions in Spain maintain a high degree of autonomy. Schools' pedagogical, organizational, and economic autonomy is officially affirmed in the country's regulations. Pedagogical autonomy is manifest in the schools' right to choose pedagogical programs and determine an educational project, thereby setting its own education priorities and objectives. Schools exercise organizational autonomy in their definition of annual programs and internal regulations. Annual programs establish the schools' organizational and curricular plan; internal regulations address student rights, responsibilities, and disciplinary requirements that are consistent with state regulations. Autonomy over economic management is reflected in schools' discretionary power over expense allocations and the sourcing of construction and materials.

The administrative and managerial work of individual institutions is supervised at two different levels. The state's High Inspection Service supervises and enforces compliance with basic state regulations. This inspection is effected not only at the school level but also within the autonomous community as a whole. The autonomous community carries out technical inspections of schools itself. These inspections evaluate the achievement of educational objectives by looking at management, administration, functioning, results, compliance with legal requirement, and education quality.

The United States: Boston, Massachusetts, and Houston, Texas

In contrast to the other countries described in this volume, education in the United States has historically been the purview of states and local school districts rather than the national government. Through legislative statute and state board policy, states prescribe the manner in which school districts are established and governed, the age of compulsory student attendance, performance standards for students, licensing requirements for school personnel, school operating requirements, and provision of funding. District boards and administrations are then tasked with translating these parameters into policies and practices for the provision of education locally. Most states also authorize the operation of publicly funded charter schools, which are free from state and district regulation but must comply with the terms of their charters, including those governing student performance.

Given the emphasis on local control in the United States, this analysis focuses on two district-state pairs: Boston, Massachusetts, and Houston, Texas. Both education systems are characterized by strong standards and assessments at the state level, combined with autonomy and support at the school and district level that fosters an array of curricular and instructional options. Both systems effectively serve diverse populations that include a high percentage of low-income students.

In the past two decades, standards-based reform has become the dominant paradigm in education in the United States. Each state develops standards for what students should know and be able to do at each grade level and for each subject area. States are required by law to annually assess and report student performance in different grades and subjects, disaggregating results by race/ethnicity, language status, and socioeconomic status, in order to spotlight any inequity in educational outcomes.

Massachusetts has been lauded for the clarity and caliber of its standards (known as "curriculum frameworks"), which encompass the arts, English, foreign languages, health, history and social studies, math, and science and technology from prekindergarten (age 4) to grade 12 (age 18) (Rennie Center for Education Research & Policy 2006).

Texas has been recognized for linking its primary and secondary education systems with postsecondary education and the workplace, through academically rigorous graduation requirements, the use of secondary-school assessments for postsecondary admissions and placement decisions, and a longitudinal data system that enables the state to track individual student outcomes from prekindergarten to the postsecondary level (Achieve 2006).

Both the Boston and Houston systems provide autonomy and support to a diverse portfolio of schools, from which students and families can choose to meet their educational needs and interests. Both Massachusetts and Texas offer charter schools, and students in Houston have the option of attending charter schools throughout the city. Houston grants traditional schools authority over their curriculum, instructional methods, personnel, and budgets in exchange for demonstrated strong leadership, a high-functioning team, and a vision and plan for the school. Massachusetts mandates participatory management at the school level. The Boston public school system aligns this decision-making authority with its broader whole-school improvement framework.[6] Each school council must approve its school's whole-school improvement plan and discretionary budget. The Boston public school system then evaluates the schools, using an assessment tool aligned to its school improvement framework. It also provides intensive support to new and existing teachers and principals. Both the Boston and Houston school systems have responsibility for intervening in underperforming schools and assisting or sanctioning personnel.[7]

Visions of Education Provision and Quality Assurance

The international review of successful institutional frameworks for quality assurance in education reveals wide differences in functions and the tiers that assume them. Policy making and administrative support are handled by two autonomous institutions in Finland, for example, while the Republic of Korea entrusts both duties to a single institution (the Ministry of Education). In England, Wales, and Northern Ireland, teacher registration is carried out by independent professional bodies (General Teaching Councils); in New Zealand this function is fulfilled by an arm of the Ministry of Education (the New Zealand Teachers Council).

These differences suggest that assuring quality lies not in the adoption of particular institutional functions but in the application of a vision, or theory of action, which in turn implies an institutional framework. Based on the sample of countries reviewed, four alternative visions can be identified: limited state, quality contracts, differentiated instruction, and managed instruction.[8] Each of these visions implies a different institutional distribution of quality assurance functions.

These visions can be placed along a continuum that describes the degree of coupling between what is dictated by the central government and what is implemented at the school level. Broadly speaking, a gradual movement from a limited state vision at one end of the continuum to one of managed instruction at the other implies an incremental expansion of central government control along with a simultaneous reduction in school autonomy.

No country perfectly applies any of these visions; although each country's education system exemplifies a particular institutional vision, each system allows for deviations from the model and the inclusion of elements of other visions. In England, for example, while the lion's share of the education system follows a differentiated instruction vision, some schools operate under conditions that are characteristic of a quality contracts vision. Although Finland has adopted a differentiated instruction vision, the state plays a very active role in maintaining some special education and language schools.

Limited State

The limited state institutional vision is based on the premise that market forces will act as a quality assurance instrument if the education system is allowed to function as a competitive market with minimal state intervention. The role of the central government is limited to establishing minimum operation requirements and reporting standards; financing schools on a per-student basis; and providing information to the market to facilitate informed school choice. Schools have discretion over the choice of performance standards, performance assessment mechanisms, and the model of instruction. Students have the right to decide which school to attend. In theory, school choice, perfect information on the quality of education provided by schools, and free entry and exit of schools should ensure that only good schools survive and that poorly performing schools are driven out of business for lack of demand. According to this vision, market forces define the quantity and distribution of schools.

Among the countries analyzed, Chile is the only one that opted for the institutional vision of a limited state. For the past 25 years, state intervention in the education system has been very constrained: the government establishes minimum operation and reporting requirements regarding student attendance, finances schools to varying degrees based on a per-student formula, and provides the market with information, arguably to an insufficient extent. While state-funded schools must follow a national curriculum, the central government mandates no performance standards or instructional models.

Application of the institutional vision of a limited state was not fully consistent in Chile. Although the foundations of the educational system laid down in the educational reform of 1980 were based on a limited state vision, many of the reforms implemented following the reestablishment of democracy introduced elements typical of differentiated and managed instruction visions.[9] Overall, however, the characteristics of the current educational system in Chile most closely align with a limited state institutional vision.

Quality Contracts

Under the quality contract institutional vision, in addition to the functions executed in a limited state vision, the state is responsible for granting and revoking operating licenses, establishing standards for performance and performance assessment, and implementing performance assessment in schools. The power to grant and revoke licenses implies that the state can actively influence the quantity and distribution of schools. Market forces, however, continue to play an important role in this allocation, because the decision of individual schools to apply for licenses is still demand driven. Although schools are obliged to comply with statutory performance standards, individual establishments still wield discretion over the instructional model and evaluation methodologies used to achieve these standards.

New Zealand is one of the most compelling examples of a coherent application of a quality contracts institutional vision. Statutory performance standards for all schools are set by the central government, but state schools, which serve 96 percent of all children, establish individual school charters with specific goals and targets for student outcomes. In order to be allowed to operate, all schools, including private schools, must register with the Ministry of Education. Registration depends on the outcome of an evaluation of premises, equipment, staffing, and curriculum carried out every three years. When a school evaluation suggests poor performance, the state exerts pressure for improvement by performing discretionary reviews. External help may be provided by trustee, principal, or teacher associations or purchased from counseling agencies; the state does not intervene directly in poorly performing schools. Students' right-to-school choice implies that market forces have a strong influence on the creation and distribution of schools around the country.

Differentiated Instruction

Under the differentiated instruction vision, the central government plays a very important role in quality assurance. In addition to the duties performed under a quality contracts vision, the state is responsible for establishing standards for staff accreditation; coordinating among schools to guarantee a balance of educational options; intervening differentially in educational establishments; and providing diverse services for schools and professional development options for staff.

The autonomy of schools under a differentiated instruction vision is generally limited to defining their instructional model, though it can also include decision making about human resources, such as the hiring and firing of personnel. The state plays a very active role in creating networks of information sharing, in order to promote successful models and programs. Although the central government determines the number and distribution of educational establishments, market forces continue to operate, because students are allowed to choose their schools. A key difference between this vision and one based on quality contracts is that in the differentiated instruction model, the state actively intervenes to improve the quality of education of a poorly performing school rather than simply revoking its operating license.

Most of the successful education systems analyzed here—including the systems in England, Wales, and Northern Ireland; Finland; Spain; and the United States—are based on a differentiated instruction vision. In all of those systems, the central government permits an array of instructional models to coexist and bases its intervention on school performance. Schools achieving good performance are granted a high degree of administrative autonomy; the state intervenes in schools whose performance is poor. Intervention options are diverse, because central governments try to account for differences in instructional and administrative models.

Managed Instruction

Under the managed instruction vision, the central government takes responsibility for virtually all quality assurance functions. Two state duties that are unique to this type of system are defining a single statutory instructional model and centrally assigning students to school. These functions affect the way in which the state serves its other functions. School services and professional development options are uniformly targeted to the instructional model in place. Intervention in poorly performing schools is also uniform. Market forces do not play a significant role in a managed instruction system. Schools act as implementing agencies for the policies centrally mandated by the state.

The educational system in the Republic of Korea is based on this vision. The central government establishes a national curriculum, performance standards, and an instructional model. The government publishes textbooks and provides them to students free of charge. Continual professional development and school improvement services are provided to ensure adherence to the instructional model. Students are assigned to schools in their residential area by lottery, impeding market forces from influencing school allocation.

Degree of Control and Diversity of Alternative Visions

The roles and responsibilities of government vary depending on the instructional vision adopted (table 8.2). In a system that adopts a limited state instructional vision, many of the responsibilities that governments typically undertake are carried out by the market. In the quality contracts vision, the government develops operating requirements and performance standards and grants or revokes licenses to participants on the basis of whether they

Table 8.2 Role of Government under Alternative Instructional Visions

Education quality assurance function	Limited state	Quality contracts	Differentiated instruction	Managed instruction
Performance standards	• Develops standards (learning, administration, teaching, teaching resources, and so forth) • Develops curricular framework • Communicates standards and curricular frameworks to all stakeholders	• Develops standards (learning, administration, teaching, teaching resources, and so forth) • Develops curricular framework • Communicates standards and curricular frameworks to all stakeholders • Evaluates adoption and implementation of standards and curricular frameworks	• Develops standards (learning, administration, teaching, teaching resources, and so forth) • Develops curricular framework • Communicates standards and curricular frameworks to all stakeholders • Evaluates adoption and implementation of standards and curricular frameworks • Develops tools to support adoption of standards and curricula	• Develops standards (learning, administration, teaching, teaching resources, and so forth) • Develops curricular framework • Communicates standards and curricular frameworks to all stakeholders • Evaluates adoption and implementation of standards and curricular frameworks • Enforces adoption of standards and curricula

(continued)

Table 8.2 Role of Government under Alternative Instructional Visions *(continued)*

Education quality assurance function	Limited state	Quality contracts	Differentiated instruction	Managed instruction
Performance assessment	• Defines general framework of system for measuring performance for all participants in system • Establishes criteria for performance assessment of all participants	• Defines general framework of system for measuring performance for all participants in system • Establishes criteria for performance assessment of all participants • Establishes levels of acceptable performance for all participants • Develops instruments for evaluating performance of all participants • Enforces implementation of performance evaluation systems for all participants • Evaluates participants' performance relative to international standards	• Defines general framework of system for measuring performance for all participants in system • Establishes criteria for performance assessment of all participants • Establishes levels of acceptable performance for all participants • Develops instruments for evaluating performance of all participants • Enforces implementation of performance evaluation systems for all participants • Evaluates participants' performance relative to international standards	• Defines general framework of system for measuring performance for all participants in system • Establishes criteria for performance assessment of all participants • Establishes levels of acceptable performance for all participants • Develops instruments for evaluating performance of all participants • Enforces implementation of performance evaluation systems for all participants • Evaluates participants' performance relative to international standards

(continued)

Table 8.2 Role of Government under Alternative Instructional Visions *(continued)*

Education quality assurance function	Limited state	Quality contracts	Differentiated instruction	Managed instruction
Performance reporting	• Provides information to market to facilitate informed choice	• Defines reporting requirements for all participants • Develops structure for reporting on participants' performance • Develops statistics and education management indicators • Maintains information systems • Informs diverse stakeholders on performance of system's participants	• Defines reporting requirements for all participants • Develops structure for reporting on participants' performance • Develops statistics and education management indicators • Maintains information systems • Informs diverse stakeholders on performance of system's participants	• Defines reporting requirements for all participants • Develops structure for reporting on participants' performance • Develops statistics and education management indicators • Maintains information systems • Informs diverse stakeholders on performance of system's participants
Impact evaluation	• Designs impact evaluations of new and existing policies and programs • Performs specialized data collection and studies • Uses information and data to evaluate impact	• Designs impact evaluations of new and existing policies and programs • Performs specialized data collection and studies • Uses information and data to evaluate impact	• Designs impact evaluations of new and existing policies and programs • Performs specialized data collection and studies • Uses information and data to evaluate impact	• Designs impact evaluations of new and existing policies and programs • Performs specialized data collection and studies • Uses information and data to evaluate impact

(continued)

Table 8.2 Role of Government under Alternative Instructional Visions *(continued)*

Education quality assurance function	Limited state	Quality contracts	Differentiated instruction	Managed instruction
Requirements to operate	• Develops broad operating requirements for all participants • Grants/revokes operating licenses	• Develops and defines operating requirements for all participants • Grants/revokes operating licenses	• Develops and defines operating requirements for all participants • Grants/revokes operating licenses	• Develops and defines operating requirements for all participants • Ensures that all participants meet operating requirements
Adequate and equitable resources	• Establishes mechanisms to ensure adequate administrative and financial operation of education establishments • Distributes resources based on legislatively approved methodologies	• Establishes mechanisms to ensure adequate administrative and financial operation of education establishments • Distributes resources based on legislatively approved methodologies • Monitors adequacy and equity of resource allocation	• Establishes mechanisms to ensure adequate administrative and financial operation of education establishments • Distributes resources based on legislatively approved methodologies • Monitors adequacy and equity of resource allocation	• Establishes mechanisms to ensure adequate administrative and financial operation of education establishments • Distributes resources based on legislatively approved methodologies • Enforces adequacy and equity of resource allocation
Autonomy, support, and intervention	—	• Develops and implements food and other welfare programs for vulnerable students	• Develops framework for providing participants with autonomy, intervention, and support based on performance	• Implements support programs for infrastructure, equipment, instructional materials, and staff development

(continued)

Table 8.2 Role of Government under Alternative Instructional Visions *(continued)*

Education quality assurance function	Limited state	Quality contracts	Differentiated instruction	Managed instruction
		• Implements assessment-oriented supervision or quality audit of support provided	• Implements diverse support programs for infrastructure, equipment, instructional materials, and staff development • Develops and implements food and other welfare programs for vulnerable students • Provides differentiated formative or support-oriented supervision • Supports and intervenes in education establishments with persistently poor performance (directly or through third party)	• Develops and implements food and other welfare programs for vulnerable students • Provides formative or support-oriented supervision to ensure adherence to curricula
Accountability and consequences	—	• Develops a framework for accountability and consequences for all participants	• Develops a framework for accountability and consequences for all participants	• Develops framework for accountability and consequences for all participants

(continued)

Table 8.2 Role of Government under Alternative Instructional Visions *(continued)*

Education quality assurance function	Limited state	Quality contracts	Differentiated instruction	Managed instruction
		• Revokes operating licenses of institutions that do not meet operating requirements	• Provides incentives and imposes penalties based on performance • Cancels operating licenses of institutions that do not meet operating requirements	• Provides rewards and penalties based on performance

Source: Author compilation.
— Not available.

do or do not meet those requirements and standards. In contrast, in the differentiated instruction vision, the government intervenes in schools to support their achievement of established standards. In the managed instruction vision, the government enforces adherence to a unique curriculum by directly managing schools.

Ensuring that all students learn requires adopting a theory of action for education provision and aligning the roles and responsibilities of all participants in the education system to ensure quality. International evidence suggests that at least three institutional visions—quality contracts, differentiated instruction, and managed instruction—can achieve good results. The challenge is to adopt an institutional vision that is appropriate to countries' individual historical, social, and political contexts and to consistently apply this vision to ensure that all students achieve at their fullest potential.

Notes

1. Rodriguez (1988), Aedo and Larrañaga (1994), and Aedo (1997) find that private voucher schools achieve better student outcomes than do municipal schools. In contrast, McEwan and Carnoy (1999, 2000) and Mizala and Romaguera (2000) find that private voucher schools do not perform differently from municipal schools, although Catholic voucher schools outperform municipal schools. The main differences among the studies include the samples used, the variables included, and the sectors categorized. Given the confounding effects of student background, peer effects, and other unobservable variables, empirically identifying the impact of competition on student outcomes is methodologically challenging.

2. As a result of political turbulence, the Northern Ireland Assembly was suspended in October 2002 and its powers returned to the national government, with the secretary of state for Northern Ireland assuming responsibility for the direction of the Northern Ireland departments.

3. Publicly funded schools in England and Wales include community schools, which are managed by local authorities; foundation schools, which are owned by school trustees or a school governing body; and voluntary controlled and voluntary aided schools, which are owned by school trustees or a funding body. In Northern Ireland, publicly funded schools include controlled schools, owned by Education and Library Boards; schools owned and maintained by the Catholic Church; grant-maintained integrated schools, which are owned by school trustees of the board of governors; and voluntary grammar schools, which are owned by school trustees or a funding body.

4. The authority of the provincial state offices does not extend significantly beyond the monitoring and evaluation of the serviceability of the school network and the satisfaction of education demand.

5. The other national agencies are Special Education Services, Career Services, the Education and Training Support Agency, and the Early Childhood Development Unit.

6. The whole-school improvement framework in Boston encompassed five "essential" activities, that included (a) full-time, on-site coach in every school; (b) a professional development model to support teachers to analyze practice together; (c) professional development for principals and headmasters so they

understand and can lead the instructional approach; (d) clear written expectations and tools for teachers and school leaders; and (e) clear written expectations for central office support for schools (Guiney and Payzant 2003).

7. Determining and imposing consequences for performance has traditionally fallen to districts and more recently to charter authorizers. The U.S. government became dramatically more prescriptive in this area with passage of the 2001 No Child Left Behind Act, which lays out a graduated set of sanctions for schools failing to meet state-established performance targets. Students attending schools that fail to make Adequate Yearly Progress are eligible to transfer to other schools or receive free tutoring services, for which districts must pay using a portion of their national funds. Schools that persistently fail to make Adequate Yearly Progress may be required to replace staff, adopt a new curriculum, decrease management authority at the school level, and ultimately face takeover by the state or other outside entity. Local school systems must comply with the accountability requirements set forth in the law, in addition to their own performance requirements.

8. The concepts presented in this section were strongly influenced by the work of McAdams (2006).

9. Since the implementation of the Program for the Improvement of Quality in Poor Area Basic Schools (Program P-900) in 1990, the state actively intervened in 900 underperforming schools to improve the quality of education, providing pedagogical materials and resources, teacher workshops, learning workshops, school administration teams, and institutional school projects. Because of the shortage of education providers, poorly performing state-funded schools were never allowed to close, however, inhibiting market forces in their role as quality warrantors. The most important impediments to the functioning of a limited state, however, were the constraints faced by municipal schools (such as, for example, teacher's statute and noncompetitive admission), which effectively raised the cost of providing education in this sector above the average cost faced by private schools, making competition unfair.

References

Achieve, Inc. 2006. "Closing the Expectations Gap 2006." February, Washington, DC.

Aedo, C. 1997. "Organización industrial de la prestación de servicios sociales." Working Paper Series R-302, Inter-American Development Bank, Washington, DC.

Aedo, C., and O. Larrañaga. 1994. "Educación privada vs. pública en Chile: Calidad y sesgo de selección." Graduate Economics Program, ILADES/Georgetown University, Santiago.

DfEE (Department for Education and Employment). 2000. "The Role of the Local Education Authority in School Education." U.K. Department for Education and Employment, Nottingham. http://www.dfes.gov.uk/learole/policypaper/pdf/localedu.pdf.

———. 2001. "Code of Practice on Local Education Authority–School Relations." DfEE Circular 0027/2001, London.

Guiney, E., and T. Payzant. 2003. Paper presented at the Alliance for Excellent Education, American High School Policy Conference," Washington, DC, November 17.

McAdams, D. R. 2006. *What School Boards Can Do: Reform Governance for Urban Schools.* New York: Teachers College Press.

McEwan, P., and M. Carnoy. 1999. "The Impact of Competition on Public School Quality: Longitudinal Evidence from Chile's Voucher System." Stanford, CA: Stanford University.

———. 2000. "The Effectiveness and Efficiency of Private Schools in Chile's Voucher System." *Educational Evaluation and Policy Analysis* 33: 213–39.

Mizala, A., and P. Romaguera. 2000. "School Performance and Choice: The Chilean Experience." *Journal of Human Resources* 35 (2): 392–417.

———. 2005. "Teachers' Salary Structure and Incentives in Chile." In *Incentives to Improve Teaching*, ed. E. Vegas. Washington, DC: World Bank.

O'Donnell, S. 2004. *International Review of Curriculum and Assessment Frameworks: Comparative Tables and Factual Summaries* 2004. Qualifications and Curriculum Authority and National Foundation for Educational Research, London.

Rennie Center for Education Research & Policy. 2006. *A Decade of Boston School Reform: Reflections and Aspirations*. (Executive Summary). Boston.

Rodriguez, R. 1988. "School Achievement and Decentralization Policy: The Chilean Case." *Revista de análisis económico* 3 (1): 75–88.

World Bank. 2005. *Chile: Development Policy Review*. Report 33501-CL, Washington, DC.

9

Conclusion

The factors that influence student learning are complex and difficult to measure. Moreover, because every child is different, as is every classroom, school, community, and nation, no single intervention will meet the needs of all students, schools, education systems, or countries. Some common lessons can nevertheless be drawn from the most recent research on student learning in Latin America and the rest of the world.

Which Policies Can Raise Student Learning?

International evidence suggests that well-crafted policies can improve student learning. These policies may target students, schools, or the education system as a whole.

Prepare Students for Primary School

The latest research indicates that the preparation children receive before entering primary school has a strong effect on their later learning. Several studies carried out in countries of different income levels consistently show that children who do not attend high-quality preschool programs are left behind even before beginning their compulsory schooling.

Household factors and the support children receive at home also have significant effects on success in school. All studies that have measured students' socioeconomic status have found it significantly correlated with learning. Parents' education and occupation are also strongly related to students' learning in the classroom. The policy implications of these findings are complicated, because they require interventions that mitigate the effects on educational performance gap of coming from a disadvantaged family.

Policies with the potential to improve learning outcomes include early childhood development programs, which help prepare children for primary school, and conditional cash transfers, which help offset the costs of schooling. Indeed, the regional and international evidence points to the fact that good-quality early childhood education programs may be one of the most effective interventions for improving learning in the long term and reducing repetition while mitigating the inequality of opportunity that disadvantaged students face.

Provide Conditional Cash Transfers

Conditional cash transfers are often lauded for their positive impacts on education and health, especially in fostering demand for these services. Evidence of the effect of conditional cash transfers on cognitive achievement and student learning is scarce, however, and limited to intermediate quality indicators, such as repetition and dropout rates. A recent evaluation finds that Mexico's conditional cash transfer program, Progresa/Oportunidades, reduced failure, repetition, and dropout rates. This type of program may also help reduce inequality in educational outcomes.

Provide Merit Pay, Evaluate Teaching Policies, and Review the Assignment of Teachers to Schools

Teachers may be one of the most important school-side variables affecting student learning. Their impact on student learning outcomes is cumulative and long lasting. Recent research suggests that investing in teachers, by providing both increased and improved incentives as well as continuous support and training, can help improve student learning.

Paying teachers for what they know and do may improve student learning outcomes, but the effect of performance-based pay appears to depend critically on how the programs are designed and linked to performance. Research suggests that pay incentives should be clearly linked to the desired behaviors; teachers must be familiar with the incentive and the desired behaviors; incentives should be large enough to merit the extra effort; and all teachers should have access to the incentive when they adopt the desired behavior.

Evaluation of teacher education policies in Latin America and the Caribbean has not received the attention it deserves, especially considering the singular role teachers play in improving student learning. Student learning in the region may be suffering as a result. It may continue to do so unless teacher education is given focused and sustained attention and rigorously evaluated for its impact on classroom processes and student learning.

How teachers are assigned to schools may also affect education quality and equity. Evidence from Uruguay indicates that schools serving the most disadvantaged students tend to end up with the least-qualified teachers, a pattern that is likely to be mirrored in other countries.

Use Resources Effectively

Research on the relation between increased investment in school resources and improved student learning indicates a tenuous relation at best. While the evidence does not suggest investing less in education, it does make a strong case for more effective use of resources. As countries in the region continue to increase their investment in education, they should take into consideration the evidence on the impact of various policies on raising student learning. For example, how many days students attend school each year, how long they spend in school each day, and the amount of time they spend on instructional activities can all affect student learning. In Uruguay, and to a lesser extent Chile, full-time schools have improved student test scores, especially for the most disadvantaged students.

Studies also indicate that how time is used in schools can contribute to—or hinder—student learning. Time on task and student attendance are mutually reinforcing, because students who see an opportunity to learn are more likely to attend class than those who are bored in the classroom or whose teachers are absent.

Increasing the length of time in school can be very costly, and the benefits are greatest among students from disadvantaged backgrounds (indeed, evidence from Latin America indicates that compensatory programs and extended school days are especially effective for indigenous students). For these reasons, it makes sense for policy makers to target the most disadvantaged students in designing school-day extension programs. While reducing the number of children per classroom is a popular education policy throughout the world, evidence on the effects of class size and student-teacher ratios on raising student learning is inconclusive. Similarly, although ICTs have the potential to improve student learning and have become increasingly popular in developing countries, rigorous evaluation of their impact on student learning is scarce and yields mixed results.

Give Schools More Autonomy

Systemwide factors play a key role in student learning. Cross-country evidence indicates that granting greater school autonomy over personnel management and process decisions—hiring teachers, selecting textbooks, allocating budgets within schools—appears to be correlated with better student performance. Decentralization can also lead to increased inequality within countries, however. To ensure that all students learn, reforms should therefore reflect the varying institutional capacities of subnational governments and schools.

Like decentralization, increased private participation in education provision through voucher schemes can both improve student outcomes and increase inequality. Evidence from Chile and Colombia suggests that per-student subsidies that differ based on socioeconomic background may be the most effective way of raising student learning and increasing equity.

The design and implementation of curricula and standards can have important consequences for what and how students learn. Because large-scale curricular reforms are rarely accompanied by evaluations, however, little is known about how changes and variations in curricula affect student learning. If curricular reforms are to have any impact, however, they must be accompanied by the support necessary to develop teaching staff and implement the reforms at the school level.

Education systems should have an instructional vision, upon which the allocation of roles and responsibilities for quality assurance functions depends. The consistent application of an instructional vision can improve the quality of education.

Suggestions for Future Research

This report identifies several gaps in the understanding of how student learning is achieved and how education policy can be most effective in improving student learning. Future research could fill gaps in several areas.

First, too little is known about what makes a good teacher-education and professional development system. The impact of various types of teacher-education programs could be evaluated in order to identify programs that yield concrete results in the classroom.

Second, more needs to be known about how student assessment information can be used for accountability. The empirical evidence has identified various problems in linking student assessment information to the performance of individuals and institutions, such as schools and school districts. However, unless all participants (individuals and institutions) in the education process are held accountable for student learning, not all children will acquire the skills they need to succeed in life. A key area for future research thus relates to improving the methodologies for providing credible and reliable information on participants' performance.

Third, an important area for future research involves understanding how to foster stronger demand for education quality. Evidence suggests that parents often choose schools based on factors other than their perceived quality and that demand for good-quality education is weak. At the same time, the evidence suggests that when parents are directly involved in schools, student learning outcomes improve. Strengthening the demand for education quality likely involves sensitizing parents and community members to issues of education quality; identifying the channels through which members of society can hold their policy makers accountable; and empowering parents and communities so that their voices are heard by policy makers. Strong societal involvement in children's education may make the difference between a region that accepts mediocrity and a region that expects excellence.

Appendix 1

Description of International Assessments

Table A1.1 Description of International Assessments

Item	Laboratorio Latinoamericano de Evaluación de la Calidad de la Educación (LLECE)	Trends in International Mathematics and Science Study (TIMSS)	Programme for International Student Assessment (PISA)	Progress in International Reading Literacy Study (PIRLS)
Implementing agency	United Nations Educational, Scientific, and Cultural Organization (UNESCO)/ Oficina Regional de Educación para América Latina y el Caribe (OREALC)	International Association for the Evaluation of Educational Achievement (IEA)	Organisation for Economic, Co-operation and Development (OECD)	IEA
Subjects covered	Language and math	Math and science	Adult literacy (math, reading, science, and problem solving)[a]	Reading
Ages/grades tested	Third and fourth grade	Fourth and eighth grade	15-year-olds	Fourth grade
Funding	Participating countries, Inter-American Development Bank, and Ford Foundation; OREALC-UNESCO provided resources and personnel	Participating countries, the Inter-American Development Bank, the World Bank, and the Ford Foundation. OREALC-UNESCO provided resources and personnel	OECD; World Bank and Inter-American Development Bank funded participation in some countries.	World Bank, U.S. Department of Education, and countries, by way of fees

(continued)

Table A1. Description of International Assessments *(continued)*

Item	Laboratorio Latinoamericano de Evaluación de la Calidad de la Educación (LLECE)	Trends in International Mathematics and Science Study (TIMSS)	Program for International Student Assessment (PISA)	Progress in International Reading Literacy Study (PIRLS)
Number of participants	1998: 13 countries 2006: 14 countries	1995: 42 countries 1999: 45 countries 2003: 46 countries	2000: 32 countries 2003: 41 countries 2006: 58 countries	2001: 35 countries
Participants from Latin America and the Caribbean	Argentina, Bolivia, Brazil, Colombia, Costa Rica, Cuba, Chile, Dominican Republic, Honduras, Mexico, Paraguay, Peru, and Venezuela, R. B. de	1995: Argentina[b] and Colombia 1999: Argentina and Chile 2003: Argentina[b] and Chile	2000: Argentina, Brazil, Chile, Mexico, and Peru 2003: Brazil, Mexico, and Uruguay 2006: Argentina, Brazil, Chile, Colombia, Mexico, and Uruguay	Argentina and Colombia
Sampling	Two weighted stratified samples: minimum of 40 students per school, 20 per grade, and 100 schools as primary unit, 4,000 students as secondary unit. Stratifications: (a) large city, urban area, and rural area; (b) public and private	Two stage probability-proportional-to-size sampling of minimum of 150 schools. Second stage samples fourth and/or eighth graders.	For population in stage 1, enrolled students defined by age, regardless of grade and type of institution. For population in stage 2, at least 98 percent of all students tested in all countries.	Identical to TIMSS 2003 at primary school level

(continued)

213

Table A1. Description of International Assessments *(continued)*

Item	Laboratorio Latinoamericano de Evaluación de la Calidad de la Educación (LLECE)	Trends in International Mathematics and Science Study (TIMSS)	Program for International Student Assessment (PISA)	Progress in International Reading Literacy Study (PIRLS)
		Stage 1: students in higher of two grades containing largest proportion of 9-year-olds.		
		Stage 2: students in higher of two grades containing largest proportion of 13-year-olds.		
Student background questionnaires	School, principals, teachers, families, and students	Country, principals, teachers, and students	Principals and students	Principals, teachers, families, and students

Source: Beaton, Martin, and others (1996); Beaton, Mullis, and others (1996); IEA (2002); Martin and others (2000); Martin and others (2004); Mullis and others (2000); Mullis and others (2004); OECD (2001, 2004).
a. The PISA 2000 emphasized reading; the PISA 2003 emphasized math.
b. Argentina did not complete all phases or publish its results.

References

Beaton, A. E., M. O. Martin, I. V. S. Mullis, E. J. Gonzalez, T. A. Smith, and D. L. Kelly. 1996. *Science Achievement in the Middle School Years: IEA's Third International Mathematics and Science Study (TIMSS)*. Chestnut Hill, MA: IEA (International Association for the Evaluation of Educational Achievement), TIMSS International Study Center.

Beaton, A. E., I. V. S. Mullis, M. O. Martin, E. J. Gonzalez, D. L. Kelly, and T. A. Smith. 1996. *Mathematics Achievement in the Middle School Years: IEA's Third International Mathematics and Science Study (TIMSS)*. Chestnut Hill, MA: IEA (International Association for the Evaluation of Educational achievement), TIMSS International Study Center.

IEA (International Association for the Evaluation of Educational Achievement). 2002. *PIRLS 2001 International Report*. Chestnut Hill.

Martin, M. O., ed. 2003. *TIMSS 2003 User Guide for the International Database*. TIMSS & PIRLS International Study Center, Boston College, Chestnut Hill, MA.

Martin, M. O., I. V. S. Mullis, and E. J. Gonzalez. 2004. "Home Environments Fostering Children's Reading Literacy: Results from the PIRLS 2001 Study of Reading Literacy Achievement in Primary Schools in 35 Countries." Paper presented at the first IEA International Research Conference, Lefkosia, Cyprus.

Martin, M. O., I. V. S. Mullis, E. J. Gonzalez, and S. J. Chrostowski. 2004. *TIMSS 2003 International Science Report*. Boston College, Chestnut Hill, MA.

Martin, M. O., I. V. S. Mullis, E. J. Gonzalez, K. D. Gregory, T. A. Smith, S. J. Chrostowski, and others. 2000. *TIMSS 1999 International Science Report*. Boston College, Chestnut Hill, MA.

Martin, M. O., I. V. S. Mullis, and A. M. Kennedy, eds. 2003. *PIRLS 2001 Technical Report*. Boston College, Chestnut Hill, MA.

Mullis, I. V. S., M. O. Martin, E. J. Gonzalez, and S. J. Chrostowski. 2004. *TIMSS 2003 International Mathematics Report*. Boston College, Chestnut Hill, MA.

Mullis, I. V. S., M. O. Martin, E. J. Gonzalez, K. D. Gregory, R. A. Garden, K. M. O'Connor, and others. 2000. *TIMSS 1999 International Mathematics Report*. Boston College, Chestnut Hill, MA.

OECD. 2001. *Knowledge and Skills for Life: First Results from PISA 2000. Publications 2000*. Paris: OECD.

———. 2004. *Learning for Tomorrow's World: First Results from PISA 2003*. Paris: OECD.

Appendix 2

Proficiency Levels for 2003 PISA Mathematics

Level 1

Level 1 includes students scoring between 357.77 and 420.07. At this level, students can answer questions involving familiar contexts where all relevant information is present and the questions are clearly defined. They are able to identify information and carry out routine procedures according to direct instructions in explicit situations. They can perform actions that are obvious and follow immediately from the given stimuli.

Level 2

Level 2 includes students scoring between 420.08 and 483.38. At this level, students can interpret and recognize situations in contexts that require no more than direct inference. They can extract relevant information from a single source and make use of a single representational mode. They can employ basic algorithms, formulas, procedures, and conventions. They are capable of engaging in direct reasoning and making literal interpretations of the results.

Level 3

Level 3 includes students scoring between 483.29 and 544.68. At this level, students can execute clearly described procedures, including those that require sequential decisions. They can select and apply simple problem-solving strategies. They can interpret and use representations based on different information sources and reason directly from them. They can develop short communications reporting their interpretations, results, and reasoning.

Level 4

Level 4 includes students scoring between 544.69 and 606.99. At this level, students can work effectively with explicit models for complex, concrete situations that may involve constraints or call for making assumptions. They can select and integrate different representations, including symbolic representations, linking them directly to aspects of real-world situations. They can utilize well-developed skills and reason flexibly, with some insight, in these contexts. They can construct and communicate explanations and arguments based on their interpretations, arguments, and actions.

Level 5

Level 5 includes students scoring between 607.00 and 669.30. At this level, students can develop and work with models for complex situations, identifying constraints and specifying assumptions. They can select, compare, and evaluate appropriate problem-solving strategies for dealing with complex problems related to these models. They can work strategically using broad, well-developed thinking and reasoning skills; appropriate linked representations; symbolic and formal characterizations; and insights pertaining to these situations. They can reflect on their actions and formulate and communicate their interpretations and reasoning.

Level 6

Level 6 includes students scoring above 669.30. At this level, students can conceptualize, generalize, and utilize information based on their investigations and modeling of complex problem situations. They can link different information sources and representations and flexibly translate among them. They are capable of advanced mathematical thinking and reasoning and can apply their insights and understandings. They use symbolic and formal mathematical operations and relations to develop new approaches and strategies for attacking novel situations. They can formulate and precisely communicate their actions and reflections regarding their findings, interpretations, and arguments and their appropriateness to the original situations.

Reference

OECD. 2004. *Learning for Tomorrow's World: First Results from PISA 2003.* Paris: OECD.

Appendix 3

Proficiency Levels for PISA 2000 and 2003 Reading

Table A3.1 Proficiency Levels for PISA 2000 Reading

Level	Retrieving information	Interpreting text	Reflection and evaluation
5	Locate and possibly sequence or combine multiple pieces of deeply embedded information, some of which may be outside the main body of the text. Infer which information in the text is relevant to the task. Deal with highly plausible and/or extensive competing information.	Either construe the meaning of nuanced language or demonstrate a full and detailed understanding of a text.	Critically evaluate or hypothesize, drawing on specialized knowledge. Deal with concepts that are contrary to expectations and draw on a deep understanding of long or complex texts.
4	Locate and possibly sequence or combine multiple pieces of embedded information, each of which may need to meet multiple criteria, in a text with unfamiliar context or form. Infer which information in the text is relevant to the task.	Use a high level of text-based inference to understand and apply categories in an unfamiliar context and to construe the meaning of a section of text by taking into account the text as a whole. Deal with ambiguities, ideas that are contrary to expectation, and ideas that are negatively worded.	Critically evaluate or hypothesize, drawing on specialized knowledge. Deal with concepts that are contrary to expectations and draw on a deep understanding of long or complex texts.

(continued)

Table A3.1 Proficiency Levels for PISA 2000 Reading *(continued)*

Level	Retrieving information	Interpreting text	Reflection and evaluation
3	Locate, and in some cases recognize, the relationship between pieces of information, each of which may need to meet multiple criteria. Deal with prominent competing information.	Integrate several parts of a text in order to identify a main idea, understand a relationship, or construe the meaning of a word or phrase. Compare, contrast, or categorize, taking many criteria into account. Deal with competing information.	Make connections or comparisons, give explanations, or evaluate a feature of text. Demonstrate a detailed understanding of the text in relation to familiar, everyday knowledge or draw on less common knowledge.
2	Locate one or more pieces of information, each of which may be required to meet multiple criteria. Deal with competing information.	Identify the main idea in a text, understand relationships, form or apply simple categories, or construe meaning within a limited part of the text when the information is not prominent and low-level inferences are required.	Make a comparison or connections between the text and outside knowledge or explain a feature of the text by drawing on personal experience and attitudes.
1	Take account of a single criterion to locate one or more independent pieces of explicitly stated information.	Recognize the main theme or author's purpose in a text about a familiar topic, when the required information in the text is prominent.	Make a simple connection between information in the text and common, everyday knowledge.

Below1: May be able to read, but have not acquired the skills to use reading for learning

Source: OECD 2001, 2004.

Bibliography

Further Reading

Allcott, H., and D. E. Ortega. 2006. "The Performance of Decentralized School Systems: Evidence from Fe y Alegría in Venezuela." Andean Development Bank, Caracas.

Altonji, J. G., and C. R. Pierret. 2001. "Employer Learning and Statistical Discrimination." *Quarterly Journal of Economics* 116 (1): 313–50.

ANEP (Administración Nacional de la Educación Pública). *Monitor educativo 2005.* Montevideo.

Bennell, P. 2004. *Teacher Motivation and Incentives in Sub-Saharan Africa and Asia.* Knowledge and Skills for Development, Brighton, United Kingdom.

Cerdán-Infantes, Pedro. 2006. "National Student Assessment Systems in Latin America: An Overview." World Bank, Washington, DC.

Eurydice. Online database. http://www.eurydice.org/portal/page/portal/Eurydice.

Ferrer, G. 2006. *Estado de situación de los sistemas nacionales de evaluación de logros de aprendizaje en América Latina.* Partnership for Educational Revitalization in the Americas (PREAL), Santiago.

Finnish Basic Education Act 628/1998. www.finlex.fi/en/laki/kaannokset/1998/en19980628.pdf.

Finnish National Board of Education. 2002. *Evaluation and Outcomes in Finland: Main Results in 1995–2002.* Helsinki.

Galindo, C. 2002. "El currículo implementado como indicador del proceso educativo." In *Análisis de los resultados y metodologia de las pruebas CRECER 1998,* ed. J. Rodríguez and S. Vargas. Lima: Ministerio de Educación del Perú.

Guiney, E., and T. Payzant. 2003. Paper presented at the Alliance for Excellent Education, American High School Policy Conference, Washington, DC, November 17.

Hanushek, E. A., J. Kain, and S. Rivkin. 2001. "Why Public Schools Lose Teachers." NBER Working Paper 8599, National Bureau of Economic Research, Cambridge, MA.

Hargreaves, A. 1996. "Teacher Training, Professional Development, and Secondary School Reform." Paper presented at the World Bank Human Development Forum, Washington, DC, November 1.

Hargreaves, A. 2007. *The Emotions of Teaching.* San Francisco: Jossey-Bass.

Hedges, L. V., R. D. Laine, and R. Greenwald. 1994. "Does Money Matter? A Meta-Analysis of Studies of the Effects of Differential School Inputs on Student Outcomes." *Education Researcher* 23 (3): 5–14.

Heñeveld, W., and H. Craig. 1995. *Schools Count: World Bank Project Designs and the Quality of Primary Education in Sub-Saharan Africa.* World Bank Technical Paper 303, Washington, DC.

IEA (International Association for the Evaluation of Educational Achievement). 2002. *PIRLS 2001 International Report.* Chestnut Hill: IEA.

Kim, G-J. 2000. *Education Policies and Reform in South Korea.* Human Development Network, Washington, DC: World Bank.

Lee, J. 2001. *Education Policy in the Republic of Korea: Building Block or Stumbling Block?* Human Development Network, Washington, DC: World Bank.

Ministry of Education and Human Resources Development, Republic of Korea. 2006. *Introduction on the Education System of the Republic of Korea.* Seoul.

National Institute for Child and Human Development (NICHD) Early Child Care Research Network. 2002. "Child-Care Structure, Process, Outcome: Direct and Indirect Effects of Child-Care Quality on Young Children's Development." *American educational Research Journal* 39(1): 133–64.

Navarro, J. C. 2005. "Las reformas educativas como reformas del estado: América Latina en las dos últimas décadas." Draft Inter-American Development Bank, Washington, DC.

Nores, M. 2005. "Quality Levels and Endowments Affecting Student Achievement in the Region." Background paper prepared for this report. World Bank, Washington, DC.

OECD (Organisation for Economic Co-operation and Development). 2003. *Attracting, Developing, and Retaining Effective Teachers: Country Background Report for Finland.* Paris.

———. 2004. *Completing the Foundation for Lifelong Learning: An OECD Survey of Upper Secondary Schools.* Paris.

Park, A., and E. Hannum. 2001. "Do Teachers Affect Learning in Developing Countries? Evidence from Matched Student-Teacher Data from China." Paper prepared for the conference "Rethinking Social Science Research on the Developing World in the 21st Century," Park City, Utah, June 7–11.

PREAL (Partnership for Educational Revitalization in the Americas). 2005. *Quantity without Quality: A Report Card on Education in Latin America.* Washington, DC.

Qualifications and Curriculum Authority. n.d. *International Review of Curriculum and Assessment Frameworks Internet Archive (INCA).*

———. 2003. *International Review of Curriculum and Assessment Frameworks. Thematic Probe: Primary Education: an International Perspective.*

Ravela, P. 2004. "How Do the Results of Educational Assessments Appear in the Media?" Santiago and Washington, DC: Partnership for Educational Revitalization in the Americas (PREAL).

Umansky, I. 2006a. "What Have We Learned? Revisiting the Education Production Function as a Tool for Understanding Education Quality in Latin America." Background paper prepared for this report. World Bank, Washington, DC.

———. 2006b. "Curriculum and Standards in Latin America: Trends and Challenges since 1990." Background paper prepared for this report. World Bank, Washington, DC.

UNESCO (United Nations Educational, Scientific, and Cultural Organization). 1998. *Supervision for the Self-Managing School: The New Zealand Experience.* Paris.

———. 2000. *The Dakar Framework for Action: Education for All: Meeting Our Collective Commitments*. Paris.

———. 2003. *Student Loans Schemes in the Republic of Korea: Review and Recommendations*. Bangkok.

———. 2004. *2005 EFA Global Monitoring Report. Education for All: The Quality Imperative*. Paris.

UNESCO Institute for Statistics (UIS). Database. http://www.uis.unesco.org/ev.php?URL_ID=3753&URL_DO=DO_TOPIC&URL_SECTION=201

United Nations. 2005. *The Millennium Development Goals Report*. New York: United Nations.

Villegas-Reimers, E. 1998. *The Preparation of Teachers in Latin America: Challenges and Trends*. Washington, DC: World Bank.

West, M. R., and L. Woessmann. 2003. "Which School Systems Sort Weaker Students into Smaller Classes? International Evidence." Working Paper 1054, Category 4: Labour Markets, CESifo, Munich.

Williamson, J. G. 2006. *Inequality and School Responses to Globalization Forces: Lessons from History*.

Wright, S. P., S. Horn, and W. Sanders. 1997. "Teacher and Classroom Context Effects of Student Achievement: Implications for Teacher Evaluation." *Journal of Personnel Evaluation in Education* 11: 57–67.

Related Web Sites

Boston Plan for Excellence: http://www.bpe.org/.

Boston Public Schools: http://www.boston.k12.ma.us/.

Broad Education Foundation: http://www.broadfoundation.org/home.html.

Finnish Ministry of Education: http://www.minedu.fi/OPM/?lang=en.

Finnish National Board of Education: http://www.oph.fi/english/frontpage.asp?path=447.

Houston Independent School District: http://www.houstonisd.org/.

Institute of Education Sciences: http://ies.ed.gov/.

Korea Education & Research Information Service (KERIS): http://www.keris.or.kr/english/index.jsp.

Korean Educational Development Institute (KEDI): http://eng.kedi.re.kr/.

Korea Institute of Curriculum and Evaluation (KICE): http://www.kice.re.kr/kice/eng/intro/intro1_2.jsp.

Korean Ministry of Education and Human Resources Development: http://english.moe.go.kr/.

Massachusetts Department of Education: http://www.doe.mass.edu/.

Massachusetts General Laws: http://www.mass.gov/legis/laws/mgl/.

Massachusetts Office of Educational Quality and Accountability: http://eqa.mass.edu/home/index.asp.

New Zealand Education Review Office: http://www.ero.govt.nz/ero/publishing.nsf/Content/Home+Page.

New Zealand Ministry of Education: http://www.minedu.govt.nz/.

New Zealand Qualifications Authority (NZQA): http://www.nzqa.govt.nz/.

New Zealand State Services Commission: http://www.ssc.govt.nz/display/home.asp.

New Zealand Teachers Council: http://www.teacherscouncil.govt.nz/.

New Zealand Treasury: http://www.treasury.govt.nz/budgets/process/default.asp.

No Child Left Behind: http://www.ed.gov/nclb/landing.jhtml.

Spanish Ministry of Education and Science: http://www.mec.es/.

Texas Administrative Code: http://www.sos.state.tx.us/tac/.

Texas Education Agency: http://www.tea.state.tx.us/.

U.S. National Assessment of Educational Progress Web site: http://nces.ed.gov/
nationsreportcard/.

U.S. National Center for Education Statistics: http://nces.ed.gov/.

Index